TRANSFORMATIONAL
THINKING
CHANGE YOUR THOUGHTS, CHANGE YOUR LIFE

ANDREW HENRY JACOBS

Transformational Thinking:
Change Your Thoughts, Change Your Life

Published by

St. Angelia Press
San Francisco, California
www.SaintAngeliaPress.com

ISBN: 979-8-218-26334-8 (softcover)
ISBN: 979-8-218-26352-2 (hardcover)
LCCN: 2023915233
Book Design: YellowStudios

Disclaimer: Please note that I don't make any guarantees about the results of the information applied from this material I share educational and informational resources that are intended to help you succeed in healing your wounds and transforming your life. You nevertheless need to know that your ultimate success or failure will be the result of your own efforts, your particular situation, and innumerable other circumstances beyond my knowledge and control.

Printed in the United States of America.

To my therapist and dear friend, Harry Flanagan.
Without your love, guidance, and selfless support,
I wouldn't be the person I am today.
I love you.

For those who have fallen hard on rock bottom
and gotten back up to rebuild your life,
on behalf of those who love you,
Thank You.

Foreword

It is an honor to call Drew my friend and colleague of more than 20 years. As with most friendships, we have supported one another along the circuitous journey we call life. There have been times of shared joyous celebrations and times of shared grief. Over these last two decades, I have watched Drew become the man you will meet in the pages of this book. He is a man who has weathered numerous storms and wisely used these difficult seasons to grow and become a more accurate version of his true self.

Drew and I both enjoy learning and have both completed our doctoral degrees during the course of our friendship. Additionally, Drew has extensive training and professional experience in workforce development, transformational consulting, and leading organizational change. Drew is an outstanding trainer and speaker who keeps his audiences engaged with his wit and humor. However, that is not the focus of this book. This book is about transformational thinking and how to change your life by changing your thoughts. Drew begins the book with the raw truth about the excruciating experience that led him to transform his thinking and his life.

As Drew has edited this book over time, we have had long and lively discussions about the process and principles of transformational thinking. As iron sharpens iron, we have been able to challenge one another and clarify what it means to transform our thinking. I trust you will contemplate, wrestle with, and learn to apply the principles that are helpful to you during this season of your life journey. Above all, I hope that you see the kind of transformation in your life that I have seen in Drew's life. He made radical changes in his thinking and his life is better for it. I hope after reading this book and applying the principles of transformative thinking, you will live the encouragement Henry David Thoreau implores us to abide by: "Go confidently in the direction of your dreams! Live the life you've imagined."

Enjoy your journey of transformational thinking!

Dr. Rhonda Lee Petrini

Contents

CHAPTER 1

MY TRANSFORMATIVE THINKING JOURNEY

"Turn your wounds into wisdom."
—Oprah Winfrey

I CAN STILL TASTE the metal. I never thought about how metal tasted until the cold steel of the implement I intended to end my pain landed on my tongue. I was terrified of going through with it, but more scared of what life would look like if I didn't. Letters were on my desk to both of my sons, explaining myself in a way that I hoped would make everything okay and knowing it wouldn't.

A hollow point round loaded in the chamber. I leaned back against the deck railing and put the gun in my mouth. Breathing in deeply, I gently squeezed the trigger as if that would make what I was doing less painful.

Then the phone rang in the house, and I thought, "I'll see who this is and then get back to the task at hand." I walked in the house to hear better. After the cursory three rings, the answering machine picked up, and I listened to my soon-to-be ex-wife saying, "Whatever you are thinking about doing, don't. You will get through this." When I went back outside, one of my closest friends, a former police officer, was breaking down my weapon. At that moment, I came to, and KNEW suicide was no longer an option for me. But my life was essentially over as I knew it. The only option was rebuilding a new life that served me better. But how?

I had no idea what to do or how to do it. How do you do that when you are broke, alone, virtually homeless, unemployable, and so deeply depressed that if you were depressed, it would be a step up? I knew I was lost at this point in my life and had nothing to lose. But I also had nothing to give. I was spent and utterly depleted. I had to get help.

We are not meant to travel this life journey alone or in self-imposed solitude. We need one another. Dear reader, you have picked up, purchased, and are reading this book that I wrote. It is a partnership. We need partners, fellow sojourners to walk with through the journey of life. I found a partner at this critical juncture in my life to help me rebuild my life; a therapist specializing in people who have imploded their life. Harry.

One of the things I told Harry when we first met was that I needed to find out WHY I did what I did. Why would I make choices to compromise everything I believed in? Why would I put myself and my family in jeopardy? Why would I cross lines that I shouldn't have crossed?

In that spirit of discovery, Harry had me take a series of expensive and detailed assessments to help him understand the root of my issues. I found out I was not a sex addict. I was not a gambling addict. I was not a drug addict. I was not an alcoholic. The news was disappointing because I thought having an identifiable diagnosis, like addiction, would make healing easier. I did have some addictive thinking tendencies and discovered I had PTSD in the 87th percentile from childhood trauma and abuse.

I thought PTSD was for war veterans. In my assessment, it felt a bit insulting to war veterans to have me classified with those who put their lives on the line for our country. Harry explained that PTSD could come from all sorts of issues and, when not dealt with, can have catastrophic results in a person's life. A skilled therapist is like a spiritual heart surgeon; they know how to go deeper and deeper, helping the client to excise intellectual, emotional, and spiritual cancers.

Everything came down to my thinking and beliefs. Most of my dysfunctional thinking and false beliefs were birthed from the childhood trauma I experienced. Some of the trauma was chronic, such as my father's emotional and physical abuse. Some of it was periodic, like the sexual abuse I experienced as a little boy. Both types of abuse resulted in my destructive beliefs, oppressive thinking, and harmful self-talk. I had no idea how pervasive the dysfunctional thinking was intertwined within my being until it was identified and excised during my healing journey. My unhealed trauma distorted my ability to make healthy decisions, maintain boundaries, and advocate for myself. This all culminated in the implosion of my life.

Most people don't change unless they have one of two motivators: pain or pleasure. I spent much of my life pursuing the pleasure of my career, thinking that would heal the wounds and quiet the demons of resentment inside me. As if accomplishments would somehow justify my existence! However, I could not do the work of diving deep inside and confronting the wounds of my childhood until I was forced to because it was time to end the pain I created.

It's like when folks decide to lose weight. Some people are motivated by the pleasure of wearing certain clothes or having a more active social life. Others are inspired by a doctor who informs them that the only way to address the physical conditions they are facing is to do the work of losing weight.

Oh, I would love to have been in the former category. If only I had been someone capable of acknowledging and identifying my unhealed wounds and dysfunctional issues before making the catastrophic choices that imploded my life. Instead, I had to come to a place where the only path forward was to be forced do the healing work once suicide was no longer an option for me.

The only way to the light was through the darkness.

For me, the only way to the light was through the darkness. And it all started with my thinking. Healing involved changing my thinking and reprogramming my subconscious and conscious minds. The coping mechanisms and beliefs that served me as a child no longer served me as an adult. In fact, these childlike thoughts and beliefs were now poison to my soul. And the only way out of my mess was through the unfamiliar path of self-honesty, inner healing, and a comprehensive restoration of my broken spirit. I needed to transform my thinking if I was to make it to the other side of peace and healing.

My journey with Thought Practice and Transformational Thinking came from a lifetime of studying world religions, respected healers, and thought leaders. I spent the first part of my career as a pastor. For as long as I can recall, I had a heart that wanted to help and protect people. I now know this was informed by two motivating factors: (a) caring for and serving others is hardwired into my personhood, and (b) deeply wishing someone had been there to care and protect me as a child.

After fifteen years in the ministry, I realized that I found fundamentalism a great foundation for spiritual growth but a poor cage. Too many of my colleagues and the faithful were more concerned with adherence to rules and traditions than the state of people's hearts. My experience with the evangelical Christian church is that, generally, it is more concerned with telling people <u>what</u> to think spiritually rather than <u>how</u> to think spiritually. I needed to learn HOW to think spiritually, intellectually, emotionally, and relationally. Teaching people HOW to think creates healthy, growing people. To transform my life, I had to learn how to think.

Harry and I began doing the work to rebuild my life. First, we looked at my trauma and wounds with brutally torturous honesty. I was too exhausted from carrying the secrets of my soul. We excised the wounds from a position of responsibility rather than victimhood. Yes, I was victimized, but my responsibility was to heal from those experiences and not live in victimhood. The process required me to accept what happened and take responsibility for the life I had created—all of it. Part of taking responsibility involved the concept of acceptance.

At this point, Harry introduced me to Alcoholics Anonymous. Although not an alcoholic, he thought the 12-step program would be meaningful to me in my journey. He was right. AA and therapy saved my life. One of the first things I learned in the rooms was about acceptance. In the big blue book, it says, "And acceptance is the answer to all my problems today. When I am disturbed, it is because I find some person, place, thing, situation, or '*some fact of my life*' unacceptable to me, and I can find no serenity until I accept that person, place, thing, or situation as being exactly the way it is supposed to be at this moment." Simple concept. Difficult to apply at first, but it soon became a transformational habit of my mind.

Once I took responsibility and embraced the concept of acceptance, then I was ready for the first step to what would become Transformational Thinking. I listed all my beliefs. The way we discovered these beliefs was to examine my self-talk and inner thoughts. I remember the self-talk list clearly. After Harry read the list of 33 statements, he looked up at me and asked, "What would you do if someone spoke to your children this way?"

"Without thinking, I blurted out, "I'd kick their ass!"

"Then why do you speak to yourself that way?"

I did not have an answer.

As I worked with Harry, it was clear that my life had become unmanageable and out of control. Due to my poor choices, there were some serious repercussions of my mistakes that I could not control; but I could control what I thought about them. Once this epiphany was birthed in my mind, I started taking responsibility for how I was responding to the crisis. I realized I had some available options to manage and some decisions to make. This gave me a small modicum of power. It all started in my mind, with my thoughts.

As I sat before Harry, I was a full-blown addict. I was addicted to work, financial security, approval, and influence. My addictive thinking was so perverse that I thought it was GOOD to be addicted to work. I justified it in hundreds of different ways. When we are addicted to anything, we end up being a slave to the object of addiction. When I was living in addiction and addictive thinking, my life spiraled into daily panic and anxiety. I was subconsciously fleeing from the life I was meant to live.

I came to understand that addiction imperceptibly begins to control and run our lives. The compulsions chip away at our autonomy and our freedom to make choices by clouding clarity and common sense. As one person stated in the recovery rooms, "I knew I was an addict when I lost the freedom to abstain."

My addiction, like many others, was the fruit of childhood trauma. I had long ago lost dominion over work and lived most of my life serving an unappeasable master. It all started in my mind, with my thoughts. I had focused my entire life on the outside world and how to control and influence it to bend to my will. Now I was reaching inward. An honest understanding or a fearless moral inventory showed me what was within my control. This process clarified my past, present, and future.

The process of discovery and healing our wounds and reprogramming our subconscious is not a step 1, 2, 3 process. Rather, it is an intermingling of principles and revelations that involve a step forward, two steps to the side or backward, four steps forward, one back. It is a chaotic and uncharted path that is different for each of us. But the principles remain the same. I advocate investing in a good therapist or coach to walk with you through this journey. They know when to hold you gently and when to push you to dig a bit deeper.

Changing my beliefs and thoughts took time, consistency, effort, and commitment. Transformational Thinking is not a promise of a quick fix to make all your dreams come true. I cannot guarantee you will win the lottery and have more money than you need. The charlatans who sell manifestation seminars and books will tell you that if you implement their specific steps, you will manifest riches beyond your dreams. They are misguided in their use of the Law of Attraction. It's not a magic elixir but a way of transforming your thoughts and therefore changing your life.

> **Rather than a magic elixir, the applied principles of Transformative Thinking are a powerful tool to help you heal and transform your life.**

Rather than a magic elixir, the applied principles of Transformative Thinking are a powerful tool to help you heal and transform your life. Please understand this. I'll say it again. Rather than a magic elixir, the applied principles of Transformative Thinking are a powerful tool to help you heal and transform your life. Meditate on that because this is an important foundation to understanding the material that follows in this book.

As you reprogram your thinking and feed your subconscious mind with healthy self-talk, you will heal inner wounds, learn your worthiness, discover how to set boundaries in relationships, maintain margin and balance in your life, and become the person you've always wanted to be. The results will be that you live a life no longer controlled by finances, relationships, or worries. What you build with that is up to you. Some people create businesses out of hobbies. Some will find that they are living their dream life already and settle into contentment. Others will completely recreate their life.

I am happy for you that you are on this journey. I am proud of you for taking the inner journey that many don't have the courage and stamina to walk through. Rather than a quick fix, you have begun the journey of genuine and sustainable transformation. I am excited for you and applaud you.

After reading this book, follow me on social media. Share your wins, big and small, with our community of fellow sojourners! (See chapter 17 for social media links.)

Now, grab a cup of coffee or tea, turn the page, and take your first step to understanding and applying the powerful truths of Transformative Thinking. Godspeed to you in your transformational journey.

A DIFFERENT KIND OF KNOWING

"Presume not that I am the things I was."
—William Shakespeare

YOU CAN HAVE THE life you've always dreamed of. You can have a life of purpose, peace, and one filled with a deep sense of connection with others. Your relationships can expand and deepen. Your work can be meaningful and doesn't even need to feel like work. You can eliminate a lot of frustration, anxiety, stress, and suffering from your daily life. The good news is that the power and ability to live this kind of life is already within you.

The transformation of Thought Practice that leads to liberation is something anyone can do—regardless of their age, socio-economic status, health, relational ability, or physical capability. All of us must begin wherever we are and accept our reality if we want to change it. If you are happy with your life and those around you are satisfied with you, then you can put this down and find another book. However, if you are ready to live your dreams, keep reading.

I know this is possible because I did it. I had to hit rock bottom before I was willing to take a long look in the mirror and take responsibility for creating the life I was living. To change our experience, we have first to acknowledge that our life isn't what we want. Then, we must be willing to change to live the life we want. Making those changes requires honesty, courage, and vulnerability. Some folks just aren't ready for that, and that's okay. Even a small desire to pursue change and inner transformation comes to mind only when we are dissatisfied, unhappy, fed up, and ready to make changes.

You can determine if you are ready to make lasting changes in your life by asking yourself a couple of questions:

- What have I contributed to creating the life I am living?
- Where do I have a responsibility here?

Changing our lives begins with changing our thoughts. Like Wayne Dyer observed, "When you change the way you look at things, the things you look at change."

The Second Noble Truth of Buddhism explains the origin of our suffering. According to their thought process, our misery is caused by behaving selfishly. Our selfish acts, in turn, cause us unhappiness and a tendency to repeat our non-virtuous behavior; thereby creating more misery for us. The cycle repeats itself as we try and soothe the wounds in our hearts. It begins with our thoughts, which are born from our grasping at the notion of *me*. This cycle creates a thought pattern that motivates us to satisfy ourselves in all possible manners and protect ourselves from any threat to our happiness.

Many people see their dissatisfaction as originating from causes outside themselves. Other people hurt them; they didn't have opportunities others did, etc. There are many excuses that run along the same train of thought as these. The truth is that all of our dissatisfaction, unrest, stress, and worry come from our thoughts. Our thinking causes our circumstances; and our thinking is entirely within our control. Your life experience is in your hands; and you control what you experience. It's all within your power and influence—all of it. You can end the suffering of living in anxious stress and create the life you want.

It's been said, "You are the master of your fate, the captain of your soul" because you have the power to control your thoughts. I want to invite you to think through this book's concepts until you understand them and set aside your previous ideas. You have to be open to the magic and excitement of a new awareness that can change your life.

There are universal truths that many people are aware of. Regardless of an individual's familiarity with these, we are all bound by universal laws. Consider the universal law of gravity. We are accountable to the confines and opportunities afforded us by the law of gravity. Whether we are aware of the law or not does not absolve us of the confines of the law. However, living unaware of the law of gravity can prove deadly. And it can also prevent us from using the principles of the law to our benefit.

When considering universal truths, you should keep in mind that virtually every religious tradition talks about waking up to the *truth*. Every path promises that the direct experience of truth sets us free. Truth brings us peace. Truth compels us to compassion. Truth ultimately brings us happiness. You see, the truth is the truth. It doesn't matter if that truth is found in Christian, Buddhist, Hindu, or Muslim scriptures. It is still the truth. Suffering is common to all of us, as is the desire for happiness and the desire to end of our suffering.

What do you want from life? To love another and be loved. To know and be known. A life freed of the shackles of stress and suffering. A life filled with good health. A very fulfilling life. All of this is well within the scope of our experience, and we never knew it. If I told you that you can have the life you always dreamed of, that it is within your power to experience the life you have always wanted, and that you already have all the resources necessary, would you be interested?

What do you want from life?

How do you live a fulfilling experience? Albert Einstein said, "Nothing happens until something moves." Your thoughts are the way you will create that movement. The power of your thoughts will allow the transfer of your ideal life from the ether into the physical world. The ether is the other dimension of the heavens, which carries energies.

You think every day. Thousands and thousands of thoughts assail your mind. Most of us are slaves and victims of those thoughts rather than being their commander. To live the life you've always dreamed, you will have to shift from being a victim of your thoughts to taking control of them. You will then learn to take responsibility for the circumstances of your life without any accompanying guilt. You will shift your thoughts to focus on what you intend to manifest.

Your inner speech is uniquely your creation. You have created it from hearing others' voices, feeding on your insecurities and doubts, and allowing your ego to keep you a prisoner of fear. Your thoughts are responsible for attracting either more of the circumstances you don't want or more of what you do want in your life. The choice is yours and only yours. Making this choice will involve discovering what is truly most important to you, who you really are, and what you authentically want out of your life experience. Most of us live with an inner dialogue that commiserates with the expectations of others. We ensure that this experience continues to flow into our lives. Taking responsibility means that these voices cease to have influence and are then replaced with the inner thoughts and dialogue that manifests what you do want in your life.

If you desire to improve your life, you must remove these inner obstacles. Shifting your inner speech to focus on what you want to create and attract into your life is the way to change your life. You must do this with unwavering intent and consistency. It takes a commitment to quit giving mental energy to what others think or feel about how you should live your life. You must not listen to the voices of the past, which seek to oppress you. At first, this can be tough because your thoughts have been in control for many years. Taking back and maintaining that control will take some practice, but you will get there. There are two fundamental, immutable facts about thoughts:

1. Thoughts are things.

2. Thoughts have a magnetic energy.

If you think thoughts such as, "I'm unattractive and I don't have enough money," guess what? People won't be attracted to you and you will always be under financial pressure. However, if you genuinely find aspects about yourself that are attractive and begin to think you are attractive; people will be drawn to you. These thoughts have to be real and not contrived. It takes time and practice to make thought transformation a lifestyle. That is why I call this work *Thought Practice*. I am continually practicing my thought work, and although it does become transformative, habitual, and more natural; it also requires focus. However, there will always be temptations to surrender control of our minds.

The temptation of this sort often appears as a person or circumstance. It can also come in the guise of something we've judged as good. We must be alert to recognize that sometimes something good is just as detrimental as something terrible. For example, take falling in love. That's a good thing. However, if it then prevents you from doing your healing work because you feel good and are distracted from your wounds—this good thing of falling in love—is preventing you from continuing your healing work. Once we train our minds, we will not be easily fooled. There is no limit to our supply and what is available to us. The sky is the limit. There is no limit. There is no such thing as having only one chance, or only two or three chances. The only question is, how much do we practice the principles until they become a living force within our lives?

The ego is that portion of our psyche where self-esteem and self-preservation reign. Our ego's role is to protect us. That is a positive aspect. However, the ego is *always* trying to protect us. It may prevent us from taking chances or leaps of faith.

Thought temptation can lead to toxic thinking if we indulge it. In general, toxic thinking is marked by seeing the bad rather than the good. Here the ego will be at work, encouraging you to avoid anything that potentially could embarrass you. However, once you begin to look for the good in everything and accept the mysterious or unknown parts of your life, your ego will lose influence over you. Toxic thinking tells you that you must make an issue out of something because your ego is fully invested in being right. If things are not going right in the way your ego thinks they should be, you have a reason for being upset. This creates internal dissonance, which is the goal of the ego. If you are internally disrupted, you are then unlikely to adopt peaceful or productive action.

Thought temptation can lead to toxic thinking if we indulge it.

When the ego is in the driver's seat of our mind, and we live within toxic thinking, even minor irritations can keep us from experiencing the peace of God. The ego feasts off anger and resentment, refusing to forgive. Anytime you value something more than you value peace, you know that your ego is exerting its influence upon you. If you want to know happiness and live in peace, you must

The ego feasts off anger and resentment, refusing to forgive.

begin a Thought Practice that removes contrary thinking from your life. You must begin to surrender the judgment of people and events and also leave behind negativity and pessimism. This will radically transform your emotional state.

Your emotions are psychological reactions to your thoughts. They are the fruit of the seeds of thoughts you have planted or have allowed to take root in your mind. Emotions flow directly from the ways you choose to use your mind. Your feelings do not just happen to you. They are the choices that you make. As noted in Proverbs 27:19, "It is your own face that you see reflected in the water and it is your own self that you see in your heart."

If your body is racked with toxic emotional responses such as guilt, anger, worry, fear, or anxiety, you must examine the thinking process that supports those feelings. To begin ridding toxic thinking from your mind, you must start by forgiving yourself. Forgive yourself for all the poisonous thinking you have indulged in this point. All your poisonous thinking, feelings, and behaviors are a way of teaching you to transcend your ego identity. Rather than lamenting the past, you must bless it for the lessons it taught you. These lessons have brought you to this point where you are ready to change.

Real transformation is not only possible, but it's also guaranteed if you change your thinking. It's not as difficult as it might seem. Change your thoughts, change your life. These three things are often seen as obstacles, but they are unrecognized opportunities for transforming your life:

- Lazy thinking
- Unhealthy self-talk
- An inflated sense of self-importance

When these three things are allowed to reside in your life, they can create almost insurmountable blocks to transformative thinking and transformative living. Throughout this book, you will explore various ways to overcome them and eliminate them as obstacles in your life. You must keep in mind that all who succeed in this Thought Practice got off to a rough start. We had all passed through many heartbreaking struggles before the transformation took place. The turning point in those who stay with it comes through the gift of crisis. It's through the crisis that we are introduced to our true selves. Often, that introduction brings focus and clarity of purpose.

It's through the crisis that we are introduced to our true selves.

Do you know your purpose in life? Often when I ask this question, I'm met with a response such as:

- A role such as a wife, mother, husband, father, etc.
- A vocation or title
- A hobby or other defense of the ego

These responses do not capture your true purpose. Relationships can change, people pass on, jobs end, etc. However, the very fact you exist indicates that you have a purpose. We will explore what that looks like for you. It is a very fascinating process. You'll discover that your purpose is not as much about what you do as it is about what you truly believe about yourself, others, and the world around you. Your second discovery will come from the power to create transformational change in your life consistent with effective Thought Practice.

Your purpose will become clear through your ongoing process of Thought Practice, time, and reflection. Our thoughts can be significant roadblocks, or they can be superhighways. We become what we think about all day long. Ask yourself the following: What thoughts do I have that inhibit me from feeling that I am living with a purpose? Your inner self knows why you are here. Still, your ego prods you to chase after money, prestige, popularity, and sensory pleasures. It is all a diversion, so you don't live on purpose. Why? The ego is threatened by your purpose and our Thought Practice. Most people focus on the demands of the ego and exist through an unfulfilled life. William James observed, "In the dim background of our mind, we know what we ought to be doing." I know I did my entire life. Unfortunately, I lacked the courage to honor my purpose.

When a purpose inspires you, everything will begin to work for you. The inspiration comes from connecting with God and your Thought Practice. When you feel inspired, what at first may have appeared to be risky then becomes a path you feel compelled to follow. The risks are gone because you are following your path, which is the truth within you. Honoring this call gets your ego out of the way. Whatever it is you want to do in life, make the motivation to bless others rather than your desire for reward. The irony is that your rewards will multiply when you're focused on giving rather than receiving. You will fall in love with what you're doing and then give the feeling of love, enthusiasm, and joy to others. Again, this begins with both your outer and inner speech.

Think of Thought Practice as a rope. A rope is comprised of many individual strands that when woven together will create great strength. The strands of Thought Practice are as strong as individual pieces. However, when intertwined with one another, their strength and effectiveness to transform grow exponentially. A small strand of nylon string is strong but not unbreakable. Weave or braid them with others, and you have a much more durable rope.

To realize your desires and manifest your purpose, you must match them with your inner speech. You should keep your inner talk focused on good reports and positive results. Your inner speech and imagination work together to create a link to God. If your inner speech conflicts with your desires, your inner voice will win. Therefore, if you match desires with inner speech, you will ultimately realize these desires.

Another strand of the rope of Thought Practice is to remain flexible. By remaining flexible and open to the magnetism that thought energy can produce in your life, you will find new opportunities coming your way. You must also stay alert and be willing to accept any guidance that comes your way. You must choose to eliminate thoughts of conditions, limitations, or the possibility of it not manifesting. If left undisturbed in your mind and the mind of God simultaneously, it will germinate into reality in the physical world. These thoughts will involve the dissipation of your ignorance concerning yourself as well as the gradual growth of your understanding. This is the beginning of the spiritual awakening of your heart and mind.

You will have to shed the layer of ignorance that the world is ANYTHING other than an abundant and generous place. Accurately viewing the Universe is a crucial strand in the rope of transformation. You must choose to see the world as an abundant, providing, and friendly place. Wayne Dyer said, "When you change the way you look at things, the things you look at change." When you think that the world is abundant and friendly, your thoughts and intentions become genuine possibilities. They will become a certainty because you experience the world from positive, magnetic energies of love, abundance, kindness, and attraction. Now you are receptive to a work that provides rather than restricts. You'll see a world that wants you to be successful and abundant, rather than one that conspires against you. I call it acting *As If*. You are acting *as if* those thoughts are already physical realities.

Johann Von Goethe said, "The moment one definitely commits one-self, then Providence moves too. All sorts of things occur to help one that would never otherwise have occurred, unforeseen incidents, meetings, and material assistance, which no man could have dreamed would have come his way."

Acting *As If* is another strand of the rope. As you live in the flow, Divine Providence will provide. Furthermore, the right people will arrive to assist you in every aspect of your life.

You will have to take action. Nothing happens if you remain in your current state, habits, and thought process. In this case, you'll have to fully let go of thoughts that question your ability to attract the right people. Otherwise, you won't recognize them when they show up in your life. Road-blocking thoughts may be difficult to recognize at first. It is how you've thought for a long time, and that is familiar to you. It is as natural as a second skin. If you believe that you are helpless to change your thinking and attract the right people, then you've invited powerlessness to your experience. If you're attached to the idea of being stuck with the wrong people, then your energy is miss-aligned with the power of the Universe, and resistance will reign. The laws of the universe are absolute and immutable. We are talking about living in the flow of alignment with these universal truths. Life flows when we live in alignment; when we are not, life is bumpy, feels forced, and is often fraudulent. God and the Universe are NOT analogous to a vending machine philosophy where you go to the universal vending machine and take whatever you want. It is not a system to be manipulated. Universal laws are based on love, honesty, and responsibility that hold true for all people. You must have trust in the Universe and then allow the right people to arrive in your living space right on schedule.

Your intentions must be clear here. You want to attract the right people to be a part of your life. And you want to have happy, healthy, and fulfilling spiritual relationships. Once you have formed a mental picture of the people you want in your immediate living space, and you know how you want them to treat you, you must be what it is you are seeking. The Universe is one of attracting energy. You attract what you think and feel magnetically.

If a friendship or partnership requires the submission of your higher nature or dignity, it is simply wrong, and you must let go of it.

Changing your thoughts and feelings is magnetic. Changing your thinking may involve certain difficult choices for you. If a friendship or partnership requires the submission of your higher nature or dignity, it is simply wrong, and you must let go of it.

Of course, the good news is that as you continue to improve your Thought Practice, it all unfolds in divine natural order. You will see and affirm that everyone you need for this journey will show up, and your resources will become available to provide for your needs. Furthermore, they will arrive at precisely the right time and moment. In this intelligent system that you are part of, everything comes from the Divine as well as through other people. That includes YOU. All of the components of Thought Practice will work if you are committed to them. There is an old legend that illustrates the kind of commitment that I am describing.

"A long while ago, a great warrior faced a situation that made it necessary for him to make a decision, which ensured his success on the battlefield. He was about to send his army against a powerful foe whose men outnumbered his own. He loaded his soldiers into boats, sailed to the enemy's country, unloaded his soldiers and equipment, and then gave the order to burn the boats. Addressing his men before the battle, he said, 'You see the boats going up in smoke? That means we cannot leave these shores alive unless we win! We have no choice. We win, or we perish!' They won." The story of Cortez burning his boats has been cited in many books over the years.

Are you facing a situation when you are being called upon to burn your boats? Consider Elon Musk. When he sold his stake in PayPal, he also sold his house. He was worth a few hundred million dollars and homeless. Why? Because he said he needed every penny to give Tesla the best chance at succeeding. Elon Musk burned his boats.

CHAPTER 2 EXERCISES

These chapter exercises are designed to help you apply the principles of TRANFORMATIONAL THINKING in meaningful and transformative ways for you. They are not designed that one should do all the exercises for each chapter. Pick and choose those which resonate with you. Record the notes from the chapter, the exercise you are doing, and the results in your notebook.

1. I am a big fan of notebooks and enjoy working through issues on paper. Something magical happens in our minds and spirits when we wrestle with ideas, plans, goals, and thoughts with a pen and paper. I encourage you to get a notebook that is dedicated to the process of Transformational Thinking.

   • Think of it in this way: If you go on a diet and obey all the principles of the diet, except you reward yourself with a piece of cheesecake every night, you will only be torturing yourself for marginal gains. However, if you forgo the daily cheats, you will see dramatic results. A notebook gives you the best chance of tracking your progress without allowing subtle subconscious cheats into your life.

   • Live the right principles long enough, and they become your way of life. One method is frustrating, while the other is life changing. The choice is yours. Take time to thoughtfully respond in your notebook to these two questions:

♦ What have I contributed to creating the life I am living?

♦ Where do I have responsibility?

2. Take a few moments to let your soul speak to you about what you need. Sit in a comfortable place where you know you won't be disturbed. Close your eyes, inhale for a natural count of four, hold it for two beats, and exhale for four. Repeat as you ask yourself, "What do I *really* want out of life?"

   • Note the answers that surface from the dormancy of your soul to the presence of your mind.

   • Repeat this exercise four days in a row, taking note of what you receive. After four days, look back on the messages you received, and ask yourself if what you wrote is what you really want out of life. Are you living that way? What changes do you need to make to live in alignment with that life?

3. Think back on the week you just lived. Did you treat your family and others around you with love and honor? Did you keep healthy boundaries and offer truth?

   • Consider a recent circumstance where you did not; what would have happened if you had offered love, honor, healthy boundaries, and truth?

   • For one day, choose to treat everyone you meet with these virtues and offer nothing but love and kindness to all. At the end of that day, note your stress levels and how you feel about the way you lived that day.

4. Answer the following questions in your notebook: who is responsible for the life you are living? Who is in charge of your mind? What are some of the voices from your past that keep you limited? What does your ego say to you to hold you back in a web of protection? Who is in charge of your emotions?

THE SLAVERY OF LIMITATION

"You can choose to be lazy or you can choose to be ambitious. Stop to think about it again. Don't you do your own choosing?"
—J. Martin Kohe

MANY OF US HAVE lived our entire lives as lazy thinkers. Lazy thinking is simply allowing your mind to be filled with thoughts that you do not choose. There are consequences to lazy thinking. You must look within your own heart and objectively ask yourself if you are at peace, joyful, stress-free, living your purpose, and experiencing the life you have always wanted. Our lazy thinking keeps us fat, irritated, worried, and merely existing. This really is not living; it is existing.

Lazy thinking is simply allowing your mind to be filled with thoughts you do not choose.

The consequence of lazy thinking is that you will just get through life rather than living the life you were intended to live. When we allow lazy thinking to take the driver's seat in our lives, we experience the shackles of limitation. Our life will have an abundance of stress and a lack of peace. Too often, we waste our life with too much worry and too little joy. This happens when we allow our ego to be in control instead of taking our rightful place as the director of our own lives.

Every experience you have in your life is your consciousness of truth unfolding. These experiences may present as love, supply, gratitude, health—or as an irritant, lack, or a repeated lesson you have not embraced. Regardless of how it seems to flow through you, it is your consciousness of truth unfolding. You cannot have insufficiency of any kind if God is your source, and you are living your Thought Practice. When you truly realize that the universe is abundant and overflowing, you will have everything you need. You do not have to apologize to others for a perceived lack of proof. Despite appearances, you need never to apologize or explain for doing your healing work and living in the higher energies. You simply, faithfully hold on to the truth of your abundance.

Giving up the sense of personal possessions will help release you from the poverty of limitation. Individual ownership is a real misunderstanding. We do not possess anything. We are stewards of those things for a time and a season. Your health, wealth, home, experience, and intelligence all belong to God. We're here only for a limited time in this world, and when we die, our possessions stay behind. To enjoy these possessions, we need to realize that possessions are meaningless. Once we harness the energy of our thoughts, we can live the life we've dreamed of living.

You must keep in mind that God is our supplier; and He set up these laws of the universe where thoughts are things. Thoughts have a magnetic pull to them regardless of their nature. Think thoughts of scarcity, such as how in debt you are, and then guess what? More debt is magnetically drawn to you. If you start thinking of $100,000, you will begin taking actions to generate $100,000. Thoughts are things, magnetic things. Look upon God as the infinite

Look upon God as the infinite source of everything. See people, things, and opportunities as manifestations of His love.

source of everything. See people, things, and opportunities as manifestations of His love. We all have the same source and opportunities to engage in a vibrant Thought Practice. We do not need to look to any manifested being for anything else. We can just look to God and look within our consciousness, where God is forever expressing His wealth. There is a common misunderstanding that supply means money, but supply involves so much more.

People naturally question the issue of money because we all have financial obligations that need to be met. The most important thing is HOW you think about money. You must remember that your thoughts regarding finances are also magnetic. Are your thoughts pulling resources to you, or are they attracting more debt, want, and stress? You must keep in mind that the foundation is God, so we don't need to have anxiety. Anxious thoughts are the worst ones we can choose. Anxious thoughts not only attract more anxiety, but they also rob God of the good pleasure He has in giving to you out of His abundance. For us to enter wholly into the source of confidence, we must understand that money is not supply; money is the result of supply. Money, clothing, cars, all constitute the effect of supply. New experiences and additions to your life prove that infinite supply is at work within you.

Since money does not equal supply, then what does? A friend encouraged me to think about it this way: consider an orange tree that is heavy with ripe fruit. The oranges do not constitute supply. When these have been eaten or given away; a new crop immediately begins to grow. The oranges are gone, but the supply continues. Within the tree, there is a law in operation. That law operates to draw minerals, substances, air, water, and sunshine through the roots, which transforms into the sap that is pulled through the trunk and distributed through the veins and finally blooms as blossoms. In time, this law transforms the blossoms into a green bud, which becomes the full-grown orange. The orange is the result of the law acting in and through the tree. The orange in and of itself cannot produce another orange. This is the law of supply, and oranges are but the fruit. They are just the result of the law.

Your consciousness partners with the universal consciousness within the guidelines of the laws of the universe. Therefore, your Thought Practice becomes the law of supply available to you. It is producing those things necessary for your well-being. As there is no limitation to your Thought Practice, there is no limit to your conscious awareness of the action of the law. Therefore, there is absolutely no limit to supply in your life. None.

We don't need to give any thought to oranges as long as we have the source that continuously produces fruit. You must change your life by changing how you think about money. Money is simply the oranges on the tree. It is a natural and inevitable fruit of the law of abundance, which is active in our lives.

As long as we are conscious of the truth that the law is operating, there is no need to be concerned when the tree appears to be bare. It will bring the fruit in the right season. When we are tuned in our conscious and subconscious, the law is at work within and for us.

We are not engaging in Thought Practice to make things come to us. We are living in the conscious stream of this truth.

As your Thought Practice develops, you will learn to enjoy the infinite supply of fruit. In the endless storehouse, there is no fear or lack to torment us. We realize this truth within our consciousness. We are not engaging in Thought Practice to make things come to us. We are living in the conscious stream of this truth. We know the truth of our own identity and our infinite capabilities. This endless supply is intertwined with our purpose. It is woven into the very fabric of our being.

Thought Practice is living in a stream of consciousness where our supply appears and then comes into our lives. Our thought energy is directed and sustained as an emanation of our inner selves. As we attune our hearing to that "still small voice" within us, we are led to our abundance where work and compensation are found. Individually, God is expressing Himself through you and your abilities. Your activities all start with thoughts. Everything begins with a thought. Remember that God has prepared for you all that is necessary for the fulfillment of your individual experience. You are never outside the harmony and energy of God's love. Thought Practice is merely cultivating consciousness of the presence and abundance of God in every passing moment. There are always good things in your path; however, they can only be brought into manifestation through desire, Thought Practice, and actions.

We can frighten ourselves with dismay and fear about what might have been or what might come. We can also forget that what is happening now is not going to happen for very long. The good news is that nothing is permanent. The bad news is that nothing is permanent.

We all experience different mind energies. These mind states reflect natural ebbs and flows, as well as the mind's standard responses to pleasant and unpleasant experiences. They are natural. They do not need to be frightening or even particularly troublesome. We are in control of our thoughts. How we program our subconscious and channel our conscious mind harnesses the mind's magnetic energy to bring about the fruit in our life. Sitting around whining for oranges when you are planting apple trees will do no good. As adults, it can be embarrassing to admit our fears. Fears spoken aloud never seem as horrifying as when they are kept secret.

However, we need to stop those thoughts of fear and replace them with what we want in our lives.

Sometimes, doubts can slip into your mind disguised as a demoralizing thought. Once past the security gate of mindfulness, doubt—if allowed to remain—acts as a double agent. It sabotages faith and trust and undermines confidence. It can blithely undercut your strength on all levels because it is entirely an inside job. Our ability to control our thoughts, choose thoughts of higher energy, and sustain our attention in the truth of the moment is the antidote for doubt. Doubt rolled in like a thunderstorm. However, suppose we do not eliminate those thoughts quickly and replace them with higher, attractive energy thoughts. In that case, those doubts will grow from a harmless storm to a category five hurricane, leaving a wake of destruction in your life.

Sitting around whining for oranges when you are planting apple trees will do no good.

Once you are in a rhythm with your Thought Practice, unsubstantiated fear will be a vapor of its former self and lose all control over you. Indecision is the seedling of fear. Indecision crystalizes when fear and doubt are allowed to take root in your mind. The two blend and give birth to debilitation. Fear is both a state of mind and a choice. You either choose to live in unhealthy, debilitating fear, or you decide to take control of your thoughts and eliminate this paralyzing fear from your being. You may be thinking, *"I'm not choosing to be afraid—I am afraid!"* However, you are choosing it because you are feeding those irrational fears rather than replacing them with rational thoughts that will manifest the kind of life you want. Fear is a state of mind. One's state of mind is subject to control and direction. We can't create anything if we don't first conceive it as a thought. Our thoughts then begin to translate themselves into the physical equivalent immediately. Thought energy is picked up through the ether and determines one's destiny. So, you must choose your thoughts carefully.

Paralyzing, unhealthy, debilitating, irrational fear is dangerous because it can kill the faculty of reason. It can destroy our capacity to imagine. It can eliminate self-reliance and undermine our enthusiasm. It discourages initiative and leads to uncertainty of purpose. Such fear can destroy accurate thinking, divert concentration and effort, and invite failure. Fear kills love and assassinates the higher energy faculties of the heart. This leaves our minds open to the negative influence of other people. Fear can be especially damaging because most people do not recognize this culprit for what it is.

The laws of Thought Practice are just that—laws. They are true whether you believe in them or not. These laws are based on principles governing the universe. Because there is a principle, a Divine law, nothing is ever an exception to this rule. We can choose to harness them for our benefit or choose to ignore them to our detriment. The choice of thought is ours. It is precisely the same as the digits one, two, three, four, five, six, seven, eight, and nine. They never get out of order and are always in their rightful place. Not one of them has ever taken anything from one of the others. Not one of them has ever crowded out the others or drawn from another. They naturally cooperate for the common good. The law is always followed. Remember the oranges?

Apples always come from apple trees. Cabbage always comes from cabbage plants. This is not an accident. So, if there is a principle, is there ever an exception to that principle? In our system of mathematics, two plus two always equals four. There is never an exception to that. Does any fruit other than apples grow on apple trees? No.

Unfortunately, many people have been hypnotized into believing a lie. Due to little understanding that thoughts are things—and they have magnetic energy—they have failed to accept that we control our thoughts and are not their victim. The moment a person knows the truth, the hypnotic spell is broken. The mesmerism may lose its hold, but that does not mean the dehypnotized person cannot fall back into it again. If one doesn't stay committed in their Thought Practice, nothing will stop those low energy thoughts from sliding back to their old, comfortable, and lazy habits.

Before you experience success with Thought Practice, you will surely meet with some temporary setback. When this happens, the most natural thing to do is to quit. That's what most people do. One of the biggest and most common causes of failure is the habit of quitting when one experiences a temporary setback. Success comes to those who are committed to success. Failure is a part of the lives of lazy thinkers and those who choose to remain failure conscious. Take meditation, for example. I began learning how to meditate five years ago. It took three years before I began to find meaningful ways to have a meditation practice. It took two more years to hone that practice. Now I do not start my day without meditating, but it required commitment, dedication, and a spirit willing to explore.

One of the biggest and most common causes of failure is the habit of quitting when one experiences a temporary setback.

Think of it this way: you have lived with mostly lazy thinking for however many years you have been on the planet. You are living at the whims of your ego-driven subconscious and conscious mind. Now, you are flexing a new muscle. It will take some time to sever the energy you have been sending across the ether and replace it with abundant, peaceful, kind, and attractive thoughts. But if you stay with it, you will have success and experience a changed life. As individuals, we have no personal capacities, and we have no personal limitations in our Thought Practice.

> ## You have been playing the game of life without understanding the rules.

Remember, you cannot have any kind of insufficiency if your source is God, who makes His resources infinite and abundant. You have been playing the game of life without understanding the rules. Now that those rules are becoming clear to you, it's a whole new ball game.

CHAPTER 3 EXERCISES

These chapter exercises are designed to help you apply the principles of TRANFORMATIONAL THINKING in meaningful and transformative ways for you. They are not designed that one should do all the exercises for each chapter. Record the notes from the chapter, the exercise you are doing, and the results in your notebook.

1. Do you allow your emotions to float like a bobber at the whim of the waves? Do you often torture yourself with phrases like, "You are so stupid!"? Do you call yourself names? How would you address someone who spoke to your children that way? The chances are that you would not be nice to them. So why do you speak to yourself in ways that are less than truthful and honorable? This week, identify two phrases that you will no longer use to address yourself. What truthful phrases will you replace them with? Write down each of the new phrases five times. Then read these new phrases out loud to embed them in your consciousness.

2. Describe God as you understand Him. You are not writing poetry—just a few words and attributes that you believe are true of God.

3. Write a short statement that shows the way you understand the truth about the abundance of the universe. Some examples are:

    • There is more than enough of the pie for everyone to be full.

    • Abundance is everywhere.

- There's plenty for all of us.

4. Do fear and doubt find roots in the garden of your mind? There is no room for either of these when the space is filled with love, beauty, gratitude, kindness, and abundance. One way to be forever free of fear and doubt is to reprogram your mind and will it to embrace love, kindness, acceptance, and abundance. Identify two or three phrases that resurface in your mind when you are afraid or in doubt. From those negative statements, write truthful statements of love. When the fear or doubt poke into your mind, replace them with the statements of love you wrote here.

5. A key to effective Thought Practice is living in the moment (i.e., being present with the moment at hand). It's also a gift and by-product of a healthy Thought Practice. Which comes first—the discipline or the gift? It does not matter. Like Albert Einstein said, "Nothing happens until you take action." Simply put, the ball is in your court. Start with being present with each moment for the morning. Flex your muscles, choose your thoughts, and live in the present from the time you wake up until lunch. How does it feel going through the process? What changes did you witness in your own experience of the day?

6. Where does doubt take root in your mind? Is it in the arena of your finances, relationships, physical body, or career? It is quite easy to determine if the doubt is based in wisdom and will lead to positive life guidance (based on healthy critical thinking skills) or debilitation (based on negative fear and doubt). Ask yourself, "What is this doubt producing? Is it protecting me from harm or is it preventing me from experiencing abundance? When the answer comes to you, you will know. Most doubts are the voices of our past or our egos trying to protect us. Once we learn to lose our ties with these baseless suspicions, they lose their power in our lives.

LEARNING TO SEE

"Listen to your beliefs, think about how you learned them, and realize that they are not genetic, nor are they the 'only way.'"
—Charlotte Sophia Kasl

MANY PEOPLE CONSIDER LIFE as a battle. But it's not a battle; it's a game. However, it's a game that cannot be played successfully without the knowledge, understanding, and application of the spiritual laws of transforming your mind so you can transform your life. We will examine these concepts together. Jesus Christ taught that life was a game of giving and receiving, *"Whatever a person sows, so shall they reap."* This means that whatever a person sends out in thought, word, and deed will indeed return to him.

- When a person gives, they receive.
- If you give hate, you will receive hate.
- If you give love, you will receive love.
- If you give criticism, you will receive criticism.
- If you lie, then you will also be lied too.

Consider Proverbs 23:7, "As a person thinks so shall they become." This means what a person imagines and what consumes their mind, sooner or later, externalizes in the material world. And if a person sends out thoughts of abundance and attraction, abundance and attraction will return to them.

To successfully enjoy the game of life, we must train our minds and engage in accurate, consistent Thought Practice. A person with a vibrant Thought Practice trained to imagine and live in the higher energies brings into their life every righteous desire of their heart. Sooner or later, we meet our creations in the physical world. Manifesting what you want requires training in the same way achieving the physical body you want requires training.

To train our minds successfully, it helps to understand how the subconscious and conscious minds work. The subconscious is simply power without direction. It is our autopilot. That is why we MUST reprogram our subconscious in our Thought Practice. That is THE key to transforming your mind and transforming your life. Please do not rush past it. The key to changing your life through Thought Practice is to reprogram your subconscious mind. The subconscious mind is like steam or electricity. It is only doing what it is told or programmed to do.

On the other hand, our conscious mind sees things as they are—or as we think they are from our perspective. It is our human mind as we know it. It generally sees things as they appear to be. It sees death, disaster, disease, poverty, and limitation of every kind. It also programs and impresses the subconscious mind. In general, our conscious mind is controlled by our ego, and our ego's job is to protect us.

The superconscious mind is God's mind. It is God's still small voice living in the realm of the Divine. It lives with perfect ideas and energies, such as love, kindness, and selflessness. There is a time, place, and purpose for you. There is something you can do, which no one else can. That is the job of the superconscious. It can be as simple as smiling at someone in the grocery store, which may result in them smiling as well. Or it could be helping a neighbor with their groceries or a chore. It may involve living a specific purpose and Divine calling like Mother Theresa did.

Thought Practice is all about giving the subconscious mind the right orders. We all have an ever-present partner listening by our side. This partner is our subconscious mind. Every thought and every word is impressed upon our subconscious. So, let's break all the old bad records of the subconscious. You can delete the files of your life that you do not wish to keep, and you can make new ones that serve you in creating the life you've always wanted. You can change your life's conditions by changing your words and your thoughts—which will in turn—reprogram your subconscious mind. Proverbs 18:21 says, "Life and death are in the power of the tongue." That is no truer than in our own life.

It is amazing what you can do when you know your powers and the workings of your mind. There is not a *quick fix* way to impress your subconscious with higher energy thoughts. Intellectual, conscious knowledge will not change your life. However, a Thought Practice that reprograms your subconscious will change your life. Thought Practice is about changing your thinking, and that starts with reprogramming your subconscious.

Our subconscious mind makes no distinctions between constructive or destructive thoughts. Our mind works with the food of thought we feed it. Your subconscious mind recognizes and acts upon thoughts that have been marked with emotion and feeling. Unemotional thoughts do not influence the subconscious mind. You will get no significant results until you learn to reach your subconscious with thoughts that have been emotionally charged with belief. You must remember that there are no free lunches. There is always a price to be paid. The ability to reach and influence your subconscious mind has its price. You cannot cheat. The price of influencing your subconscious mind is the persistent application of these principles. Here is the most significant fact: The subconscious mind is fertile and will act on any instructions that are charged with emotion.

The orders must be presented through repetition before they are imprinted onto the subconscious mind. This process is called autosuggestion. It is how we reprogram our subconscious. We can voluntarily feed our subconscious mind thoughts of positivity, health, creativity, maturity, or we can neglect it. If you permit thoughts of a destructive nature to find their way into this abundant garden of the mind, weeds will grow in your life. The choice is yours alone.

Your subconscious mind receives and files sense impressions or thoughts, regardless of their nature. You can voluntarily plant any plan, thought, or purpose in your subconscious. It can be anything that you want to create in the material world. The subconscious acts first on the dominating thoughts it is fed that have an emotional feeling and energy. Our subconscious works day and night. Through the procedure of Thought Practice, our subconscious draws upon the forces of infinite intelligence to bring our thoughts, goals, and dreams to fruition. It's worth noting that you cannot entirely control your subconscious mind. However, you can freely hand it any plan, desire, or purpose that you wish.

All negative thoughts, such as those of fear and poverty, serve as stimuli to your subconscious. They are seeds planted in fertile soil. Unless you master this aspect of Thought Practice and feed your mind more desirable food, you will live in a garden of weeds. You cannot feed your mind junk food and expect the same results as if you had fed it healthy, nutritious food.

Your subconscious does not remain idle. Ever. If you fail to plant the desires you want for your life, your subconscious mind will then feed upon thoughts that reach its fertile soul because of your neglect. Your thoughts serve as a magnet, pattern, and blueprint to influence your subconscious mind. What is created in the physical world is that which your mind has been drawing into your life. All this happens, even while you are sleeping. Your subconscious is always at work.

Your subconscious mind is more susceptible to influence from thoughts charged with emotion than those solely based on rational thought. This programming and the influence of the subconscious mind is the basis of Thought Practice. It based on understanding the essential connection between your conscious mind and your subconscious mind. Sometimes we have the flash of a dream that crosses our minds. We think of it as a fantasy, something unattainable. In reality, may be a glimpse of your destiny conveyed to you from God. Many people are living in ignorance of their purpose. They strive for things and situations that do not belong to them and would only bring failure and dissatisfaction if attained. Many people simply try to get through life. It is much better to find your purpose, program your mind for the life you've always wanted, and then truly live.

It is much better to find your purpose, program your mind for the life you've always wanted, and then truly live.

Life offers so much potential for those who understand the power of self-talk and implement the truths of Thought Practice. Dream big and follow your God-given intuition. Transform your thoughts; put into action the Divine unseen forces in the ether; and confidently rebuild your life to reflect your best, most authentic self. To accomplish this, it's essential to choose the right words and thoughts that you wish to catapult into the universe.

Too many people limit their supply by limiting their vision. If a person continues their destructive thinking of deficiency, hate, fear, lies, and condemnation, this negativity will fester and grow. So, choose positivity.

This is why it's essential to cleanse your subconscious mind of all the lower energy attitudes like judgmentalism, depression, lack, stress, anxiety, unkindness, etc. This is important for permanent healing and freedom. We must choose to cease the mental energies that do not serve us. Many people magnetically attract disease and unhappiness through the condemnation of others. What we condemn and judge, we then attract into our lives. When we condemn and judge, it's like picking up a live electrical wire; we should not be surprised when we are shocked. Our relationships can provide a good barometer of this principle.

Our relationships can be helpful teachers because they often illuminate the most painful and unhealed aspects of our lives. When conflict arises, we feel threatened and often forget that relationships can be vehicles for awakening and healing. We tenaciously hold onto our views, judgments, and our need to be right. All the while, we project and defend our self-image. We shut down or we lash out. When we believe all these reactions are justified, we perpetuate our suffering. As we continue down this path, the disappointment we cause ourselves and others becomes a pain we can no longer ignore. The pain motivates us to awaken. Heartbreak and humiliation are often motivations to heal and change.

Part of the problem is that we are taught relationships are supposed to give us security; they are supposed to save us. We assume that relationships are supposed to make us feel good through being supported, appreciated, loved, nurtured, and pleasured. We imagine that being in a perfect relationship will relieve us of all our ailments. This is simply not true.

To transform our lives and create healthy relationships, we need to face our issues and work through them. It is time to incorporate introspective questions into our Thought Practice. Instead of being reactive, we can begin to ask to take an honest, self-reflective inventory of our life. What questions can you ask yourself to clarify your dreams, longings, goals, hopes, expectations, requirements, desires, and fantasies?

The philosopher Soren Kierkegaard said, "Perfect love is to love the one through whom one has become unhappy." To put it another way, the more we work with our reactions, the more the path is cleared for love to flow through us.

To transform our lives and create healthy relationships, we need to face our issues and work through them.

The more we remove conditions that we impose on our relationships, the more open is the way to unconditional love. We do not have to open our hearts. The heart is already open. We just need to clear the obstructions that get in the way and then experience that openness. That opening begins with forgiveness.

Forgiveness is forgiveness, just like love is love, and grace is grace. Period. Forgiveness is often tainted with the idea that there should be some form of magnanimous acceptance by the other person, even though they did us wrong. This understanding of forgiveness is not what it is about. Forgiving is about working through and healing resentments. These resentments block our desire to live the life we want to be living. Forgiveness is most often about losing our hold on the one thing we most want to hold onto—the suffering brought on by our resentment.

Sometimes we wonder, what am I to do with this resentment? You may get a response like this: *"It's not good to hold on to resentments. Why don't you just let it go?"* But can we just let it go? The answer is yes and no.

Even when we understand how much resentment hurts us, we often do not have the ability to let it go. If we could just let it go, we wouldn't be stuck in resentment. Healing this pain can take time. Simply saying you're letting go of resentments isn't an authentic Thought Practice. It is a cheap fantasy. It is a fantasy based on how we would like things to be. Authentic Thought Practice is not magical or delusional thinking.

As we consistently focus our Thought Practice on the energies of love, kindness, gratitude, non-judgment, grace, forgiveness, and peace, we understand each person is on their own journey. When we have this focus, we begin to let go of our resentments. We embrace the freedom that forgiveness brings. This will bring us to a point where we can say words of forgiveness with love, grace, and understanding.

It is crucial to realize that saying words of forgiveness has nothing to do with condoning another's actions. It's about forgiving the person, not about what they did. It means seeing those actions as coming from the person's pain. We don't do this by looking at the other person's pain, but by attending to our own. Once we've healed our pain, we're more open to genuinely seeing others' pain. At this point, saying words of forgiveness helps us open our hearts and free our minds for a more energetic and effective Thought Practice. Forgiving and letting go of resentments is a fundamental key to our freedom. However, there will be other opportunities for growth that will continually be laid in our path.

A fundamental switch that happens is that we no longer see problems as problems. We shift our thinking and choose to see problems as opportunities. There comes a stage for most of us in our Thought Practice, where we begin to see the effects and enjoy life. We are removed from our resentments, hates, and fears, as well as any doubts about the principles we may have had about Thought Practice. Every problem in our lives is an opportunity for us to:

1. Learn lessons that God and the universe have been trying to teach us.

2. Flex the muscles of our Thought Practice in the laboratory of our life.

It's an opportunity to live the consciousness we have attained. At this stage of our development, it can be exhilarating as we see growth after growth. There are still issues in life, but they are now genuinely viewed as opportunities.

When we gain an understanding of this, there will be long periods of conversation with ourselves. We try to make it clear to ourselves that if we have temptations that do not seem to yield results immediately, that's okay. We will realize that no opportunity or demonstration can rise higher than the Thought Practice from which it emanates. It is like lifting weights. Someone who has been training with weights for years can do more than someone who is just beginning. In proportion to our Thought Practice and meditation, we do manifest less and less of the natural man. We demonstrate more and more of our higher conscious self, which is being revealed to us in our Thought Practice.

As we grow in Thought Practice, we are no longer chained to the past. The degree of freedom we experience becomes exponentially greater as we learn to see the world with new eyes and healed hearts. Most of us are called to a discipline of Thought Practice by a desire and need to change

As we grow in Thought Practice, we are no longer chained to the past.

our life. Indeed, in the early part of our practice, we all spend time trying to change. Our sense of dissatisfaction drives us toward fitting ourselves into whatever image we have of being more awake. We try to be stronger, calmer, more positive; or less reactive and less stressed. Yet as we implement our strategies and flex our Thought Practice muscles, we see that we are changing. We try to be nice and pleasant and patient. Still, almost always, we experience the disappointment and futility of this approach to change. Most of us are seeking to ask expansive questions, not find restrictive answers.

Thought Practice involves understanding the energy of the mind, the power of our thoughts, and the laws of the universe. I call this boomerang thinking. We receive what we give. The game of life is similar to the game of boomerang. Our thoughts, words, and deeds return to us sooner or later, with astounding accuracy. This is the law of karma, which is a Sanskrit word meaning *"come back."* The Christian Bible states it this way, "Whatever a person sows, so shall they reap" (Galatians 6:7). Healthy obedience always precedes authenticity and freedom.

The laws of electricity must be obeyed before electricity becomes our servant. When managed ignorantly, it becomes deadly. So, it is with the Laws of Thought. The subconscious mind is simply power without direction. It carries out orders without questioning. So, it is vitally important to program it with the right orders. Our inner spiritual work is all we have when our pilgrimage on earth is finished.

It has been said that you can know someone by their fruits and actions. This law of the universe applies most aptly to gratitude. A demonstration of our inner journey of Thought Practice is our state of gratitude. Gratitude reflects itself in actions and words. The higher the concept of gratitude, the more loving, kind, attractive, and magnetic the actions reflect that gratitude. The act of expressing gratitude is in recognizing and acknowledging within yourself the source of all the good in your life. To express gratitude, there must be an element of love. It is impossible to express gratitude without some level of love through your consciousness. Gratitude has meaning far beyond the word gratitude itself or even the ideas connected with gratitude. It goes deep into the reality of your being.

As it is generally understood, gratitude is an outpouring of appreciation for that which we have received. Gratitude is closely related to supply and the energies of attraction. There is no limit to the gratitude we can express.

You can go on a rampage of appreciation. Gratitude is vital for manifesting your intentions. It's the surest way to stop the incessant inner dialogue that leads you away from your Thought Practice and into lazy thinking.

If we want a changed life, our Thought Practice must include an understanding that God is love. Period. Gratitude flows out of that thought, and it is the oil that keeps the machine of Thought Practice running smoothly. Let's say that you are cash-strapped now. Don't apologize for the lack of cash flow, and don't minimize the lack of funds. Let what you have go forward with all the love and expectation that you can feel. Send it out without apologies, excuses, or explanations. Send it with trust and gratitude and expectation. Again, you can resist these universal laws to your detriment, or you can live your life actively within them. The choice is yours.

As noted earlier, when you change the way you look at things, the things you look at change. Moreover, your intention to feel successful and experience prosperity and abundance depends on your understanding of yourself and God. Your Thought Practice, from which your success and abundance will come, is a highway to achieve those. The way you look at life is a barometer of what you expect which is informed by your current beliefs about your self-worth and capabilities. Can you change the way you look at things? Can you see the potential for prosperity when you've previously seen scarcity? Can you reframe your thoughts about what is, simply by changing the way you see it? YES! But it takes time and practice.

A paradoxical line in the book, A Course in Miracles says, "Infinite patience produces immediate results." This means that you are a co-creator of your life. You know that the right people will show up on a divinely ordained schedule. The immediate result that you'll receive from your infinite patience is a deep sense of peace. You can move away from hoping, wishing, and begging for the right person or people to show up in your life. You should know that this is a universe that works on energy and attraction. Remind yourself that you have the power to attract the right people to assist you. This step is crucial. If you cannot banish doubt about your ability to attract helpful, creative, loving people, then the rest of this book will be of little use to you. It all begins with knowing in your heart that it is not only a possibility, but a certainty. You want to accept the truth that there is a divinely ordained timing to your life—more explicitly—your best life.

Act on your inner picture. Practice mindfulness to attract ideal people into your life. Only you can do the work of attracting the right people into your life. Share your needs, dreams, prayers, and desires with trusted people in your life. Then be alert for signs of synchronicity as your dreams come to fruition.

Don't make the mistake of evaluating your intentions as successes or failures based on your ego and your schedule. You should create a knowing within and let the universe handle the details. As you harmonize your thoughts, your intellect, and your feelings, you will need to give yourself grace as you practice. Like any new skill, it takes time and consistency.

You can change your life and attract the resources, relationships, and rewards that you dream about. Those dreams can come true if you choose to manifest them. Only you can do the hard work of your Thought Practice. No one can do it for you. It is a wonderfully fulfilling journey if you are willing and consistent.

CHAPTER 4 EXERCISES

These chapter exercises are designed to help you apply the principles of TRANFORMATIONAL THINKING in meaningful and transformative ways for you. They are not designed that one should do all the exercises for each chapter. Record the notes from the chapter, the exercise you are doing, and the results in your notebook.

If you were victimized, it is time to refuse to live in victimhood. Don't give your abuser any more power over your life.

1. It is true that as a person thinks, so shall they become. No matter when this book came into your hands, at this point, your life is a product of your subconscious, voices from the past, and possible lazy thinking. Remember, your subconscious mind is powerful, and reprogramming it will take consistency and time. But like everything else in life, the more you do it, the easier and more natural it becomes. First, you must own your life—all of it. It is a powerful step that puts you in the driver's seat of your life.

   • If you were victimized, it is time to refuse to live in victimhood. Don't give your abuser any more power over your life. If you have offended, hurt, or damaged others, take responsibility and make amends. If you have blamed others for circumstances in your life, choose to look at what you did to place them in a position to influence your life.

- Accepting responsibility for your life and thoughts is a powerful first step, and the rest won't work if you don't accept these facts now. Make a list of those who have damaged you and those you have damaged. Next to each person's name write down the following:

  ♦ The nature of the wound

  ♦ Steps you can take to forgive that person and let go of resentments

  ♦ How you can make amends with those you wounded. Making amends is important but we don't want to do more harm through the amends process.

2. Our subconscious mind makes no distinctions between constructive or destructive thoughts. Whatever thoughts we feed our minds, it accepts them and grows them. Your subconscious mind also recognizes and acts upon thoughts that have been marked with emotion and feeling. So, how do you use this information to reprogram your subconscious?

   - Decide what you want. Are you ready to choose peace instead of stress, gratitude instead of anxiety, and love instead of worry? You must have clarity on what you want in your life.

   - Commit to reprogramming your subconscious mind by ridding it of doubt and fear. You must refuse to let these two weaknesses have any room in your mind.

   - Embrace the beauty of uncertainty. You have no power over all of life, but you *do* control your mind, your actions, and your reactions.

3. Think of reprogramming your subconscious as threefold: Thinking, Feeling, and Believing.

   - Begin with a snapshot in your mind of who you currently are, and then imagine yourself achieving the goal. Be specific in what you're going to become—not just with the end in mind—but see yourself as your life unfolds and you become that person.

   - As you envision the change—don't just see it—but feel what you'd experience as that person. Allow the feeling to enter your mind and flow through you as you envision the self of the future. Recognize that feeling and become familiar with it.

   - After thinking and feeling comes doing—it's time to put your envisioned self into action. The power to create is in the present. Always. Repeat this flow often and throughout the day. As you drift off to sleep, let your mind focus on the future self you are creating. Smile at the daydreams. Feel it. Your subconscious mind will begin to feed on that food as you sleep.

4. Your subconscious mind is like a computer hard drive. Just as we can erase and put new software into a hard drive, we can reprogram the data in your subconscious mind. It is very easy to do. In fact, the technique is so simple, you might think, *is that it*? Here goes: the best and most effective technique to alter your negative subconscious mind patterns is **awareness**. That's right. Once you become aware of the messages you feed your subconscious, you can reprogram the messages. Subsequently, the additional principles of Thought Practice will flow more naturally.

5. Experiences and circumstances tend to repeat themselves and reappear in our lives until we learn the lessons they intend to teach us. If you feel a sense of déjà vu about certain situations, ask yourself what happened. Do not judge or console yourself by building a story around it. Stick to the facts and then ask: What

did I do or think that brought this into my life? What lesson does the universe want to teach me? Check with intimate friends and ask them what they believe these recurring circumstances are trying to teach you. Identify your emotions in these situations without assigning blame to others.

6. Your inner picture shows how you foresee your life and what kind of person you want to be. To achieve your desired future, you must first see it through the application of Thought Practice. Find a quiet place where you won't be disturbed. Now close your eyes and take a few deep, relaxing breaths. Choose a higher energy such as love, peace, encouragement, honesty, kindness, abundance, expansion, receptivity, or beauty. Imagine yourself in your day-to-day life *being* that chosen higher energy. Specifics are very important here. What do you see? What do you feel? What do you hear? How do you respond to people and situations in that higher energy? Visualize yourself feeling happy and energized. Smile. When you are ready to return to your day, come out of your visualization the same way you entered by taking several deep, conscious breaths. When you are ready, open your eyes, give thanks, smile, and go about your day with that vision at the forefront of your mind.

7. Remember, no one else can do it for you. The good news is that Thought Practice is so intimate and unique to each of us and that you are the only expert on your own heart and mind who can transform your life. That is exciting. Who knows you better than you know you? The way you apply the principles and practices is unique to you and holds the power to transform your life experience. As you embark on the week ahead, write down three practices you will make part of your day. For example:

    • Start each day with the visualization, choosing the same higher energy for each day this week.

- Select one traumatic event from your past and choose to see it each day as a gift. Note the good things that came into your life as a result. Forgive the perpetrator and let go of all resentments.

- Treat the people at work, even those who irritate you, with love and compassion.

- End each day with the pre-sleep visualization, daydreaming until you fall asleep to reprogram your subconscious.

NOTHING TO PROVE

"Whatever we have to be is what we are."
—Thomas Merton

I WANT TO INVITE you to rearrange your thoughts about who you are. This will help cultivate the infinite aspect of who you are. Your eternal being and your soul all help to release the creative energy that flows through you. Ultimately, this culminates in your Thought Practice as an absolute knowing that whatever you need will come to you in the right form and time. Living in the law of abundance means that thoughts of shortage or lack are not a part of your thinking and perspective on life. You will then begin to expect that what you imagine for yourself is not only on its way; it's already here. Unfortunately, many of us have lived a good portion of our lives, having not seen the traffic sign of the universe saying, "Wrong way."

Several years ago, I was driving with Kevin, a good friend of mine, in the Bay Area. Kevin and I always enjoyed deep and thoughtful conversations. So, it was not uncommon for me to be deep in thought with him when we spoke. We came to a four-way intersection, and I came to a stop in the far-left turn lane. I was the first person at the intersection. We chatted, and I looked up, waiting for the light to turn green. We talked for several minutes. Cars were coming and going on each of the four points of the intersection. People honked and waved me forward. I was not going to break the law and run a red light, so I politely declined and waved them forward. I commented several times on the length of the light, to which Kevin only smiled.

Unfortunately, many of us have lived a good portion of our lives, having not seen the traffic sign of the universe saying, "Wrong way."

Finally, I noticed something to my left.

A stop sign. I looked at Kevin and said, *"What's a stop sign doing at an intersection with a traffic light?"* He smiled and said, *"There's no traffic light. It's a four-way stop."* I was so deep in thought that I assumed there was a stoplight that wasn't there. That's how many of us live our lives. We wait at self-imposed, non-existence red lights. Now you know the basics:

Thoughts are things.

- Thoughts have energy.
- Thoughts are magnetic.
- You control the programming of your subconscious.
- You choose what thoughts you have.

Now you are aware of lazy thinking and the pitfalls of living life with lazy thoughts. It's your choice and only your choice to engage your Thought Practice and live the life that you've always wanted. One of the changes you will notice early on is that as you flex the muscle of your mind, you will see an increase in synchronicity or coincidences in your life.

The universe uses everything for your eventual good, if you allow it. Everything that comes across your path is an opportunity. Everything and everyone that presents in your life is a teacher. Changing your thoughts to accept that everyone and everything can be an opportunity for you to learn and bless others can ultimately transform your perspective on life.

You will notice coincidences lining up in perfect symmetry in your life. Events that seemed to be unconnected become interconnected in their alignment and timing. With your Thought Practice aligned with the universe's higher energies, you will even begin to create these situations and connections. Then one day, you will know deep in your soul that you are the co-creator of your life along with God. You no longer see yourself as a victim of haphazard circumstances. Not everything that happens to us is good. However, there is a good that can come from the circumstances of our life as we embrace our healing journey.

As part of your growing Thought Practice, begin to look for and say yes to meaningful coincidences. Visualize in your mind a clear picture of something you want to bring about. It can be a new attitude you wish to adopt, something you want to create, an opportunity you'd like, or anything else that you want to manifest into your life. You need to form a clear picture in your mind. Very clear.

Hold your inner focus on what you pictured and send energies of love and attraction to it, smiling and feeling the love as you do so. You should send this love as frequently as possible. If doubts peek into your mind, don't give them any energy. Simply stop those thoughts and replace them immediately with the thoughts of love, attraction, and faith that it will happen. As you flex this muscle of your Thought Practice, you become proficient at keeping your energy on what you are manifesting. As you live in love, kindness, and honesty, you will attract coincidences that complement your desires. As you notice these coincidences aligning in your life, you will find yourself growing in awe and anticipation. As your awe and anticipation increases, you will begin to see the beauty in the interconnectedness.

Think of it like this: You take your six-year-old on their dream trip to visit Disneyland. During the trip, your child is sullen, disinterested, uncommunicative, and disengaged from you. Once you return home, you ask them how it was for them, and they respond with a shrug. They do not express any appreciation for the trip—or any love for your generosity. How do you feel about the trip? How would you feel about saving for another trip to bless them next year?

Now, take the same scenario, but the child is full of engagement, wonder, and presence during the trip and repeatedly says, "Thank you." They throw their arms around you at the end of the trip, squeeze as hard as their little arms can, and exclaims, "Thank you, thank you, thank you!" How do you feel about the trip? How would you feel about saving for another trip to bless them next year? The universe operates in a similar fashion. Remember the boomerang? We reap what we sow which is aligned to our energies of gratitude, appreciation, and love.

As your Thought Practice expands, you will have an increase in your love, appreciation, and gratitude for God and for life. The feeling of love will permeate your thoughts, attracting more of what you are putting out. The love will overflow in your life, filling your thoughts with purpose.

As you focus on the higher energies of love, honesty, kindness, intention, attraction, generosity, and gratitude, you will begin to receive more of those energies into your life and surroundings. With practice, your Thought Practice will find a cadence and rhythm that becomes a source of strength in your daily life. The mystery of life continues, but you will live in the experience of accepting guidance and live with a heart full of spiritual nourishment. You will see a rise in your desire to do what is right and to make amends for the pain you have contributed to others. Your Thought Practice will build upon itself and release increased fruit into your life.

As your Thought Practice matures and deepens, you will find yourself living more authentically than ever before. You no longer have difficulty being yourself. You learn that a life lived authentically leads to deeper universal truths, heightened awareness, and an increase in the flow of blessings into your life. You will accept yourself knowing that whatever behaviors you exhibited in the past were who you used to be. Even those that were destructive or immoral were a part of who you were at that time. You will no longer be able to compromise who you are. Some folks will self-select out of your life, and that is okay. Let them go with a blessing. In radically accepting yourself, you will see a decline in defensiveness in your life because your inner knowing is healthy.

It was surprising to me as I embarked on Thought Practice to see how I intuitively became healthier physically, emotionally, spiritually, and intellectually. Evidence of your inner healing includes being less judgmental, more forgiving, and more understanding of yourself and others. Maturing in your Thought Practice erases judgmental tendencies as you recognize that others are at their own place on the sacred path. You will come to understand that judging others says very little about them and a tremendous amount about you. You accept others on their very own path.

The qualities of others that previously irked you come to be seen as reflections of gaps in your own life. As Carl Jung put it, "Everything that irritated us about others can lead us to an understanding of ourselves." I was shocked at how judgmental I was for a person who prided myself on non-judgment. The result was tranquility and peace. These are natural fruits of our realigning with universal attraction and intention in our Thought Practice.

> **"Everything that irritated us about others can lead us to an understanding of ourselves."**
> **—Carl Jung**

Part of the healing of our mind and living in a vibrant Thought Practice is counterintuitive to us.

Thought Practice is all about proactively choosing your thoughts and harnessing the accompanying energies. However, Thought Practice is also about letting the world unfold without attempting to control it all or figure it out. It is trusting the Divine and trusting that everything will work out without your controlling and forcing. It's living in a state of allowing instead of finagling to make things work. It's recognizing that some of your thoughts are about how you think your world should be rather than accepting how it is. Becoming open-minded is a big part of Thought Practice.

Many people live in a ready defense of their opinions. That determination of your ego serves no purpose in your Thought Practice. To grow and harness this powerful tool, you will find yourself living in a state of allowing. Allowing life to unfold naturally in the appointed time. Allowing others to be themselves on their journey. You will find yourself accepting what comes your way as part of the plan and looking for the lessons and opportunities within the unfolding. It's living without labeling, explaining, or defending. It's a subtle shift at first, and you have to accept responsibility to identify it moment by moment.

It's both effort and non-effort at the same time. It's an effort to control your thoughts and choose what thoughts you allow to take seed in your mind. It's a non-effort in letting the universe unfold your path each step of the way. It is an effort without attachments. Non-effort may sound like a prescription for laziness, but this is not about laziness, inactivity, lack of planning, or abandoning purposefulness. It is about losing control of our ego over things that we have no authority over, so the higher energies can guide us. It's about trust. Proverbs 21:31 in the Christian Scriptures reminds us that we do the preparatory work, but ultimately victory comes from God.

The ego is a huge part of our lives. It's essential for those of us drawn to Thought Practice to understand the ego if we want to quit living in anxiety. The ego's job is to protect us from real and perceived threats. That is a good thing. Unfortunately, the ego is a poor judge of what differentiates danger from opportunity. It cannot tell the difference. As a result, the ego keeps us chained to the lower energies of the false self and fights against our living daily in the higher energies. We each allowed the ego to take leadership in our lives as a way of protecting ourselves. We adopted subconscious ego protections to guide us. It starts early.

When I was very young, about four or five, I remember my mom's dear friend commenting on how handsome my brother was. She turned to me and said, "Don't worry, you're funny, so you'll do fine in life." Notice that she didn't say I wasn't handsome. But my young ego heard that as something to defend.

Throughout my life, I learned to use my senses of humor to deflect, flirt, negotiate, and connect. Nearly every time a woman has commented that she thought I was attractive, my subconscious immediately roared with a shout, "*LIAR!*" It is completely illogical, but it is protective.

Another example is what I learned about wisdom. In my mid-twenties, I was in a business meeting with experts in their field. I had an opinion on the topic at hand and shared my insight. One of the elders turned to me, paused, and then scanned the room. At the same time, he addressed me. "That is a common misunderstanding which I would have expected from someone who hadn't had the experience you've had, not from you." For years, I adopted a policy of ego protection that I did not share in meetings until everyone shared. Then if there was something missing from the discussion, I shared my thoughts. Over time people began to comment on how wise I was because of this practice. It wasn't wisdom; it was ego immaturity and protection.

Several years into my Thought Practice, I now share my opinions when appropriate, and others' comments no longer have the power to hurt me like they did. A few years into my Thought Practice, I was in a meeting and shared an opinion on the issue at hand. One of my colleagues responded dismissively and arrogantly. I smiled and replied to him, "You know I appreciate you killing that idea before we spent too much valuable time on a dead-end road. I appreciate it because I do not care if I am right. I care that WE are right as a team." I meant every word, and I felt nothing at that moment but the higher energies of love, peace, and gratitude.

How do you know if your ego is in an inappropriate place of leadership? Here are a few common signs your ego has been in the driver's seat of life:

- Do you have a desire to pull attention towards yourself by exaggerating your experiences?
- Do you rewrite history so that you are painted in a better light than you were? Maybe you state facts as you would have liked them to be rather than they were.
- Do you make up scenarios to save face?

Our ego uses all of these are methods to remain in control. It attempts to control how we want others to see us, how we want to see ourselves, and how we protect ourselves. It's an exhausting way to live, and it prevents us from living in peace and purpose.

Reminding yourself that you are not in charge helps keep the ego in its proper place in our lives. Putting your ego aside in your Thought Practice is simple. It's as simple as telling your ego that you will trust in the loving power that created the universe rather than your self-indulgent assessments for how you want things to be right now. Each day practice letting go and seeing where you're directed. Take note of who shows up—and when and how. Observe the strange coincidences that seem to collaborate to steer you in a new direction. Notice situations that occur spontaneously and out of your influence. When you begin to put your ego in its place, it will use one of its most potent influencers to try and regain control over your life. Self-doubt.

It is easy for many of us to dismiss the effect that self-doubt can have in our life. The insidious nature of self-doubt allows it to become thoroughly intertwined into our belief system. When ego is in control of our life, we can see the evidence by our doubts manifesting to stop before we start. The doubt comes out in thoughts like the following:

- If only I were this or that
- I am too much of this or not enough of that
- It would be easier if I did not have to
- I could never

And many other thoughts that limit us or prevent magic before it ever had the chance to begin. Be on guard for the attack of self-doubt. When self-doubt is banished, we come to a knowing that leads to creative and inspired solutions far beyond what we believed was possible. The more you are on guard to the roadblock of self-doubt, the more you will live in the higher energies. I want to be clear on the issue of self-doubt. You will need to deliberately and actively work at banishing self-doubt from your inner world as well as Thought Practice. When self-doubt rears its ugly head, stop. Stop the thought and replace it with accurate, intentional thoughts about your value and worth. Remember: *As you think, so shall you be.* Permitting self-doubt a seat at the table of your mind allows a traitor to be on the leadership team of your life. Self-doubt leads to a form of imprisonment by keeping us a slave to the ego.

If self-doubt keeps us imprisoned, irrational fear is the guard of that prison. What would you do if you were never afraid? What would you attempt if you knew you couldn't fail? God is not about fear. Bringing this pure awareness into consciousness will help you to banish this doubt and fear from your life. When you are afraid of experiencing uncertainty, stop those thoughts and replace them with thoughts of truth. Everything you do produces results. Some results are what you intended, while others are not. If you learn from them and adjust and grow, you didn't fail. Labeling yourself as a failure is meaningless and serves no positive purpose to transform your life. When you are doing the work of living in the higher energies and your Thought Practice, you are living purposefully and can experience newfound freedom.

To be live a life of freedom, let go of the ego's hold on you. You can do that by:

- **Stop being offended by pettiness.** The person is merely expressing opinions out of their ego wounds; it has nothing to do with you unless you engage with your ego.

- **Let go of needing to be right in non-consequential discussions.** Who cares which dish soap is best or what online stores have the best this or that. Going to google to prove a movie quote or sports statistic is a waste of energy.

- **Practice contentment and appreciation for what you have.** Let go of your need for more. More stuff. More territory. More, more, more. You will discover that oftentimes, less truly is more.

- **Quit introducing yourself by your occupation and achievements.** Just let go of your reputation. Who cares what anyone else thinks of you.

- **Cease being judgmental of yourself and others.** When you notice thoughts of harsh judgment, stop them, and do your Thought Practice. Replace them with thoughts of love, kindness, and gratitude.

All five of these obsessions of the ego will evaporate as you quit feeding them and refuse to give them attention. The more you consistently starve these thoughts and feed higher energy thoughts, you will notice your stress, anxiety, and worry decreasing. Your joy, contentment, and peace are growing. Perhaps you are familiar with these statements, "Do not give in to petty problems; don't worry about insignificant matters." And, "Don't sweat the small stuff and it's all small stuff."

One of the most common tactics of the ego is to create and then feed off stress and anxiety. Thomas Merton once remarked, "Stress and anxiety is the mark of spiritual insecurity." A result of effective Thought Practice is a more stress-free and tranquil life as you manifest your purpose. Stress is a tool of the ego. Living in stress can trick us into feeling like we are doing something when—in reality—our negativity, worry, anxiety, and stress do nothing to solve our issues.

There are many reasons we choose to embrace, welcome, and invite stress into our life. For me, it was an addiction. I lived in fear and felt unworthy. This increased my stress and anxiety. When I felt stressed, I felt important because I had things to be stressed about.

Perhaps stress is a habit, a custom, an expectation, or a belief on your part. The fact is stress is familiar to the ego, and peace is unfamiliar, so the ego craves and creates stress. If you stop the thoughts and inner dialogue of negativity and stress, you will eliminate stress' physical symptoms in your life. Instead choose the peace in your life that passes understanding.

Choosing to bring Thought Practice to the presence of your stress is a crucial decision. On any given day, you have hundreds of opportunities to choose your thoughts and eliminate the potential for unnecessary stress. When you notice stress-producing incidents in your day, you always have a choice. Do I stay with the thoughts that produce anxiety, or do I choose fresh thoughts to overcome this downward spiral? The choice is yours and only yours. You can avoid the downward spiral of stress from your life by engaging in a consistent Thought Practice. You live in a universe that has limitless potential for joy built into the process of living.

Stressful thoughts and uneasy feeling are an indicator on the dashboard of life.

Stressful thoughts and uneasy feelings are an indicator on the dashboard of life. They can (a) indicate areas of inner resistance and hard-fought control you are holding onto or (b) they can indicate that attention is needed to an issue that requires thoughtful alertness. Spend time in calm silence to determine whether you are dealing with your ego or a legitimate warning.

Like anything else, you will get better and better at this the more you commit to Thought Practice as a regular part of your life. Remember, nature abhors a vacuum. When you ruminate in stressful thoughts of worry and anxiety, you leave no room for thoughts and feelings of joy, peace, and contentment. This happens when you allow thoughts such as:

- *I cannot*
- *It will never happen*
- *I am too this or not enough of that*
- *I am afraid, etc.*

These thoughts become like a computer program, which will result in stress and anxiety in your life. However, you can also choose to activate thoughts that make stress impossible in your life. Would you like to live a life free of anxiety and stress and full of peace and joy? The choice is yours and only yours.

Your thoughts trigger stressful reactions to the conditions of your life. Stressful thoughts create resistance to joy, peace, and mindfulness. Stop unhealthy tapes from playing in your mind that ultimately prevent you from manifesting your desires. Instead, program your mind's computer to live in tranquility and purpose.

When you are faced with the choice to be right or be kind, be kind, and you will be right. Choosing kindness doesn't mean that we validate others' opinions. It does mean that we differentiate between our ego and living in the higher energies. Living in kindness is not about pleasing or placating others; it's all about what's happening inside ourselves in those altercations. Your ego whines and pushes to be right, but it is usually at the subtle expense of another. When you choose to be kind instead of right, you eliminate the possibility of stress in that moment of kindness. The more you do this, the more comfortable and more natural it will become for you. Your ego will resist your Thought Practice because it knows it's losing control. Remember, your ego is designed to protect you, and it fears the loss of control. The shape and frequency of your ego's demands will create the intensity of the resistance you feel to your Thought Practice. It is a little different for everyone. However, you can determine resistance easily.

Thoughts that generate stressful or bad feelings are resistant. Any thought that creates a barrier between what you would like to have—and your ability to attract that into your life—is resistance. Giving your opinion and trying to convince others that your opinion is the correct one is a resistance thought. Putting down another's opinion is a resistant thought. We may do this frequently with sports teams. We razz and put down a friend's team just because it's not a team we like. All of these opinions, assaults, and defenses are ego based. We all know people with an insecure need to be right. How much do you enjoy being around those people? Sometimes what we are talking about is far more important than a favorite sports team; so, the power here is living kindly while you discuss instead of arguing. The key determinant is if you find yourself in an ego defense.

Your ego is a demanding force that is never satisfied. It wants you to continually seek more money, power, security, acquisitions, and prestige. These are the fuel that it feasts on. The more you pursue appeasing the ego's hunger, the more peace and contentment allude to you. However, when you live life through your Thought Practice and allow life to unfold and come to you, you will find peace and fulfillment. Try letting life come to you, and you will notice the clues of what you crave is on its way to you. Let go of your attachment to your stuff and accomplishments. Try instead to enjoy what you do and all that flows into your life. Come to the realization that you own nothing. Nothing.

You are a steward of certain possessions, but they will go to someone else when you physically leave the earth. Most people cannot name all our presidents, celebrities of generations past, or all of history's heroes. People are not generally remembered for their ego satisfaction. People are remembered by those whom they loved and were loved by. Remember that your ego makes up a tiny portion of your mind but has adopted the role of the boss with the lie that your physical life is what is most import-ant. It's from this role as the boss that your ego breeds toxic emotional behaviors and reactions. People do not want to be around toxicity. They may not be able to identify why they don't want to be around you, but they know they don't. So, they self-select out of your life or engage minimally. However, if you cultivate your Thought Practice and live in the higher energies, you will become an attractor to others in your life. They will naturally be drawn to you.

When you live in the higher energies of your Though Practice, your presence will begin to instill a sense of attraction in others. They will want to be around you. Living authentically in the higher energies of optimism, forgiveness, understanding, honesty, creativity, and kindness will draw others to you. When you are living in the higher energies and consistent in your Thought Practice, you will notice that people are affected by you and the energy you radiate. This is true with everyone, from the barista at Starbucks to your family. As you become more proficient with Thought Practice, you'll see your dreams fulfilled almost magically, and you'll see yourself creating ripples in the energy field of others. Your new way of seeing will enable others in your presence to feel comforted and peaceful. Indirectly, these folks will become loving accomplices to your connection.

Living authentically in the higher energies of optimism, forgiveness, understanding, honesty, creativity, and kindness will draw others to you.

As you review the universal attributes of Thought Practice and simultaneously work to implement those attributes in your life, you begin to see the significance of what you desire for others. It's been said if you want to be at peace, be peace. If you wish peace for others, you'll then receive it as you live peace. If you see beauty and worthiness in others instead of irritation, you become beautiful and worthy. You can only give what you have in your heart; you attract what you give away. Transformation begins when you live the higher energies in real-time throughout your day through your Thought Practice. You choose your thoughts.

CHAPTER 5 EXERCISES

These chapter exercises are designed to help you apply the principles of TRANFORMATIONAL THINKING in meaningful and transformative ways or you. They are not designed that one should do all the exercises for each chapter. Record the notes from the chapter, the exercise you are doing, and the results in your notebook.

1. Remember, there are no idle thoughts. Thoughts are palpable things charged with energy; they are magnetic. And you control them by programing the hard drive that is your subconscious mind. You choose your thoughts. By maintaining a vibrant Thought Practice, you connect your thoughts to energies. Approach your day without being critical and judgmental towards yourself or others. When critical, judgmental thoughts emerge, learn to transform them with ludicrously lavish thoughts of love, compassion, and understanding. Notice that your lazy mind judges far more often than you might realize. Transforming critical, judgmental energy will exponentially increase your peace. Capture in your notebook your experiences of transforming judgmental thoughts with thoughts of compassion.

2. We are often lost in our thoughts throughout our day-to-day lives. The goal is to detach from your thoughts for a few moments and watch them as a neutral observer. This practice can help you become aware of negative thought patterns. You will find yourself

questioning your beliefs, thereby weakening negative thoughts and consciously replacing them with those of higher energy.

- Here's what you can do: sit comfortably, take a few deep breaths, and calm yourself down. Take the time to observe your mind as it produces thoughts, but don't let yourself engage with them. If you do find yourself replying to those ideas, take a second to recognize that and get back to quietly watching.

- If you feel strong emotions bubbling up inside you, acknowledge them instead of trying to suppress them. It's okay to listen to your body as you feel the energy and intention behind those thoughts. But continue to observe them as they emerge from your brain, and you will start to see negative thought patterns that power some of them. Simply becoming conscious of these patterns is enough for them to begin crumbling.

3. The trouble with confirmation bias is that you knowingly filter the information you are willing to pay attention to. So, not only do you actively look for signs that confirm your current views, but you question any information that opposes your viewpoint. This can be dangerous. Confirmation bias can be particularly challenging to identify. Following are steps that will help:

- When you disagree with someone, suspend your disagreement and hear them out. When they are done, don't defend your view or discredit their view. Instead, look for areas where they may be right and where you could grow from accepting their opinion. You see, confirmation bias is a disease that plagues your ego. We hate to be wrong, and we are desperate for others to validate our position. Prioritize truth over being right because if you ignore the truth too many times, you'll be proven wrong sooner or later.

- Nurture an environment where it is okay to disagree. Asking others, "Am I right?" will likely only get those who approve of you to speak up. You'll get better answers with a question like, "Why am I wrong?"

- Constantly seek alternate views and opinions in print, on TV, and in person. That might mean visiting websites, reading newspapers, and watching shows that you previously avoided. Remember, seek the truth and not evidence that you're right.

4. Let go of the need to be right. Who cares which dish soap is better or what online stores offer the best deals. Going to Google just to prove a movie quote or sports stat is a waste of energy. This level of ego defense does not endear you to others or help them in their life. It's petty and a waste of time and energy. The exercise here is simply to let it go. Let go of your need to be right. At home, it's more important that you and your spouse make the right decisions for your family, not that you are right more times than they are. At work, it is more important that the team make the right decision for the business, not that you are always right. Letting go of the need to be right makes life a lot more peaceful, and the irony is that others will respect you more.

5. Thought Practice is all about changing yourself, not others. If you often feel offended, it can be challenging to change your mindset. Very few people who have mastered living in the higher energies get easily offended. Choosing to change ourselves requires humility, open-mindedness, and keeping our ego in check.

- Consider what triggers you to feel offended. Often taking offense to a person or a situation is a choice.

- Ask yourself what you are really reacting to. Often, we can get easily triggered because we let assumptions—or our unhealed wounds—color our perceptions of others. Perhaps you are making an unfounded assumption when you claim to know other people's motivations.

- So, where do these assumptions come from? Take a long, hard look at your relationship with yourself. If your ego gets bruised easily and you often feel defensive, perhaps others are not to blame. Your own insecurities and mistrust of self can you behave this way. Are you hurt because you allow others to inform how you feel about yourself? Consider that not everyone is being deliberately malicious toward you. Perhaps we are misreading the room.

- Question the influence of your past. Another major trigger is seeing a behavior or hearing a phrase that reminds us of a negative experience, thus offending us. We associate specific actions with pain even if the person doing it means no harm. Just seeing them do those things is enough to put us on the defensive.

- Write out your values. Journal your values to determine which problems you really consider worthwhile. This will help you figure out what's worth raising a fuss about and what can be released and forgotten. Additionally, having a stronger sense of your values will help you feel less threatened when they are challenged. Trusting your values makes others' opinions less important.

6. One of the gifts of a vibrant Thought Practice is the ability to choose to live in a state of contentment. This week, flex your muscle of contentment by practicing these three steps every day:

- Be grateful even when things go awry. Instead of bemoaning the circumstances, be thankful for the lessons you have learned and those you will learn. Welcome the opportunity to solve a dilemma; also welcome the gift of being at peace.

- Stop comparing yourself with others. In the 12-step program, it has been said that comparison leads to despair. This is true. Their journey is theirs, and yours is yours. Refuse to get sucked into the trap of keeping up with the Joneses.

- Live your life in the here and now. Refuse to indulge thoughts of if / when or if / only as they serve only to keep you in a state of fear and unrest, creating anxiety and frustration.

7. Stop indulging in critical judgments about yourself and others. When you notice thoughts of judgment, stop them, and do your Thought Practice. Replace them with thoughts of love, kindness, and gratitude.

YOUR MOST IMPORTANT CONVERSATION

"Your self-talk is the channel for behavioral change."
—Gino Norris

ONE OF THE SIGNIFICANT gifts of a consistent Thought Practice is that we truly love ourselves and become the healthiest versions of ourselves. My journey in a 12-step recovery program and therapy informed the principles I am sharing on Transformational Thinking. Before that, I liked myself, but I did not love myself. I could not love myself, and no one else really could either. My self-talk was a reflection of my lack of love and it was atrocious. You may recall, when my therapist, Harry, and I began to explore my self-talk, he asked me to share some of the loops that played in my head for as long as I could recall. They were the following:

- Stupid!
- What is wrong with you?!
- Why would you say that?
- You idiot!

The list was much longer, and when I concluded, he paused, looked into my eyes, and asked me, "What would you do if someone spoke to one of your children that way?" Without thinking, I responded in a protective rant for my boys stating how no one would talk to them that way and how they were worthy of love and protection. When I was done, I was breathing hard. I was exhausted from protecting my lads against the attack of a non-existent foe. Again, in his wisdom, he asked, "Then, why would you talk to yourself that way?" Now I was mad. Harry has that effect on me sometimes. "I'm not talking to myself that way; those ideas are what I've heard for as long as I can remember. At some point, those voices became my voice!" That is the crux of self-talk for many of us. We adopt the voices of others as our own.

The voice of others, which I adopted as my own, was a significant problem in my lazy, unhealed thought life. The people who owned the voices of the past no longer recalled repeatedly saying those phrases to me. Some of these people were now dead. Others would not even remember that I was ever in their life. For most of my life, the tapes that played daily in my mind were mine. I was responsible for playing them and for allowing them a foothold in my life. You can argue that the abusers bear responsibility for their actions, and they do. But only I can be responsible for my own life and healing journey. Only you can be accountable for your life. Everyone in our life is a teacher. Everyone. Those who hurt us. Those who blessed us. Those who walked away and those who stayed. You will notice that the universe has a habit of bringing the same type of people and circumstances into your life until you learn the lesson you need to. Self-talk, accepting responsibility for our lives, and embracing the lessons we need to learn are all part of Thought Practice. The gift they give us is that we come to a point where we finally both like and love ourself. We have come to accept and appreciate who we are.

> **We adopt the voices of others as our own.**

Loving ourselves is activating spiritual solutions by converting inner thoughts and feelings from disharmony to love. You will start to see anger, judgmentalism, and discord as invitations to surrender to love. You will see them as warning lights letting you know ego is still in the driver's seat.

You will see them as doorways to taking responsibility for your thoughts, feelings, and life.

Awakening in your Thought Practice begins with a step Buddha called, *Right Understanding*. In fact, Right Understanding is at the beginning of the Buddhist eightfold path. In the context of our Thought Practice, Right Understanding means that we understand how the universe works. It means we accept the power of our minds, the energy, and the results our thoughts produce. Right Understanding means that we know and embrace that freedom of choice exists and is ours. Life is going to be what it is—sometimes pleasant—and other times, unpleasant. We will be thrilled and disappointed. We will live the expected and the unexpected. What a relief to know that whatever waves come our way, we can ride them with grace and excitement.

Loving ourselves is activating spiritual solutions by converting inner thoughts and feelings from disharmony to love.

When we get good at our Thought Practice, we can be like surfers, delighting in the most complicated waves. We gain this freedom when we translate our daily actions in the resolve to behave in ways that stretch the boundaries of our conditioned response. We can think of it in terms of weight training. If you want to build bigger biceps, you need to use every opportunity to practice lifting weight consistently and push yourself just beyond yesterday's capabilities. If you are going to live in loving, kind, and fearless ways, you need to practice eliminating the tendencies to be angry, rude, and afraid. Life is a terrific gym for Thought Practice training. Every situation every day is an opportunity to practice and become more and more skilled.

A great place to practice this is in the area of forgiveness. This applies both to forgiving ourselves and forgiving others. Forgiveness is the price you pay for freedom. Forgiving others is a key component of loving ourselves. Perhaps, you've heard others say something like, "I am never going to forgive so and so." What a terrible choice they are making. The other person has already hurt them. They are now planning to continue the hurt long after the event by enshrining it in memory, reliving it repeatedly. The image that often comes to mind is from the Westerns of the 1950s. The Sherriff puts the town drunk in a jail cell and shuts the door but doesn't lock it. The joke is that the prisoner shouts and rattles the bars of the cell, and all of us know he only needs to turn the handle to get out.

Some of us live one step beyond rattling the bars. Instead of rescuing ourselves, we maintain our position of righteous indignation by recounting and reliving our grievances and hurts. It's the equivalent of having the key to the cell in our hand, reaching through the bars and locking ourselves in, and then throwing the key across the room. Remaining a prisoner or enjoying freedom both start with the right understanding and then using our Thought Practice to live it out.

Our thoughts and our speech matter. Jesus Christ and the Buddha both taught that our thoughts and speech are critical and must be managed carefully. Today, start to speak to yourself like you would another person you love and cherish. Words are potent. Words are powerful. The old nursery rhyme, "Sticks and stones may break my bones, but words will never hurt me," is complete hogwash. Far more people limp through life wounded by words than by

Today, start to speak to yourself like you would another person you love and cherish.

physical violence. More people carry baggage from words than sticks and stones.

We are obliged to tell the truth but should be mindful of doing so in such a manner as not to cause more harm. Telling the truth to ourselves and others is a form of love and care. Almost every major religious leader taught that we should be honest, kind, truthful, and helpful. When correcting someone, we can choose to do it fast and loose, or we can consider where the other person is and how best to communicate with them. One way to do this is to check our motives. If we respond out of frustration, our speech could tear the other down instead of building them up. We want to make suggestions in a way the other person can receive them. Otherwise, we are wasting our energy and likely causing more harm to the other person.

Remember, words have power and thoughts are things. Words carry thoughts. Never forget that. Right speech simplifies our lives because we will have less clean up and repairing to do. James Russell Lowell observed, "Light is the symbol of truth." Conversely, darkness is the symbol of deceit. You can hide the truth in the dark while in the light, there are no hidden things; everything is revealed. Darkness conceals what light reveals. When you bring light into darkness, you bring an attitude of openness that does not allow fear of exposure. There is no fear of exposure because you have nothing to hide.

As you cultivate your natural self through your Thought Practice, you will begin to live more authentically with who you are. As you start listening to your higher self, you start relaxing, and the pressure lifts and fades. You eliminate harmful thinking patterns and destructive self-talk. You realize people do not need to be controlled or dominated by your opinions. Others are not obligated to live up to your expectations or abide by your wishes. Their choices do not determine your peace and happiness.

One way you can live in this freedom is to change the self-talk tapes to the voice of gratitude. You can change your life by consciously choosing to live in a state of gratitude. Life will shift as you emphasize all you are grateful for in your life. Be grateful for all you are instead of dwelling on what you're not or wish you were. Be grateful for all you have accomplished rather than living in angst for what you have not completed. Be grateful for those who are in your life and the opportunity to love them. Do not dwell on those who chose to leave your life. Express gratitude by surfing the wave of life and allow it to be your ally rather than fighting it. This is true for every aspect of your life. The more you push against it, the more resistance you create. Living in a state of gratitude can turn tragedies into triumphs.

Pain can be a great teacher. Life can be difficult and painful, and it is okay to admit it. Amidst the pain and difficulties, you can still be genuinely happy and at peace. Pain is inevitable; deep ongoing suffering is optional. Suffering often comes when we struggle and fight the wave of what life brings rather than accepting and living open to the lessons these circumstances have for us. We suffer when we struggle with our circumstances and refuse to choose our thoughts and embrace the lessons the universe yearns to teach us. When we accept pain as an inevitable aspect of life, we can decrease our suffering.

Too many of us try to control the present, thinking it will somehow ensure our satisfaction with the future. But life is always changing. Ram Dass said, "We should make friends with change." Perhaps we should also make friends with the pain as a teacher and an avenue to personal growth. When faced with difficulties, remember our ego tends to blow up the pain to be much worse than it is by future tripping, living in righteous indignation, and trying to control the narrative. Let it go. We cannot control all aspects of life, other people, and nature.

Seeing pain as a teacher and as a gift will transform your life. Living in peace for the difficult lessons life is teaching can ease the journey. It's an important part of Thought Practice because we all experience pain in our life. And because we all experience pain, the transformation of your pain is part of learning to love yourself.

Although pain can be a teacher, we should not minimize the pain of others. Every pain is difficult to the person experiencing it. We need not evaluate the pain of others by comparing it to our experience. We are all sojourners experiencing the mysteries and ups and downs of life. If someone says you hurt them, you don't get to decide you didn't.

As you practice living in the higher energies within your Thought Practice, you will see your thoughts' magnetic attraction. As you learn to love from a place of healing and health, you will notice more love coming into your life. You will attract into your life all that you are thinking and manifesting. To accomplish this, notice your thoughts that create resistance to the higher energies of love, gratitude, and expectation. When your self-talk begins to focus on lack, stress, and anger, stop those thoughts.

Just stop them.

There is no magic trick to this. Just stop those thoughts. Mid thought. No explanation or saying, "I shouldn't think this way about myself." Just stop. Then replace those thoughts with thoughts of intentionality, accuracy, and attraction. The more you practice, the more you will notice others experiencing calm and peace in your presence.

The power of your loving energy puts them at ease. As people feel the higher energies of love, peace, kindness, and truth in your presence, they will feel safe. When you are living in the higher energies of self-love, your presence soothes and energizes others. People feel better about themselves.

Have you ever been around others that made you feel better when you were just in their presence? Did you like to be around them? I would wager that they were not negative, angry, frenetic, and stressful people. I would be willing to bet that they were mature, calm, loving, kind, and honest people living in the higher energies.

People will have a deep sense that they genuinely care about them. They are less likely to focus the conversation on themselves, nor will they use you to massage their ego. Most of us don't want to be around people who are frenetic, stressed, anxious, and living in the lower energies making comments at our expense. They leave us feeling insignificant.

Once my Thought Practice hit the tipping point and became more of a habit than a struggle of embracing a new skill, my boundaries became naturally healthy. The boundaries were a seamless extension of loving myself. The higher energy of love has interesting effects on our lives. You will notice that those who live in the higher energies, due to the Thought Practice, bring something to others. Your presence magnetically attracts others through love, acceptance, and wisdom. Your presence becomes a catalyst for others to heal. By living in the higher energies, you radiate warmth which benefits others. It's natural and saturates others with a positive energy they may not be able to describe. As your Thought Practice grows, your self-love increases your love for others as well.

As you continue to change your thoughts, you will see your life change. You will become the higher energy attributes of love, optimism, wisdom, kindness, understanding, truth-telling, and peace. As you begin to live in these higher energies, you will want those attributes for others. As you see others with kindness, truth, understanding, and compassion, you will see them as worthy thereby decreasing your spirit of judgmentalism. Remember, you can only give

> **As you continue to change your thoughts, you will see your life change.**

away what you have, so how can you love and accept others fully if you don't love and accept yourself?

Our self-talk or inner speech is a significant component of Thought Practice. Self-talk is the most important conversation you will have in your journey of Transformational Thinking. Transformation requires honesty, consistency, and persistence. It will take time to reprogram old habits and let go of thoughts that do not serve you any longer. These old thought patterns have been around a lot longer than you have been trying to change them. Time takes time so be patient with yourself.

CHAPTER 6 EXERCISES

These chapter exercises are designed to help you apply the principles of TRANFORMATIONAL THINKING in meaningful and transformative ways for you. They are not designed that one should do all the exercises for each chapter. Record the notes from the chapter, the exercise you are doing, and the results in your notebook.

1. One exercise that can eliminate lazy self-talk is making lists. In your notebook, make a three-column page.

   - In the first column, write down the specific phrase that is part of your negative self-talk.

     ♦ *You said the exact wrong thing to your friend when she asked for your opinion, because you never think before you open your mouth.*

     ♦ *You dominated the conversation. No wonder everyone thinks you are a loudmouth.*

     ♦ *You are an idiot.*

     ♦ *What is wrong with you?*

And on and on. Usually, the loops return to the same half a dozen phrases for most of us. The phrases may be unique, but the patterns are not.

   - In the second column, write the cognitive distortions—no matter how many there are. In the examples we're using, there are at least four: overgeneralizing things, jumping to conclusions too quickly, all-or-nothing thinking, and mental filter. Others include "should" statements and labeling.

- In the third column, write a statement counteracting the lazy, negative thought. For example:

  ♦ Instead of saying, "*You said the exact wrong thing to your friend when she asked for your opinion because you never think before you open your mouth.*" You could replace that with options such as, "*You don't know if you said the wrong thing; your intuition is usually correct.*" Follow up with your friend and explain that you were speaking out of love and concern, you intended to help, but you are concerned that you may not have communicated effectively. Ask them for their impression of the conversation.

  ♦ Instead of saying, "*You're an idiot!*" you can say statements such as: "*Everyone makes mistakes, and you are brilliant in the areas of XYZ.*" Then choose to dismiss and ignore those thoughts of stupidity when they resurface.

  ♦ Instead of saying, "*What's wrong with you?*" you can replace that with statements such as: "*Nothing is wrong with me. I really appreciate my XYZ, and the areas to be improved are my teachers.*"

2. Another step towards treating yourself better is to notice when you are self-critical. Many of us are so used to hearing that nagging little self-critical voice that we cannot hear the good things that others say about us. Don't do that to yourself. Whenever you feel bad about something, and that inner voice starts to say something mean, stop. Think about what you've just said to yourself. Write down that internal dialogue as accurately as possible. Now read it. What words did you use when being self-critical? Are there any phrases or insults that come up again and again? How do

you sound—cold, angry, or aloof? Do the words remind you of someone else who used to talk to you this way in the past? Learn as much as you can about this self-critic who hides within you.

3. Do your best to soften that inner critic. But be compassionate with it instead of being self-judgmental. That voice is you, so don't tell it that she's a bitch. Instead, tell it that she's causing you pain and making you feel unsafe.

4. Anytime you start to say something hurtful to yourself, acknowledge what you really mean by it and speak it in a positive way. Imagine what a compassionate and kind friend would say in that instant. Don't curse but use terms of endearment for yourself and envision feelings of warmth and care (and not in a schmaltzy way!).

5. Write down the phrases of lazy self-talk you use, and underneath each one, write an accurate thought that is positive and displays living in the higher energies of love, honesty, and compassion. Consider the following examples:

   - **Negative:** Everyone will be angry at me if I change my mind.
   - **Positive:** I am allowed to change my mind. People will understand.

   - **Negative:** I failed and got myself humiliated in front of others.
   - **Positive:** I am proud of myself for even trying.

   - **Negative:** I am fat, and I look weird. Why am I even trying?
   - **Positive:** My body is good to me. I should get healthier for me.

6. Positive self-talk is not a natural instinct for you if you have always been self-critical. But it's time we change that. It's possible to shift that inner dialogue to be more encouraging and productive.

However, like all new habits, getting in the flow of more positivity will take time. These tips may be helpful to you:

- **Recognize negative self-talk traps.** Certain situations may increase your self-doubt and lead to more destructive self-talk. Workplace events, for example, may be particularly challenging. Identifying the times when you experience the most negative self-talk can help you forestall and prepare the answers.

- **Register your feelings**. Stop and assess your self-talk on a predominantly difficult day. Is it becoming too harmful? How can you make this situation better?

- **Find the funny side.** Laughter can help get rid of worry and tension. When you need a pep talk for positive self-talk, find reasons to laugh, such as watching funny animal videos or a video of your favorite comedian.

- **Surround yourself with an optimistic crowd.** We all have the ability to mimic our surroundings. You can absorb the attitude and sentiments of people around you. This applies to negative and positive people, so select positive people.

- **Use positive affirmations.** Don't underestimate the power of a positive word or image. It's all you need to redirect your thoughts to better things. But we all know how hard it can be to do some positive self-talk when the negativity comes so easily. So, write down the positive affirmations on little post-it notes and put them in areas you frequently visit. Every time you come across one, read it, and you'll find yourself smiling a little more.

7. Self-forgiveness is an essential part of changing our lazy self-talk. But it is important to understand that self-forgiveness does *not* absolve us of personal responsibility. We must make amends and fix our conduct as needed. It's important here to clarify what self-forgiveness does not mean. It does not mean that everything

you've ever done is acceptable, perfectly okay, and without repercussions. Actions do have consequences. It does not mean that you have never made a mistake.

- Self-forgiveness is about offering compassion to your past self for the mistakes it made and paving the way for a better future because that's the only thing that we can do. Beating ourselves up and staying in shame is not helpful or constructive. Engaging the process of self-forgiveness begins with identifying your judgments.

- Judgmentalism turned inward are the statements that are causing you mental and emotional pain, and they are the things you hold against yourself. So, as an example, you might tell yourself that, "I should never have driven so fast and aggressively. That was so stupid of me." It is time to forgive that judgment. This may take several passes, like peeling the layers off an onion. The next step is to forgive the judgment that you hold against yourself. You might write, "I forgive myself for judging myself as stupid, and the truth is _____," and then you put in that blank what love, connection, and compassion would say about you.

- And maybe the truth is that you were doing the best you could in that moment, at that time. Perhaps the truth is that you were in a lot of pain, and you made a poor choice, and maybe the truth is that you've learned from it and that you're not the same person now that you were then. Play with it and see what feels true for you.

8. If you want to let happiness into your life, first, you'll have to make some space for it by letting go of things that make you sad. If your heart is filled with pain, it will be difficult to let in anything new. Here is what we suggest:

- **Decide to let go and stick to it.**

  ♦ The upsetting feelings in your heart won't vanish on their own. You must commit to letting them go; otherwise, you might end up self-sabotaging your conscious and subconscious effort to move on from a hurtful past. Being mindful about the decision to let go also means accepting that you have a *choice* to do it. It is possible to stop reliving the past pain, but you must stop yourself from reliving the painful stories and events of the past.

  ♦ The trigger could be a person or an event that automatically brings your pain to the forefront. It is time you learn to rise above that. It can be incredibly empowering to know that it is your choice to either hold on to the pain or live without it.

- **Express your pain—and accept your responsibility.**

  ♦ Yes! It is okay to express the pain you feel. Do whatever you need to do to get it out of your system. Talk to a friend; hire a therapist; fill out the pages in your journal; or write a letter to yourself as you make sense of the hurt that hides within your hearts. This will help drive out the pain as you also get a deeper understanding of it.

  ♦ The world isn't black and white; there's a lot of grey area in between. Similarly, not all blame can go out to others. While you may not be responsible for all the pain, some part could be attributed to you.

  ♦ Think about what you could have done differently to get a better outcome. What will happen if you are faced with the situation again? How will you handle it? Are you merely a victim or a hopeful participant in your own life? Don't let your pain become your only identity; you are so much more than that.

- **Stop being the victim and blaming others.**

  - ◆ It feels good to let go of all control and be a victim. It feels like you versus the world, and you are the winner. But here's a newsflash: The world doesn't care. Yes, you are special, and your feelings are important, but your feelings don't get to override everything else.

  - ◆ Your happiness is your responsibility. Do not give others the power to dictate your thoughts and feelings. Why would you let another person—one who hurt you in the past—dictate how you feel in this moment? No amount of contemplation can fix a severed relationship or turn back time. So why ruminate on events and people who have wronged you?

- **Focus on the present and the joy.**

  - ◆ Let go of the past and stop thinking of yourself as the forever victim to someone's horrible decisions and actions. Realize that you can't undo the past. However, you can move forward in your healing journey. So, do what you can to make today the best day ever. Divert your attention to the here and now, revel in the laughter and joy of those around you in this moment. When sad memories start to creep back into your consciousness, acknowledge them and tell them you are growing and healing. Then bring yourself gently back to the present.

  - ◆ Give yourself a conscious cue to stop living in the past every time you slip back into it. You can tell yourself, "It's fine. The past is past, and now I must live in the present where I can focus on my own happiness and do _____." Remember, you are just trying to make space in your mind for happiness and other good things. And for that, you must choose not to feel the hurt and instead welcome joy into your life.

- **Forgive them—and yourself.**

  ♦ It is not easy to forget someone's bad behavior and the consequences it has inflicted on your life. However, it is in your best interest to work toward forgiveness. Sometimes we get so overwhelmed in our pain that forgiveness requires the help of a therapist.

  ♦ It is crucial here to understand that forgiveness isn't a weakness. When you forgive the person who did you wrong, you are essentially saying that you are a good person and acknowledging that the person also has some goodness in them, which didn't quite come through when they hurt you. Now, you want to be over whatever happened then and open your heart up for better things. And to do that, it is essential to let go of the pain they caused.

  ♦ Forgiveness is a way to let go of all the bad so that you have the space in you to let in the good. It is the first step to moving on. When you forgive others, you give them a fighting chance to do better.

  ♦ This also applies to forgiving yourself. Sometimes we blame ourselves for a situation we hardly had any control over. There is no reason to keep beating yourself up over it either way.

  ♦ No one should ever be solely defined by the mistakes they make in life. Similarly, our pain shouldn't be used like a sword hanging over people who have wronged us. It is not healthy. Every day you choose pain is another day everyone else around you has to live with that decision. So do yourself, and everyone else, a favor. Let go. Forgive and move on. Life's too short to be miserable.

THOUGHTS ARE THINGS

"As a single footstep will not make a path on the earth,
so a single thought will not make a pathway
in the mind."
—Henry David Thoreau

NAPOLEON HILL ONCE SAID, "Thoughts are things and powerful things at that." Boy, was he right. If we knew and understood how powerful our thoughts were, we would quit our negative thinking. When our thoughts are intertwined with purpose, persistence, intentionality, and clarity, they create power and transformational change. They create the life we want to live. Every one of us becomes what we are because of our dominating thoughts and desires.

Our desires seek expression, and our thoughts are transformed into reality. The good news is it is all our choice. Each of us can do it. Harnessing the energy of our Thought Practice is available to every human being. You are not an exception to this law of the universe. We are all the product of our thoughts. What we think, we become.

When we live a vibrant Thought Practice without worrying about the results, the proper results come to us. They find their way to us as a means of fulfilling our thoughts and desires. Debilitating doubt and fretsome worry block our dreams from manifesting. As a recovered professional worrier, I realized a few years ago that so much of what I worried about never happened. Realizing it was a waste of energy helped to free me.

It's like being thirsty on a hot day and drinking nothing but vodka sodas to quench your thirst. It may taste good for a moment, but the alcohol and soda water dehydrate you. The results are that you will be sick from dehydration at the end of the day, even though you drank. This, of course, is because you drank something that worked against you. Worry has the same effect on our Thought Practice. It makes us feel like we are doing something in the moment, but it prevents what we want from manifesting.

Think of it this way—both success and failure begin in your mind. They are the offspring of thoughts. Within the universe's inexhaustible storehouse, our thoughts continuously attract that which is in harmony with the thoughts we choose to hold in our mind.

Any idea can be placed in our mind through repetition of thought and connecting those thoughts to feelings. Attaching feelings to thoughts creates additional energy. We are who and what we are because of the thoughts we choose to hold in our minds.

> **We are who and what we are because of the thoughts we choose to hold in our minds.**

Think of your mind like a muscle. Muscles grow and becomes more effective with proper training and use. Creativity and imagination become more alert when we use them. Positive thoughts of higher energy increase as you choose to hold them in your mind, believe them, and become aware of their presence in your world. Keep in mind that temporary defeat is not a permanent failure. As your Thought Practice grows, you will begin to see that thoughts backed by a powerful desire tend to manifest in the physical world.

Thought Practice is not a quick fix. It is not a voodoo magical incantation. It is a practice that takes skill and effort. Think of it as a lifestyle change. For Thought Practice to change your life, it has to become a way of life. It becomes how you live. Thought Practice is merely becoming aware of the laws of the universe and then living in harmony with them. This system is available to every person who dares to use them. The starting point for all change is a desire. You think every day. It's only a question of if you will live a life that results from lazy thinking or an experience you choose through specific thoughts.

Think of Thought Practice like food. If you want to lose weight and eat nutritiously, watch your calories and exercise regularly, you will likely transform your body. If you eat well two days a week, and the other five you eat pizza, cheeseburgers, and ice cream, you will not meet your physical health goals. Spasmodic effort and lack of focus will be of no value to you. It will frustrate you. To get the results you want, you must apply the principles of Transformative Thinking until their application becomes a way of life for you.

If you focus on what's ugly, you will attract more ugliness into your thoughts, emotions, and ultimately into your life. By choosing to hold onto the higher energies of love, peace, faith, trust, kindness, and intention, we can process our circumstances even in the worst situations where we feel disappointed.

The truth is that disappointment is a part of life. Rather than focus on it, choose to look around for the lessons and let disappointment be your teacher. What is the frustration saying about your journey? Your ultimate goals? Your habits? Where do you bear responsibility in the circumstances that led to the disappointment? Remain determined in your Thought Practice with the attitude of, "I will burn my boats and stake my entire future on my ability to live in the higher energies." And then, you will. Your persistence is key to Thought Practice transforming your life.

Without persistence, you are defeated before you begin. With persistence, you will change your life. It is that simple. With persistence, it doesn't matter how many times you stumble because you will get where you want to go if you never give up. If you remain persistent in lazy thinking, you will live a life of distress and anxiety. If you focus your Thought Practice on the higher energies, you will live a life of purpose and peace, free of anxiety. Thought Practice is about changing your mind and changing your life.

Your mind, like a vacuum, cannot have open space. You either fill it with thoughts that hold your life back in the mire or catapult it into what you dream. The choice is yours. Every thought you have is either strengthening or weakening your ability to harness the energy of the universe. Every thought you have has an energy that will either strengthen or weaken you. Weakening thoughts are obstacles to creating the life you want.

We attract what we think and emanate. Therefore, you must become conscious of your thoughts. Every thought impacts your life. You attract into your life what you think and feel inside. For example, if you know you are a liar and therefore do not respect yourself, others will not respect you. They may not know why, but they will not. So, living in the higher energy of truth-telling will increase your self-respect, which will attract others to respect you.

Do you remember our earlier discussion about the subconscious mind and the conscious mind? The subconscious acts on its programming. The programming begins at birth with all sorts of stimuli; your subconscious mind is in a constant state of programming. The only question is, what do you want to program it with? Do you want to program it with thoughts that give you the life you want? Or do you want to program it by lazily letting whatever comes inside you to program it? Do you want peace and prosperity—or anger and anxiety?

You can reprogram your subconscious through the repetition of affirmations. Any thought and impulse that is repeatedly passed onto your subconscious mind is ultimately accepted and becomes a program in your mind. Your conscious mind then translates those programs into the physical equivalent in the most practical ways available. It's the natural way our brains work. If someone believes they are doomed to failure, they will fail. They are living a self-fulfilling prophecy.

You can reprogram your subconscious through the repetition of affirmations.

Their negative beliefs program the subconscious mind to attract failure. If someone believes that they will live their dreams, they ultimately will. They will subconsciously and consciously make choices that lead to energy magnetically coming to them. Opportunities will open up in alignment with their thoughts, and stepping stones will appear taking them where they want to go.

To reprogram your subconscious, remind yourself that our universe is a good place, that God has an unlimited abundance, and that abundance is available to you. You will have to believe that living in the higher energies of faith, love, kindness, non-judgment, attraction, and peace is possible. You must have faith that the higher energies exist and are for you even when your circumstances don't demonstrate it. You must believe this when your enemies surround you, and they seem to be winning. You must believe this when you are in financial need and don't see relief coming. You must believe this when you are seriously ill. It is such moments of darkness that you still must have faith. You must believe that the higher energies are yours, and abundance is on its way.

I heard it described once like this:

> It is like waking up in the dark and lying there with your eyes open. In a minute or so, your eyes adjust to the darkness, and you can see…dimly. Or

you can choose to turn on the light and see much better instantly. Your ability to see does not change a thing about the truth of what's in that room. The only difference is your ability to see.

Reprogramming your subconscious through Thought Practice does take time, patience, and consistency. One of the first areas to reprogram is the issue of fear that many people struggle with. In the Christian Scriptures, there is a warning and encouragement from God 365 times that says, *"Fear not"* or *"Be not afraid."* Interesting that God gives us one every day. He knows we are creatures prone to fear.

Remember your mind abhors a vacuum, so it will be full. What it's full of is up to you. Fear and faith cannot occupy the same space at the same time. Wouldn't you like to eliminate fear from your life?

For most of my life, I lived in fear, worry, and anxiety. Crippling. Debilitating. Unfounded. Yet real, palpable, and fed. You cannot simultaneously live in faith, peace, and happiness…..and fear. One way you can eliminate fear is to realize you cannot fail. Every action produces a result. If these results are not what you wanted, then you have an opportunity to learn and grow, regroup, and take different actions.

You will grow far more from these types of results than from the results of *success*. I'd encourage you to eliminate the concept of failure from your thinking and vocabulary. Focus on faith, not fear.

Your thoughts are like electricity. Electricity can power your appliances and lights, dramatically enhancing your life. Electricity can also kill a person instantly if they ignore the laws. How one uses electricity is up to each individual. If you want to harness electricity, it will best serve you to learn and understand its laws and obey them. Your subconscious mind is the same. The rules exist whether you are aware of them or not.

Now that you are becoming aware of them, it gives you responsibility and opportunity. The responsibility is yours alone. No one can do it for you—you alone can harness this power to transform your life. For example, if you think you are beaten, you are. If you think you shouldn't, you won't. If you want to win but think you can't, you won't. However, if you KNOW you can never be beaten, you won't be. If you know you can win, you will. It may take time to learn and apply these lessons, but you will achieve your goals if you think you can.

When my boys were little, they each played a lot of different sports. I felt that it was important for them to try and find what they liked. For a few years, they both played little league at the same time. There was one boy who was far better than any other players on any other team. He worked hard and loved baseball. He would not be beaten when something did not go as he intended. One day after practice, I asked him, "What would you like to do when you grow up?"

Smiling big, he said, *"Play baseball!"*

Before I could respond, another dad interjected, "That won't happen. One out of forty thousand kids will make it to the major leagues." Knowing that father, I don't think he intended to be cruel. I was perplexed by his answer, though. Why on earth would you kill the dreams of an eight-year-old boy? I looked at the boy and said, "He's right in that it's very tough, BUT look at how good you are now. If you keep working hard and get better and better, who knows what could happen. Plus, you are having fun, right?" The little boy looked up at the other Dad and said, "I could be the one in forty thousand if I keep working hard."

Who knows what will come of our dreams. I do know what will come of dreams whose seeds are plucked while they are still germinating—nothing. Absolutely nothing at all. People always ask if the little boy made it to MLB. No, he did not, but he played ball throughout his youth and loved it. It gave him purpose and a tribe of like-minded people who helped him stay focused. He learned hard work, discipline, and reality. At some point, he realized MLB would not be in his future, but you know what, he still lived his dream. It just looked a little different than the eight-year-old version.

Remember, if you think you can't, you won't. If you think you can, you might. Your subconscious mind is working all the time. It never sleeps. It is your choice to make it start working for you or allowing it to work against you.

- Thought Practice is not difficult.
- Everyone can do it. It all depends on our willingness to practice.

If we are willing to put in the effort, we will be able to do it. Not only that, but we will learn to do it well. Pain and pleasure will come and go. Celebration and disappointment will ebb and flow. Your thoughts and emotions will remain tranquil and at peace. It is incredibly freeing to know you do not need to be pleased to be happy. Thought Practice makes it not only possible—but probable—to live in peace and happiness every day. You can cultivate a mind so spacious that it can be powerfully passionate and awake and involved and at peace and content without a struggle.

Your conscious mind is key to reprogramming your subconscious mind. When the Buddha taught his eightfold path, he said it had a specific number of parts. People could be sure they were going the right way if they saw one of the eight markers. These signposts are:

- Right View
- Right Intention
- Right Speech
- Right Action
- Right Livelihood

- Right Effort
- Right Concentration
- Right Mindfulness

Travelers seeing these signposts will know they are headed in the right direction of happiness. The order in which the traveler sees the signs don't matter. It can be slightly different for each of us, depending on our temperament, experience, and maturity. If we look at a sign carefully, it becomes apparent that each one has all the others intertwined inside of it. On your journey of Thought Practice and happiness, you can start anywhere. You start wherever you are.

Thought Practice strengthens and softens your mind. That is the paradox of Thought Practice. By softening our mind and accepting the rules of the universe, we enhance our intention to use it rather than lazily abdicate this responsibility to our ego. We soften our minds to deeper truths, strengthening it as a tool to live the life we want.

You start wherever you are.

Through consistent Thought Practice, we can eliminate all mind hindrances from our life. These hindrances are anything that sucks us back into the fearful control of the ego. These hindrances obscure our clarity resulting in confusion and apprehension. That is part of why you are reading this book; you want to live in peace and clarity and purpose. These hindrances get in the way of us living in our natural, peaceful, and loving state because they thrive on doubt and anxiety.

Once we see these hindrances as thoughts, we can deal with them skillfully. We stop feeling attacked by them and can act wisely. I once heard it described as a gyroscope. Our mind, like a gyroscope, is moving towards a place of balance. It is also constantly shifting and changing in response to circumstances. There will be periods of more energy and focus and work to maintain the stability and focus and times of less intensity and energy. There are natural energy shifts of the mind, and they will dim and become less and less intensive as our practice gains strength. Once we eliminate toxic thinking from our subconscious, it is like adding rocket fuel to the engine of our life.

CHAPTER 7 EXERCISES

These chapter exercises are designed to help you apply the principles of TRANFORMATIONAL THINKING in meaningful and transformative ways for you. They are not designed that one should do all the exercises for each chapter. Record the notes from the chapter, the exercise you are doing, and the results in your notebook.

1. Repetitive thinking gives birth to our beliefs. A personal belief is the repetition of the same thoughts and ideas over a long period of time. Simply put, this means that when you repeatedly revisit your positive beliefs, they become a part of your belief system. The more time and weight you give to positivity, the quicker your brain rewires to accept it as normal.

   • Sure, it will be difficult to see the bright side at first; the negativity will pull you with all its might. The best thing to do is acknowledge it, see it, and then turn your attention to the positive thoughts that want to come in so badly. Enable them, make space for them, and listen to them. Do this exercise for a few weeks; it has the potential to rewire your brain and significantly change your mindset.

   • When you act upon these positive thoughts, you feel better while doing it. This improves your confidence and helps you believe that whatever you do will have considerable consequences, even if they aren't what you expect. But this starts when you take responsibility for your thoughts. As Jim Rohn said, "You must take personal responsibility. You cannot change the circumstances, the seasons, or the wind, but you can change yourself".

2. *Remember one key thing: be consistent. These exercises require daily consistent effort. Be patient. Changes will not happen overnight. Transformational change takes time.*

- Practice visualization. For example, imagine yourself in a car. You are in the driver's seat. You're at the wheel, and you know exactly where you are going. You feel a cool breeze on your face and see a calming sunrise over the horizon that fills you with hope and warmth. Point to the place on the horizon where your goals are. You drive towards it with confidence and courage.

- Use positive affirmations to empower yourself. Come up with a few phrases and mantras that speak to you: "I deserve to be happy, and nothing can stop me," or "My worst enemies are within, and they no longer have power," or "I control my thoughts and will only think thoughts of the higher energies of love, honesty, kindness, and abundance."

- Live in the now. Live consciously connected to what is happening in your life in the present moment. If you focus on the past or future, your subconscious can betray you with regret and anxiety. Choosing the opportunity to live in the present is a pathway to peace and happiness.

- Focus on one thing at a time. Reprogram your subconscious to avoid multi-tasking. The stress of doing multiple things at the same time is an enemy to inner peace. The result of multi-tasking is stress, and you, therefore, cannot bring your best to everything. When you learn to focus on one thing, you will find you accomplish more in less time.

3. Would you let someone dump a truckload of rotten food, dirty diapers, and smelly trash in your living room? Then why do you

let people dump garbage in your mind? Only *you* can choose what to feed your mind! You must remember that bad thoughts are like junk food for the brain. We all know that junk food is bad for us and has no value whatsoever. Similarly, do not indulge in and fill your mind with bad news, drama, negativity, hate, or any other destructive thought. Henry Ford said, "Whether you believe you can or you can't, you're right." If you don't believe you can do something, how can you expect to follow through with it? So, this is another solid example of why you and I need to be careful about what we think and what we say. When bad thoughts enter your head, reframe those thoughts. Picture yourself doing what you want to be doing, and you can start taking steps to do it. The mind has a way of revealing plans and thoughts to you as you begin taking more actions.

4. Self-fulfilling prophecies are just that: self-fulfilling. They are not good or bad, they simply are, and they operate on whatever we feed them by thinking, holding those thoughts in our mind, and then acting on them. Understand that self-fulfilling prophecies are real and a lot more common than you would think. But there's nothing magical about it as it involves declaring something and then fulfilling that declaration. If you slept poorly, the chances are that you are about to have a bad day. This is a small thing, but these seemingly negligible thoughts have the power to upend your day.

   - Some people believe that they need to speak things out loud for them to make a prophecy valid. But the fact of the matter is that quiet self-fulfilling prophecies take shape in your thoughts all the time. And they are just as effective at turning into real words and actions.

   - The exercise here is to strive to make your self-fulfilling prophecies positive and full of the higher energies of love, abundance, expansion, kindness, honesty, grace, and non-judgment. If you can train your brain to operate with positivity as a fuel, the prophecies you make will be more in line with the results you are looking for. This week, rewire one of your lazy self-fulfilling prophecies with one of the higher energies and resolve to stop the lazy thoughts when they occur. Replace them with those of the higher energies.

TOXIC THINKING

*"Be careful what you think. Your life is shaped
by your thoughts."*
—Proverbs 4:23

MANY OF US SUFFER from toxic thinking. We flog ourselves needlessly. We limit our potential by limiting our beliefs. We destroy our peace with stress and worry. We cause ourselves worry, anxiety, angst, and depression, all with our lazy, toxic thinking. There are many forms of toxic thinking, but in general, they fall into four categories:

- Self-flagellation
- Procrastination
- Judgment
- Living in the past

A key to launching effective Thought Practice is to change the way you look at yourself. The habit of thinking in self-flagellation and judgment is a result of your subconscious' training. You learned that joy was possible only when life was going the way you thought it should. Of course, you will experience sadness and disappointment at times in your life. It's healthy to experience your feelings and express them appropriately. Understanding the nature of your sadness helps to accept it, honor it, and heal it.

In the end, when you want to dissolve it and be free of it, you must bring in the higher energies of love, kindness, and acceptance. Sadness cannot survive in the same moment as the higher energies of love and joy. You replace low energy thoughts with those of higher energy, and you do that by changing your self-talk. Does your inner speech match what you want out of life? You do this by catching yourself when you are doing it. For example, when you catch yourself thinking about what's missing from your life, stop.

Change your focus from what's missing in your life to what you want and intend to bring into your life. If it's finances, don't think, "I wish I had more money." Instead, replace it with, "I will generate xx number of dollars by doing such and such." If you don't like a specific circumstance of your life, don't think about it. All of that mental energy you spend complaining and worrying is a magnet for attracting more of what it is into your life. Does it bring the object of worry into your life specifically? Does it bring the object of worry into your life specifically? Sometimes. It does bring angst, anxiety, and stress while robbing you of joy, focus, and peace. Focusing your thoughts on what you want and are creating fills your mind, which prevents your mind from filling the vacuum with worry.

Self-flagellation usually happens inside us, and no one will likely see when it's happening within us. Thought Practice changes the way you look at yourself, and for Thought Practice to be effective, you will have to start changing the way you look at yourself. Did you catch that? A key to changing your life is to change the way you look at yourself. The person who is centered and established in the right thinking and only sends out goodwill towards themselves and others cannot hold negative thoughts. It's natural at this point to ask, *What about things I've done in the past?*

People new to Thought Practice are sometimes filled with remorse for having done someone wrong. If the wrong can't be righted, its effect can be neutralized by doing a kindness to someone else in the present. It's important to forget those things behind you and focus on what's before you. Our ego doesn't want us to do that. Our ego wants us to hold onto the regrets and replay the tapes of how we have wronged others. Our ego wants to shackle us to our regrets and sorrow. Start to pay attention to your thoughts. Specifically, pay attention to the judgment you direct towards yourself and others. Then, make a conscious effort to shift to compassionate thoughts and feelings. Remember, your thoughts are magnetic and attract into your life what you think about and send out.

One way you can stop the self-flagellation and shift away from thoughts of self-judgment is to let it go. Yes, that is correct. Detach yourself from your thoughts of anger, self-pity, or whatever, and just love yourself as the temple that God gave you to house your soul in this journey. The journey and the ability to extend forgiveness become natural when you don't carry hate within you. Change the way you look at yourself.

Grab a common problem you face and hold it in your mind. Often when considering a problem, two streams of thought permeate our consciousness. One is that we start to beat ourselves up. We allow our inner speech to be overrun with thoughts such as:

- How could you be so stupid?
- If only you would have done this instead of that

Another way we harm ourselves is by ruminating on thoughts such as:

- What if this or that happens next?
- How am I going to solve this or that?

All these thoughts serve us in no positive way and, in fact, deplete our energetic resources. They magnetically draw more of what already exists in our life to us.

There is a way out. Relax. Rest. Choose peace. Let peace be rooted firmly in your mind and heart. Choose thoughts that let grace take over the situation. There is an invisible energy that is produced by your thoughts. You choose the energy you send out by the thoughts you choose to hold in your mind. You choose what you want in your life by your Thought Practice. These energies work in and through you. They end up living on the superhighway of life. We do not have to be dependent on circumstances or external conditions for our happiness. We can begin to live the consciousness of fulfillment. We see that universal abundance is available to all of us and that although it can manifest as material things in our life, it goes beyond those things.

When we live this way, we live in peace, knowing that whatever comes our way in life will not threaten our peace. We live every day naturally in peace and love knowing that whatever comes our way will be a teacher and guide.

Until we tear the weeds of our thinking up by their roots, we will not escape the hypnotic rhythm of our lazing thinking and the unhealthy programming we have received.

Until we tear the weeds of our thinking up by their roots, we will not escape the hypnotic rhythm of our lazy thinking and the unhealthy programming we have received. We can stop the self-flagellation and its balms with their false promises. These balms soothe us for a time through their seduction, but, in reality, they feed the beast of our self-flagellation. We become like a dog chasing its tail; we go mad trying to comfort our restless hearts. Like our physical yards at home, the weeds tend to come back. The more we tend the garden and consistently eliminate and prevent weeds, the more room we have for peace and anticipation.

Years ago, I bought a home whose large yard had gone unattended for years. The back yard grew consumed with blackberry bushes that were eight to ten feet high and as thick as a brick wall. It took us four months of evenings and weekends to clear those weeds from the yard. It took another four months of digging blackberry root balls that we missed. It took another three years before they were eventually defeated. I had to change up my methods. I had to be vigilant. Finally, the back yard was thriving with native plants, shrubs, and trees. But it took time, attention, and consistency.

Eventually, the good plants took over the yard, and it required little attention to thrive. The new plants became the natural state of the yard. It is the same with self-flagellation and our Thought Practice. At first, it is a battle to stop talking to ourselves in ways that are not healthy and feed healthy thoughts. If you work the muscle of your mind to reprogram your subconscious enough, those thoughts will take over the garden of your mind.

All of us use our thoughts to create the world we choose. The question becomes, are we choosing the life we want or settling for the life of lazy thinking? Remember, you hold power over your life through your thoughts. You have everything you need to transform your life and are gaining the tools to manifest into the physical world what you want and need for your life. Like a good parent who is passionately in love with their child, God is in love with YOU.

He is not offended by your humanity. He created it. You are loved by God now. As is, now. Not when, or if, or because. Stop flogging, and you will see a dramatic increase in your joy and peace. Do not put off starting your Thought Practice. There is no better time and place to start and continue your practice than now. Right now. At this moment, as you read these words.

PROCRASTINATION

It's okay to not be very good at it. You are learning and working on reprogramming some deeply rooted thoughts. Lance Armstrong wobbled on his bike as a little boy when his training wheels were first taken off. Jimi Hendrix didn't begin by playing the national anthem. He started by learning one chord, then adding another, and another. There are bound to be unknowns and obstacles along your path, but there are no reasons to procrastinate or stop your Thought Practice. Remember, when you change the way you look at things, the things you look at change. Choose to view the events you once considered *obstacles* as **opportunities** to grow as a person. Choose to keep your thoughts and how you are living in alignment and harmony. If you think one way and live another, you activate your ego-dominated attitude of fear and protection. This will always distance you from peace.

> **Choose to view the events you once considered obstacles as opportunities to grow as a person.**

Your actions need to be in harmony with your thoughts. Trust in those thoughts that harmonize and be willing to act on them. In the same vein, choose to eliminate actions from your life that are incongruent with your thoughts and what you want in your life. Refuse to view yourself in terms such as inauthentic or cowardly because those thoughts will keep you from acting on what you know you were meant to be and how you were meant to live. For example, say you are at the grocery store, and that still small voice inside of you nudges you to take a specific action. Do it. Don't hesitate, just do it.

At one time in my life, I had minimal financial resources. I had lost everything and was nearly homeless. I was in the grocery store buying ramen because it was all I could afford. The lady in front of me was frazzled. She was frantically going through her purse, looking for more money. Finally, she looked at the clerk and said, "Um, just put the milk back." Without thinking, I handed the clerk my five-dollar bill and said to her, "The milk is on me." The woman looked up at me and said, "You have no idea what that means to me." All I could say was, "Glad I could help," as I walked away without my ramen. And I meant it. I wasn't thinking anything other than, "Well, this will be fun to see how God feeds me." I arrived at my apartment empty-handed, and I noticed something in front of my door. As I approached, I realized they were bags of groceries. Four bags full of veggies, meat, cheese, and milk. Thank God, not a package of ramen in sight. When your actions are in harmony with your soul or higher thoughts, these beautiful surprises in life can happen.

Your actions need to be in harmony with your thoughts. If you are thinking healthy, high-energy thoughts and getting pissed off at other drivers, you will see that whichever you feed will gain control. If you feed the higher energy thoughts, your driving will become peaceful. If you feed the beast of indignant driving anger, you will reap stress and anxiety and frustration. Trust in those thoughts that harmonize and act on them. Refuse to give any energy to thoughts of discouragements such as:

- I should not.
- I may look stupid.
- What if they think I am flirting.
- It is none of my business.

Look at the entire kaleidoscope of your life, including all of the people who have crossed your path. See all the jobs, successes, apparent failures, possessions, losses, wins, everything from a perspective of gratitude and as an opportunity for your growth and enlightenment. Look upon everyone who has ever played a role in your life as someone sent to you for your benefit. This includes those who hurt you, walked away, abused you, took advantage, etc. Everyone was assigned to teach you something that you needed to learn. All of those events served a purpose for you to arrive at the place you are on your path.

One step at a time, you will find grace and peace replacing anxiety and frustration. You are creating a new energy field for yourself. As Albert Einstein observed, "Nothing happens until something moves." You are coaxing habits out of your life one step at a time. One thought at a time. Begin by capturing individual toxic thoughts the moment they occur. One moment at a time. One day at a time. And you will begin to see the transformation from toxic to clear thinking in your life.

Your Thought Practice becomes more comfortable and more natural as it grows into your way of life. The only task is figuring out what's wholesome and attracting what you want into your life. Buddhists talk about actions conditioning other actions; and any non-action conditioned as a determination to do better.

In your Thought Practice, it is essential to put first things first. What are the first things? Only you can determine that. One guiding principle is that all thoughts and actions must be in alignment with the higher energies of love, honesty, kindness, right behavior, right speech, and gratitude while avoiding the lower energies of judgment, anger, lying, hate, and greed. Relax into the future and let it go. Make an active commitment to enjoy your day. This day, today. Just enjoy it without worry about tomorrow. The more peaceful you are with your life today, the more productive you will

Relax into the future and let it go. Make an active commitment to enjoy your day.

be in your life tomorrow. It is challenging to accomplish anything lasting when you are in a frenetic state of anxiety and stress. When you relax and are peaceful, you become inspired and efficient.

You have the power and everything you need to end procrastination in your life. Remember, power is defined as organized and directed knowledge. Power is the ability to choose your thoughts and actions and convert your energy to manifest what you want into your life. Knowledge is converted to power by organizing it into plans and practices and expressing those plans in actions. One of the most freeing ways you can exert this power in your own life is to stop judging yourself and others.

JUDGMENTALISM

The way to cease being judgmental toward others begins with changing the way you look at other people. Practice the art of allowing others to be themselves and be where they are on their journey. When we resist the temptation to judge and criticize others, we can see them as teachers, as those hurting and wounded on their journey. They remind us that we can only have peace when we forgive rather than judge. By radiating this forgiving energy outward, you will find the same kind of respectful, positive energy flowing back to you. The most simple and immature way we often judge is by appearances.

When we judge others, we limit our capacity. It is not in our purview of responsibility to change others. It does not fall within our ability to change people. All we can change is our demonstration in the life of our thoughts. And in that, we can change the energy and attraction in our life, which will likely inspire others to change. There is an old saying, "No one is your enemy or friend. All are your teachers." Judging another's appearance is as shallow as life can get because we typically know very little of their experience, depth, pain, or journey.

Finding a way to bring non-judgmental harmony to a situation is a mark of a maturing Thought Practice. Living in this mature Thought Practice eliminates the ego's needs. Proving someone else wrong so you can be right only exacerbates the problem. One of the most compelling ideas regarding judgment comes from Wayne Dyer. He said, "When you judge another person, you do not define them. You define yourself."

I invite you to look at your heart and determine what is truly important. When you update your view of the essential things in your life, the world around you will seem very different. You will begin to see the senselessness of exhausting yourself in pursuit of what keeps you trapped in a vicious cycle of striving and never arriving—pursuing stuff to fulfill the hole in your heart. If you live like this, you know you have signed up for it. This becomes a life of frustration and dissatisfaction because the search itself becomes the jailor. By practicing cessation, you'll move into prioritizing what's important in your life. The pursuit of more and more comes from lazy thinking and judgment. We judge our satisfaction with what we have compared to others. It's crazy when you stop to think about it. It's important to be aware of the conditioned responses that lead you to label people, places, and circumstances as less than perfect. See the flawless behind the supposed flaws.

All judgment comes from a violation of the higher energy law of love. Our boomerang of hate, resentment, and criticism come back heavy with sickness and sorrow into our life. Without love, our lives are about as welcome as crashing symbols on a quiet Sunday morning. When we stop judging ourselves, we can begin to stop judging others. Jesus once said, "He who is without sin cast the first stone."

Lazy thinkers who are controlled by their ego, cast the first stone. Judgment is a misguided attempt to deflect from their issues, thinking that throwing stones at others will make them feel better. Those involved in active Thought Practice can't take those actions. An enlightened mind is not a mind driven by judgmental or critical spirit. Judgmentalism prevents transformation, and this magnetic energy pulls lower energies to manifest in our life. A judgmental attitude makes the user feel they are operating from a superior position. This, of course, is entirely false.

So, what happens when you are on the receiving end of judgment? It has very little to do with you. It's a gift when others do this because it clarifies that you likely don't want them in your life. The laws of the universe are universal. That low, dark energy is magnetically drawn back to them.

As you flex your Thought Practice, you will experience miracles of love, provision, and abundance. Your perspective on life will change as you view others as being on their path. Some will join you, and others will need to be let go of—all without judgment. Once you focus your Thought Practice on judgment, you will see how often we tend to judge. As you flex that muscle to shed thoughts of judging yourself and others, you will feel free and peaceful.

LIVING IN THE PAST

Living in the past is a form of toxic thinking. This traps many people, shackling them to a life they didn't intend; thus, preventing them from living the life they want. A grand illusion is putting energy into your past, even if you find it objectionable. You are then acting on those thoughts serving only to produce more and more of what's always been. To break free of this, you must begin to see what makes living in the past an illusion in the first place. Remember, the wake of a boat doesn't drive the boat; the wake is a result of the boat making forward progress. The wake has no bearing on the boat's future. Your past does not drive today or your future.

> **Living in the past is a form of toxic thinking. This traps many people, shackling them to a life they didn't intend; thus, preventing them from living the life they want.**

In the same way, explaining, excusing, or justifying your past actions doesn't serve you today. The past is the past. Let it serves as your teacher. The more and more you live in healthy Thought Practice and the higher energies, the fewer messes will be created that need to be cleaned up.

Many people are comfortable wallowing in the experiences of the past. They propagate their victimhood and allow the past pain to become a large part of their identity. Feeding past drama and using energy to remind ourselves of all that transpired serves to shackle us to the past. Certainly, we need to make amends where possible. We need to take responsibility for our actions. We need to forgive those who have harmed us. But we should not live in the past. No one said it better than William Shakespeare when he reminded us, "What's done is done." One day I realized that I no longer needed to be ashamed of my past. I was done wishing for a better past and began to live for a better future. That decision has made all the difference. In reality, all any of us have is now, the present moment. Now. The past is done, and the future is hasn't been created.

Hindrances to living your Thought Practice are generally present for two reasons. First, you are blaming the past for your difficulties. Or second, you are caught up in the personal history, refusing to let it go. Know in your heart that everything in your past and the personal account had to take place for you to be where you are today. How do you know that to be true? Everything DID take place, period. Rather than curse it, bless and embrace it. Bring it love and acceptance.

Stop looking at the past as an anchor to your future. In your automobile, is the windshield or the rearview mirror larger? A rearview mirror is a tool for perspective. It was not designed as the object to navigate forward. Change your perspective regarding the past. This is not excusing our past actions, which may have caused others pain and difficulty. If you have amends that you need to make, make them. Instead, this is focusing on living in the now and the higher energies. It's living in perspective rather than judgments of good or bad. What you may have called "bad" had "good" hidden inside the experience.

Some of those lessons waiting to emerge only manifest as we let go of limiting beliefs. Living in the past can distract people from attending to the real matters at hand.

As you continue to grow in your Thought Practice, you will find eliminating the following four forms of toxic thinking will be like rocket fuel for your practice. These include self-flagellation, procrastination, judgment, and living in the past. As you eliminate these, you will find fulfillment and peace previously unknown to you. Remember, the robbers of time are the past and the future. We should bless the past, learn from it, and forget it. We should bless the future, knowing it has opportunities for growth and blessing in store for us. The support system for all of this is your choice of thoughts. It is your Thought Practice. If you are engaging in a toxic thought process, you will be producing emotional responses that put your body in a state of anxiety. To live in higher energies and fulfilling emotions, you must control and choose your thoughts.

CHAPTER 8 EXERCISES

These chapter exercises are designed to help you apply the principles of TRANFORMATIONAL THINKING in meaningful and transformative ways for you. They are not designed that one should do all the exercises for each chapter. Record the notes from the chapter, the exercise you are doing, and the results in your notebook.

1. Self-flagellation or self-criticism is all too common, unfortunately. People indulge in such negativity for several reasons. It could be one or more of the following:

    - **Family history**. When someone lives with parents where one or both frequently and harshly criticize themselves, this trait can pass on to the child.

    - **Parenting style**. If a child is unnecessarily punished by the parents and is blamed for everything that goes wrong, the child begins to internalize this experience. The chances are that the parents implied or stated outright that the child is bad. This criticism is often accepted by the child and this unfortunate perception becomes a part of the child's reality.

    - **Low self-esteem**. The above factors combined with external elements, a constant lack of achievements, and others' negative statements all come together to make a person self-critical.

- **Cynical view**. Some people are naturally inclined to have a pessimistic outlook of the world. This attitude naturally extends to themselves.

- **Lack of accountability**. Some people simply do not want to be responsible for their own lives and decisions.

2. If you want to enhance the quality of your life, start by changing the way you indulge in Thought Practice—transition from being lazy to being dynamic. Put all of your focus on the higher energies of love, kindness, honesty, grace, abundance, expansion, and non-judgment. This week do the following in your Thought Practice:

   - **Accept yourself**. This does not mean you should stop trying to become better or doing something about the aspects of your life that make you unhappy. But also, do not set ideals that are too high and inaccessible; you'll only end up disappointing yourself. Do not set yourself up for self-criticism. Be slow and deliberate with the change.

   - **Do not compare**. Comparing yourself with those above you is a recipe for despair. Anytime you feel bad about not being good enough, remember everyone has flaws. All those social media celebrities and influencers who show off their so-called *perfect lives* have their own trials and tribulations. They are just more skilled at hiding their issues. So don't be upset if someone is good at pretending that they are better than you.

   - **Comfort yourself**. Instead of blaming yourself, try to say that things aren't so bad after all. When unsure in a situation, don't automatically start criticizing yourself.

   - **Live in the now**. Thinking about all the actions that have already passed keeps you from paying attention to the present moment.

If you want to get over your past mistakes, come back to where you still have opportunities to excel.

- **Act when ready.** Instead of sulking and blaming yourself, it is time to sit up and act on whatever is bothering you. Rectify the situation, apologize, work, talk it out, and do whatever else you need to do to feel like you are above the blame.

3. If you don't stop the self-blame, it will eat you up inside. The negative emotions and guilt will make you want to punish yourself over and over again. But nothing is worth that kind of self-flagellation. That is why the sooner you change your approach to your issues, the lighter you will feel at the end of this exercise. But before you begin, it's time to become truly aware of your issues. Ask these questions that are meant to take you on a journey of self-discovery.

- Questions About Values and Life Goals

  ♦ What do you consider the ideal you?

  ♦ What are some of your dreams and goals?

  ♦ What makes your dreams or goals so important?

  ♦ What is keeping you from achieving these?

  ♦ What are the most important things in your life? (e.g., Family, children, career, friends, love, or anything else at all.)

  ♦ How much time do you give to each of these things?

  ♦ What are some of the values you'll try to instill in your children?

- Questions About Personality

  ♦ Describe yourself using only three words.

  ♦ How has your personality changed since childhood?

♦ Do you feel like you have taken after either of your parents?

♦ What qualities do you most admire in yourself?

♦ What do you consider your greatest strength?

♦ What would you say is your greatest area for improvement?

♦ What scares you or keeps you up at night?

♦ What is your approach to decision-making—logical or intuitive?

♦ How would you complete the question: "What if…?"

- Questions About Relationships

♦ What does your ideal intimate relationship look like?

♦ Are you satisfied in your current relationship?

♦ Who would you call if you only had minutes to live? What would you say to them?

♦ Who do you think you love the most?

♦ What is the absolute best moment you have experienced during a relationship?

♦ Describe a devastating moment that you experienced in a relationship.

♦ Do you believe that you treat yourself better than you do others?

4. When things don't go as planned, it is only natural for people to react negatively, get angry, or become anxious. While many of us can't help but feel the worry, try to keep away from a pattern of constant worrying. It has a way of seeping into our lives even when things are going well, making you feel unnecessarily negative and even unsafe. Future tripping, officially known as *anticipatory anxiety*, can result in overwhelming stress. When you feel anxious

about the lack of control over life and your future, the coping mechanisms you reach out to may not be very healthy. This can include unhealthy eating patterns, overspending (retail therapy), isolating yourself, over-indulging in alcohol, using drugs, and possibly even self-harm. And where is the good in all that? Future tripping isn't going to prepare or protect you from whatever the future holds, whether it's good or bad. So why worry about it and increase our stress?

- Don't start your self-talk with, "If only....." Any thought that begins with those words is bound to take you down an unproductive path.

- Explore all available options when making a decision. Then leave it up to the universe or God to direct your steps.

- Learn what you can control and what is out of your reach. If you want to avoid future tripping, know what is under your influence. For instance, you decide how you present yourself and what you wear. But you can't control how someone reacts to you or what they think about your clothes. As much as we want others to react the way we want, it's just not going to happen.

- Be at peace with what you can control as well as the things you can't. This way, it becomes easier to let go of the useless need to regulate your life and enjoy things as they come. Here's a good affirmation: "If it is meant for me, it will come."

5. Procrastination is never real. The consequences of procrastinating are very real. And it all starts with our thoughts. All those thoughts that keep you from being productive are just that, thoughts. They are not real. They never were. That's because they aren't about what's happening in the moment. Those thoughts are merely telling us a story about what could have been or what could be. To deal with procrastination, we must practice mindfulness,

which involves hearing, understanding, and editing the stories we tell ourselves.

- If you often find yourself procrastinating when there are tasks that need to be completed, you are actually practicing your creativity... but for all the wrong reasons. A creative mind like yours can come up with some amazing reasons not to do things you are supposed to do. It can also give some truly scary outcomes of getting something done. For example, your self-talk might include: It won't work. It is not the right time. No one will care. I am late anyway. It will not be good enough, etc.

- Think about something you procrastinated about recently. What were some of the thoughts moving through your mind at the time? What kind of emotions do you remember feeling? They would not have been very optimistic.

- Here's a simple process to change that procrastination habit:

  ♦ Take a few deep breaths and focus your thoughts.

  ♦ Now ask yourself what you'd need to feel differently in a situation when you are bound to procrastinate?

  ♦ Now, imagine a person who can do those tasks with ease and without second-guessing themselves. What enables them?

  ♦ Imagine that you have been working on what is needed to make advancements in your life. It might be confidence, trust, joy, or an inner hope that all will be all right.

  ♦ All you need to do is take a small step to get things flowing. When you choose to take even the smallest step, something magical happens as your body and mind come together to make it happen. Try it a few times, and you'll find that the negative voices start ignoring you; you aren't listening to them after all. Accomplishing your objectives is very much possible; just start small and move towards your goals.

6. If you want to make over your life and attract what's missing, Thought Practice can get you there. As we move through the day, we send our energies out into the world and receive the same from others. Our spirits are also composed of energy; they vibrate and are felt by others. Have you ever noticed how you feel happy, calm, and cheerful in the presence of some people, while others make you feel sad, anxious, or cold just by their sheer presence? That's because the vibrations of others resonate deep within us. Good energy boosts positive feelings as it removes all anxiety. But bad energy brings in conflict, resentment, and discord. You are here to reprogram the hard drive of your mind, which is the subconscious. Here's how to do it through the conscious mind:

- **Pay attention to the energy you put out into the world.** You can't attract good energy if all you ever give off is negative energy. Think about the vibes you are putting out there and how you make others feel when they are around you. Do you exude peace and happiness? Or are you all about the doom and the gloom? Negativity impacts your relationships as well as strangers around you. It may be subtle, but they can feel it in your approach to the world. What kind of impression would you like to make on people? If you naturally draw others to you, and people love to hang out with you, chances are you've got great energy. But if you feel like people try to avoid you and don't even take you up on your offers of assistance, the vibrations are pretty negative. So, focus your energies on the good and the positive for better outcomes.

- **Change the tone and attitudes that you use in your thoughts.** It's hard to stop negative thoughts once they start. The pessimism comes easily to many of us, and the rest would rather feign indifference than actually feel something good. But if you don't want to attract negativity, it's time to eradicate it from your thoughts and attitudes. Let positivity be your guide. As the Dalai Lama says, "See the positive side, the potential, and make an effort." Do everything you can to change the tone of your thoughts to the positive. For starters, you could reframe the thought, "It's impossible for me to adjust to this new situation," into "I know this new situation will be challenging, but I have it in me to find solutions and adjust to the changes." Do not let yourself wallow in pessimism and negativity. Stop looking for ways to exaggerate things that could go wrong. Replace negative statements with realistic, yet positive statements.

- **Remove all negative influences from your life.** Negative vibes not only repel others but also disrupt your happy feelings and drain you of the goodness still inside you. Low energy negative feelings could be brought on by people, places, things, or even jobs that have an unfavorable hold on your life. These may be toxic, enhancing the toxicity within you. Don't be apologetic when cutting out of your life all the external factors that bring on the negativity within you. Look for the negative influences and remove them. Then work to limit accidental exposure to them and mentally fortify yourself against possible encounters.

- **Practice compassion and kindness.** The smallest acts of kindness can have a poetic impact on both the giver and the receiver. Studies show that people who are kind to others live healthier and happier lives. That is because giving to others creates a feedback loop that continually brings your goodness back around to you. The more positivity you put out there, the more good feelings come back to you. Showing compassion does not have to be a grand gesture. It could be as simple as a note to someone to tell them something nice about themselves, buying a cup of coffee for the person in line behind you, or simply taking a moment to smile at someone close to you. These simple yet powerful actions can fuel your and other people's happiness as you send out heaps of positive energy out in the world.

- **Show gratitude.** Take some time every day to find things to be grateful for. This will allow you to let go of any toxicity and negative emotions that pull you down. Here is a quick exercise: every morning, think of five things you are thankful for. Then think of at least one person that you are grateful to have in your life.

  ♦ It might also be a good idea to keep a gratitude journal. This is a place where you jot down all the little things that made you happy and helped you feel a sense of contentment during each day.

  ♦ When using it, remind yourself that you've been through a lot and that you deserve all these little and big reasons to smile. When you realize how you have weathered the many storms, it will make you so much more appreciative for what you have right now.

- **Align your current self with your future self.** When you spend your time, money, and other resources on something, rest assured that it will impact you for days to come.

  ♦ All of your choices are directly aligning you with the type of future you are choosing for yourself. This is why it is important to make decisions that will help you become the kind of person you want to be. Ask yourself:

    - What are my desires that I should be working towards?

    - What are my goals and dreams?

  ♦ Now imagine getting it all and living that life. Who are you in this ideal future? How do you behave? What do you do?

Align your current thoughts and actions with this future self that you wish to become. As you continue to take steps towards making your wishes come true, you will feel the motivation and the energy to control other parts of your life as well. Reaching out to more positive experiences is a great way to create a favorable reality for yourself.

- **Always act in good faith**

In business, there is always an assumption that all parties are acting in good faith. While we all know that we should treat each other with kindness, many of us do not always live by this principle, whether acting in a personal or professional capacity.

Make it a policy to be civil and respectful towards everyone you meet. Be nice to people, and they may choose to reciprocate in kind. And more importantly, don't retaliate or be harsh with people, especially when they've done wrong. Maybe they were just having a bad day. Reinforcing the negativity and reminding them of their shortcomings isn't going to help. Show compassion and be gracious even if the other party is a little short on those qualities.

ONE DECISION

"Everything in your life is there as a vehicle for your transformation. Use it."

—Ram Dass

AS YOUR THOUGHT PRACTICE grows, you will become more tolerant and less controlled by your false self. The false self is controlled by your ego and living in lower energies of anxiety, judgment, and worry. You will notice that you grow in satisfaction with what is. The voice of your ego dims and has less influence in your life. The ego will still whisper and shout from time to time, as your ego is never quite content. If you choose one thing, your ego will persuade you to consider something else. If ego is in the driver's seat of your mind, it will always obstruct your ability to live in the higher energies of love, peace, contentment, and purpose. Your ego will whisper things to you and will try to convince you that your Thought Practice isn't working. These whispers will come when you have indulged the lower energies of anxiety, judgment, and control.

In this fast-paced world, we want instant gratification. If Thought Practice is viewed as a tranquilizer whose effects are felt instantly, it will fail. I have seen this struggle with some clients who are unwilling to consistently do the hard work of transforming their minds through their Thought Practice. Thought Practice is not an instant cure. Thought Practice is, in its essence, the choice to cultivate the mind to achieve insights that lead to the liberation of living in the higher energies.

As you flex the muscle of your mind, you will notice that an initial transformation is an awareness of impermanence. It is liberating to realize the temporary nature of life. It helps us to recognize that holding onto the past, in addition to being painful, is futile. The fact that we will all be lost to one another at some point encourages us in our Thought Practice to be kind to one another and live in grace in the now.

As an example of this, consider your breath. Rest your attention on the experience of breathing. Notice that each breath rises and passes away. Notice how the oxygen feels as it enters your nose and fills your lungs, circulates, and then takes the off-ramp as you exhale. Notice the temperature of the inhale and then the exhale. Fresh and then warm, and each component of breath has a beginning and an end. A rhythm. Everything that arises also passes away. As you walk, notice how your foot meets the ground and then passes. As you eat your next meal, notice how you sat to enjoy and felt hungry, how each bite felt in your mouth, and how the end of the meal satiated your hunger. Everything is temporary. Everything begins and ends and must begin again. Thought Practice is the same.

Your Thought Practice and experiencing REAL transformation comes down to decisions. Each of us can only decide for ourselves about our Thought Practice. No one can do it for you. You cannot do it for another. Each of us must decide for ourselves. And each of us must choose over and over throughout each day, every day. The choices change as the muscles of the mind grow. But decisions still need to be made. If you don't make them, your ego will prepare them for you, and you will once again live in anxiety, worry, and stress.

We are all free to begin from wherever we are. There are no better or worse places to start. We have freedom from our self-chosen suffering to reach inner peace where the pain is our teacher and suffering ceases. This is, of course, the ideal state of mind, so how do we achieve it? Most of us limit ourselves by the confines of our philosophies and religious bents. By clinging to one system in the search for freedom, we can only experience that which the system allows. But the truth is infinite, unpossessed, and unbounded. All religious and philosophical systems are improvised by people and are attempts to guide us on the path of truth. Unfortunately, the path is often mistaken for the truth. In Thought Practice, when our mind is searching for its freedom, we must assume an impersonal attitude. All options are open. This leaves us free to explore, investigate, examine, and—most importantly—experience the joy of the peace of moment-by-moment freedom.

Freedom is not just a result. Freedom is not something waiting at the end of our Thought Practice. Freedom is instantaneous, right now, from the beginning. We can experience freedom in the very process of exploring and expanding our Thought Practice. We can experience freedom in every step of the way. To live in this freedom in our Thought Practice requires two things:

1. An open heart

2. Consistency

Freedom and peace are the results of retraining your mind. Part of Thought Practice is accepting life as it is rather than as you think it should be. As you think, so shall your life be. Beautiful thoughts build a beautiful life and soul. Successful thoughts attract a successful life. Kind thoughts lead to a rich life of kindness. Loving thoughts pull more love into your life.

Lasting transformation can arrive quickly in your life as you stop attracting the low energies of depression, lack, judgment, and fear; and instead, magnetically attract the higher energies of kindness, abundance, grace, and faith into your life. This process has its seed in being present and mindful in your Thought Practice. In choosing to be mindful, you feed correct thoughts and thought energy into your subconscious, which gives birth to your conscious thoughts. Your thoughts are things, and they give birth to the circumstances of your life. Therefore, remaining present and mindful is the initial key to your Thought Practice providing real transformation in your life. So how do you retrain your mind to live in this space?

Your thoughts are things, and they give birth to the circumstances of your life.

You retrain your mind through your daily Thought Practice and a specific avenue of that practice. It's a state of consciousness where your mind is free of scattered thoughts, and you can find moments of clarity that produce peace. We call that avenue meditation.

Just the word suggests all sorts of ideas, biases, and questions for many people. So, what is meditation? In its purest form, meditation means to focus the mind and choose your thoughts. It can also have a contemplative portion and a relaxation component. Regardless of the structure, mediation transforms our thoughts. There are many, many forms and traditions of meditation. Regardless of the method, reflection marks an alteration in appearance, condition, and function as it changes a person's systematic thinking. Mediation is the transformation of our minds, and it produces clarity and peace.

My physician encouraged me to meditate years ago. I tried with all my heart, and I…fell asleep. She explained to me that mediation was about emptying your mind. My struggle was that as soon as I realized my mind was empty, it was full of the thought of being empty. Then, I realized that the idea that meditation is emptying your mind is inaccurate and self-defeating. Meditation is not emptying your mind. Meditation is focusing your mind. There are thousands of ways you can do that.

Meditation can be challenging to master. That is why it is called a practice. It takes time and exploration to find a method that works for you. If it weren't difficult, everyone would do it. Have you noticed that the components of your life that are the most fulfilling take the most practice and effort to figure out? It took me three years before it clicked, and I found what worked for me.

When you begin, you will not be a master. At the very least, you will find a space in yourself where your soul can breathe. In the beginning, learn to be friends with your mind and to come to peace with your emotions. As a part of your Thought Practice, you will find that meditation helps you make peace with your feelings, heal them, and learn from them.

As you give yourself the grace to explore meditation and begin to discover what it may look like for you, you will find yourself loosening up inside. As you loosen up and you let go, the emotional tension inside you will relax. When you loosen up, you can look at yourself with a higher capacity for objectivity and healing and becoming. You will begin to experience your emotions rather than being controlled by them. As your Thought Practice grows, you will create your feelings and responses.

Explore meditation without expectations. If you put expectations on yourself, you may feel unnecessarily discouraged. Refrain from comparing your experiences with meditation with another person's experiences. I am competitive by nature, and when I began meditating, I learned the Dali Lama mediates for three hours in some sessions. I could barely do five minutes. Then it hit me: he is the Dali Lama, and I am not. He has his experience, and I have mine. I began to approach my time of meditation without any expectations except to breathe. I closed my eyes and paid attention to my breath. I did not control it, expect it to be something, count it, or anything other than notice it. As I focused only on my breathing, something happened. It was just a glimpse, a peek of what was to come, but it did pop up very quickly. I relaxed. When I emerged from that first session, my problems were still all knocking at the door. Nothing had changed, and yet somehow, I knew everything had changed.

Becoming aware like this is like discovering a new lifelong friend—that person you meet and instantly know you will be friends for years. Peace shows us that our feelings have no control over us unless we give them that privilege. They are impermanent and have no power on their own. This encouragement is powerful because it helps us realize that we no longer need to experience living with overwhelming feelings. The tidal waves cease. It's as if we fed what we had and created more by trying to get rid of our stress and anxiety. However, by changing our thoughts, we ultimately change our life. Stress and anxiety need no longer have a place of power in our lives.

Meditation is a paradox. It's a letting go and a concentrated holding. When you concentrate and begin the process of changing from one energy to another, you quit giving energy to the things you don't want in your life. Therefore, be very careful what you think about it.

- **BE** very careful what you think about.
- Be **VERY** careful what you think about.
- Be very **CAREFUL** what you think about.
- Be very careful **WHAT** you think about.
- Be very careful what **YOU** think about.
- Be very careful what you **THINK** about.
- Be very careful what you think **ABOUT**.

All of your thoughts, not just the ones you want, form a bastion of energy that you radiate outwards to create the circumstances of your life. That's how you can use your Thought Practice to avoid getting what you don't want.

Stop giving energy to the things you don't want. Surprisingly, this is where most people put their thought energy. They maintain anxious, worried, and stressful energy by focusing their thoughts on anxious and stressful worries. The universal law of magnetism applies, no matter what your thoughts are.

Remember the seven immutable words from the book of Proverbs in the Christian Scriptures? "As you think, so shall you become." When you attach passion and emotion to those thoughts, you charge them energetically, which gives them power. Remember, every action began with a thought. Every illustrious career started with a thought. Every life-changing conversation started with a thought. You began with a thought. Sometime in the past, perhaps your dad thought of approaching a woman. One thing led to another, and you are the energetic result of that initial thought. Nothing happens until an idea occurs, and actions take place. It is precisely the same as you explore meditation.

Meditation brings to our attention to this present moment. We always have the choice to spin off into thinking about something, focusing on our breathing, or being present with whatever the moment brings. It's natural to spin off into planning, fantasizing, and self-judgment at the beginning. You are in the fundamental stages of changing your mind to change your life. Notice, as you begin do you tend to regret or explain the past, or worry and fantasize about the

You are choosing to flex the muscle of your mind and show it who is in charge.

future? As you notice your patterns and return to the present, you are choosing to flex the muscle of your mind and show it who is in charge. Doing so allows us to have thoughts and emotions flow through us without getting hooked on them and spinning our focus off on a tangent.

Meditation begins with a thought. How do you get started meditating? Perhaps the easiest way is to download some guided meditations from iTunes. There is also the Calm app, which offers hundreds of 8-12-minute guided meditations that cover numerous topics. Some meditation snobs look down their "enlightened" noses at guided meditations, but who cares? Are you trying to change and improve your life or win the approval of others? These guided meditations can help you address and remove lower energy thinking and build higher energy thinking patterns into your life.

Regardless of the methods, you begin to discover how meditation works in your life. There are drainers and enhancers to any meditative practice. The drainers will derail your meditative experience quickly. The enhancers will create more peace in your Thought Practice and meditative experience. There are numerous drainers, but the three most common are fear, anger, and judgment.

One of the most common energy drainers impacting many people is fear. If you do your Thought Practice, living in fear becomes a distant memory. It may seem impossible now as you are beginning. Still, consistent Thought Practice wipes out the low, draining energy of fear. Instead of living in fear that you have to make a sale, you will come to know that the right person who needs what you provide will show up at the right time. Our fears are birthed when the ego is in the driver's seat. If you feel fear, use it as a check to determine if your Thought Practice is targeting the thought you want in your life or if you have slid back into lazy thinking. When controlled by the ego, our minds are masters at taking mostly neutral information and spinning it into worry and fear. It's a result of our boomerang thoughts of hate, resentment, and criticism. The energies return to us as fear. Without the higher energy of love, life becomes a gauntlet of surviving fears.

Another energy drainer that is closely related and often birthed out of fear is anger. Fear and anger are invited into the subconscious by permitting seeds of lazy thought to lay dormant, take root, and produce their fruit. We preclude space for the higher energies of attraction, peace, and love when we do that. This begins with lazy thinking and forgetting to do the work of our Thought Practice. We create openings for fear and anger with lazy thinking. By doing nothing, we create the soil for them to flourish. Remember, we remove fear and anger from our life by acknowledging them and then letting go. Forgive, accept, and give thanks to the teachers who we have had in our lives. Seeing them as beings on their journey with love and warmth changes fear and anger into love and gratitude. It's only when you choose to consistently move away from the lower energies of fear and anger that you eliminate them—and the problems created by them—from your life.

The third energy drainer that will derail your meditation is judgment. Most of us don't think of ourselves as people who judge. Many of our problems, concerns, and pain result from how we judge others' actions. This judgment infests our hearts, relationships, homes, and work. We then contribute and accentuate those actions by judging others and ourselves. The drainer and delayer of judgment start in our thoughts.

Judgmentalism begins in the thoughts we hold of ourselves and others. Do we view others as good or bad, smart or dumb, attractive or unattractive? When we choose to see people through the eyes of love, acceptance, and understanding, we preclude a lot of judgmentalism. Transform your thoughts and actions by focusing on love and acceptance.

Even though I have prided myself on being non-judgmental and accepting of people, I became aware that I still had work to do. One day, I decided to tackle this issue in my life. I noticed the judgmental thoughts as they crossed my mind. I was shocked at the thoughts I had flooding my mind, which came from my ego and subconscious mind. There was one specific issue that stood out. I was highly critical and judgmental when it came to people who cut in line.

Once I realized that I was judgmental about line cutters and decided to work on it, I noticed cutting everywhere. It was a scourge on society. Every day I experienced cutting in line at least once and sometimes two or three times. At the grocery store, driving, everywhere. I was shocked as the problem had never been so acute. Once my brain keyed in on the line cutters, I was given a tremendous gift. I was given the gift of tangibly working on a judgment in my Thought Practice.

I worked on this every day until it became a non-issue, which took just over eight months. Once I came to the point of not judging the cutters but responding to them with honest love and clarification, the cutting stopped. The gift was that I dramatically improved my thoughts and eliminated many judgmental tendencies from my life. Becoming conscious of your thoughts, choosing your thoughts, and living in thoughts of love is the solution to the derailer of judgment. It takes time and consistency, but gradually and inevitably, love transforms the judgment into joy, acceptance, and beauty.

It's important to note that after an episode of judgmentalism, refrain from the urge to discuss it and share this offense with others. The more you focus your conversation on the other person's transgression, the more judgment will flood your thoughts. Don't feed this temptation. Additionally, if you are speaking to another who is not as far along the path of Thought

Practice as you, they will likely validate your judgment. This does nothing to further your growth and power in Thought Practice.

This would be analogous to two depressed people sitting over coffee talking about how depressed they are and then wondering why they are depressed. It's been said that small minds discuss people, while healthy minds discuss ideas. Many people who do not consider themselves judgmental spend most of their conversation time talking about other people. On and on, they prattle about what someone said, how terrible it was, and how it affected those around them. Meanwhile, the present moment is degraded to the low energies.

When you talk about another person, make an earnest effort to send direct, loving, and honest support to them. Encourage other people and send love to those who seem lost in their gossip, hatred, and judgment. Kindly let them know that you won't participate in those lower energy discussions. You can do this by simply not encouraging them to continue in the gossip or feeding into it.

The cast of characters that derail our meditation and Thought Practice includes far more than these three. However, all of the others tend to be borne out of these. Some of the offspring of fear, anger, and judgment are the following:

- Worry
- Guilt
- Shame
- Vanity
- Envy
- Greed
- Hypocrisy

- Pride
- Self-centeredness

Regardless of the derailer, it is telling you something is not yet healed in you. These derailers can also be your teachers if you let them. As you replace those thoughts, you can also heal those wounds once and for all through meditation and Thought Practice.

Just as there are derailers to our meditation and Thought Practice, there are enhancers; remember what energy will be returned to you. It is a fundamental universal law. Once you accept that you are responsible for what happens in your life, your Thought Practice will grow by leaps and bounds. As you learn to choose your thoughts, you will move to a state of realization in which you experience power, freedom, and peace. You can see it in a person's appearance who is living at a higher level of Thought Practice. They seem to be in a state of peace and happiness, no matter the circumstances. So, anything that enhances your higher energy thoughts is an enhancer.

One of the first and most powerful enhancers in your Thought Practice to mediation is to be emotionally excited and enthused. Charge your thoughts with the accompanying emotions. That gives them energy and power. When you are meditating and thinking thoughts of love towards another person, inhale and feel the love. Let it permeate every fiber of your being. On the exhale, relax into the gratitude for that love. You may find yourself smiling inadvertently. That is an indicator you are feeling the higher energy of love.

When you feel the emotional excitement of the higher energies of love, honesty, beauty, kindness, peace, and others, you want to attract them into your life. This transformation will leave your time of meditation feeling energized, excited, and thankful about life. You will also see this energy creating magnetically more into your experience. You will see that your problems take on a different hue and tone. They are less charged, without stress or anxiety, and full of opportunity. This magnetic law is true because lack begins in your thoughts. If you have love, kindness, and peace as your thoughts, you will not have room for judgment, worry, or anxiety. They cannot inhabit the same space simultaneously. When you enter the lower energies of judgment, anger, and anxiety in the life of another, meet them with love, kindness, and honesty. Without ever having to preach to the person, you will have opportunities to use the higher energies to transform the lower energies in their life. When you live with love in your heart, you radiate faster, healthier energy. It may mean some difficult conversations, but love is not always easy.

When you live with love in your heart, you radiate faster, healthier energy.

I had a friend consumed with anxiety. She asked me to coach her on her Thought Practice to transform her mind and life. For the first couple of months, she was a keen student, applying the principles and choosing her thoughts. As one cause of her anxiety fell off the plate of life, she replaced it with another. She was livid. I explained that the pattern in her life was clear. There were three areas of anxiety consistently present. When one fell off, a new cause for anxiety joined her life. The universe was trying to bring her the opportunity to learn a valuable lesson. One day in our conversation when I pointed this out to her, she responded, "As soon as so and so is taken care of, I will not be anxious any longer." I smiled because it was the same pattern she lived for years and years. At that moment, I brought the highest energy of honest love and kindness to her with a question. "You must like or get something from living in a constant state of anxiety because you are continually choosing to live there and not address it. How does living in anxiety serve your life? What do you get out of it?"

Several days later, she came back with an answer saying, "Living in anxiety gives me an identity and makes me feel like I am doing something." BINGO! She took a significant step into living in the higher energies and eliminating the lower energy of anxiety from her life that day. With clients who struggle with worry and anxiety, I often ask them what those emotions have accomplished. I have yet to receive a lasting, higher energy answer. You see, they serve only as a distraction and a derailment.

It takes considerable strength and courage to live in the higher energies. Experience with higher energies is key to transformation and can occur in your time of mediation. Experiencing how all this works in your life encourages you to keep going and flexing the muscle of your mind. You can learn how to do Thought Practice through other guidance, like from this book. But that guidance cannot transform your life—only you can through your experience.

Take riding a bike, for example. You instantly can relate to that statement not because you read about it but because you have ridden a bike. Your experience gives you all kinds of references, energy, and memories to build on. It is not because of evidence presented to you on bike riding that persuaded you. It is a knowing because of your direct experience with bike riding.

It is with all knowing that you are transformed. You come to know the power and energy of your thoughts. Go to a place where fear is harnessed and peace is tangible.

Transformation takes place incrementally through our Thought Practice. Thousands of little variables change, and then we have a moment of epiphany.

But the epiphany experience is not the only part of the experience. It is the tip of that iceberg. Your experience in life depends on the state of your thoughts. Let go of how you are perceived, detach from the results you produce, and instead immerse yourself in the experience of your life. Don't pursue happiness, but instead bring happiness to all you are and do. Be happy.

Expect the higher energies of love, kindness, and gratitude in your life. Look for them. This is quite different from the default setting of lazy thinking, which is habitually looking for ways to feel hurt, angry, and offended. Expecting love and kindness helps you perceive your thoughts' power and manifest them as realities in your life.

Expect the higher energies of love, kindness, and gratitude in your life. Look for them.

When you choose transformation, you will come to find your mediation as a time of centering your thoughts and encouraging your mind. It's like giving your day a pep talk. You will be provided what you need rather than searching to fill self-created holes of what's missing.

Living Thought Practice gives you freedom. Freedom comes when you notice the opportunity to defend or explain yourself, and you choose not to. Instead of protecting yourself, turn within and sense the texture of misunderstanding, feeling it through your body. Don't get caught up in the apparent quality of being right or wrong. Congratulate yourself for choosing to be in paradoxical unity, an oneness where all the higher energies are. Silently appreciate the opportunity and your willingness to practice living in higher energies.

Each person who has a healthy Thought Practice finds freedom from the lower energy thoughts and emotions which have held them in bondage.

Practicing living in higher energy brings them into manifestation. The Christian Scriptures states, "Be transformed by the renewing of your mind." A key to that is stopping the outward verbal expression of what you don't want. The second you catch yourself doing this, examine the thought behind your expression. If you place energy on what is, you will see more of that continuing to show up in your life. Even if you detest your life's circumstances, if you place energy on what you despise, you will attract it magnetically into your life. Remember, you get what you want, and you get what you don't want. The choice is yours—day and night, dream of what you intend to do and be. Choose your thoughts, and you choose the life you live.

CHAPTER 9 EXERCISES

These chapter exercises are designed to help you apply the principles of TRANFORMATIONAL THINKING in meaningful and transformative ways for you. They are not designed that one should do all the exercises for each chapter. Record the notes from the chapter, the exercise you are doing, and the results in your notebook.

> **Tell your heart and mind that it is time to learn from it so you can do differently next time.**

1. How do you deal with your feelings when your expectations remain unmet, and you feel decidedly disappointed? Do you let the disappointment stop you from going on with your life? Here are various strategies that might help you:

    - **The event that disappointed is just a small blip in your life.** It's unimportant in the greater scheme of things. Learn what you can from this setback instead of letting it affect your life and decisions in negative ways. Do not make that disappointment bigger than it needs to be.

    - **Don't give the event any more importance than it deserves.** People have a habit of unnecessarily enlarging small negative events and turning them into huge stories. But if you'd only share these stories with others, they'll tell you that they are essentially inconsequential. Hanging on to the disappointments will bring in more of them; that's just the way the world works.

- **Learn to let things go.** The longer you hold onto displeasures and distresses—rehashing the event over and over in your mind—the harder it becomes to move on from it. So do not do that. Give it one last thought and tell your heart and mind that it is time to learn from it so you can do differently the next time. Tell yourself to let it go. Focus on what you want from life, not on the failures that hold you back.

- **Do something.** The best you can do when things are not going your way is to get back to work. Rejected by a literary agent? Missed a step during your dance recital? Kids acting up at the school? Clients who just don't get it? It's okay. Do something now so you'd know that you are fighting the challenges head-on. This could mean writing your next book, hitting the studios for more dance practices, taking the kids to counseling, refining your marketing plan, and doing everything else you can to get back on track. Ask for help. Tweak your goals and do something.

- **Learn from experience. For most** people, unmet expectations automatically translate into *failure;* therefore, they want to avoid it at all costs. But here is the deal: failure isn't such a bad thing. It offers a unique opportunity to learn, improve, and grow. Yeah, so what if you failed. The people who love you won't love you any less because of it. Do not linger too long. Just take the time to learn the lesson and move on.

Take the time to learn the lesson and move on.

- **This one's an important lesson—that's why you'll see it repeated several times in this book.** F-O-R-G-I-V-E. When others disappoint you, it's only because you had high expectations of them. Move on.

And when you feel disappointed because of your own self, do the same. Everyone fails eventually. There is no use beating yourself up about it. Accept whatever happened because the only other alternative is wallowing in self-pity, and that's not going to get you anywhere either. At least with forgiveness, you can breathe a sigh of relief and look toward the future.

- **Let go of the shame.** When you feel disappointed, do not sit around and stew in the anger and frustration that follows. Instead, tell someone; talk to a friend about the disappointment you feel. This will help you release the feelings of indignity. If you ignore it, the resentment for having been shamed can grow inside you like a poisonous vine that will slowly eat away at your confidence. Don't let it have that power over you. Instead, share it, laugh about it, and diminish it, so it leaves you for good. Listen to others as they share their foibles with you because you are not the only one who has ever have messed up.

2. Low energy thoughts and emotions can derail us from our goals and keep us from living in the higher energies. Regular Thought Practice is a great way to continue vibrating with the higher energies that keep the derailers at bay. This is important because those derailers take us away from all that we want in life and lead us towards fear, anger, worry, vanity, envy, greed, pride, and shame. Here's what we should do to deal with these elements:

- **Step One: Turn toward acceptance**

  ♦ As you become aware of an emotion rearing its head within you, notice where in your body it originates. It could be a tightening of the throat, pounding heart, or knots in your stomach. Where in your body do you feel the tension? Sit with this emotion and identify it, don't ignore it. It could be anger, anxiety, grief, depression, sadness, or any other emotion. Get up and walk around if it gets too difficult. Do whatever you need to do without pushing your emotion away. Bottling it up inside will only make it explode that much more violently later. So give your emotions the attention they deserve no matter how difficult they are.

- **Step Two: Identify and label the emotion you're feeling**

  ♦ Instead of saying, "I am feeling anxious," say, "This is anxiety," or, "This is anger." This way, you acknowledge its presence while also empowering your own self to stay detached from it.

- **Step Three: Accept your emotions**

  ♦ When you feel a particular emotion, accept it and acknowledge its presence. It is only through this mindful acceptance that you can embrace your feelings with compassion and understanding towards yourself. Think of a loved one who is having a hard time. What would you say to them? You know that the answer is something kind and uplifting. Why don't you say the same to yourself? "I am okay. I don't deserve the blame. I already did the best I could with the resources I had."

  ♦ Extend kindness to yourself and be mindful of what's going on within you. This is the way to empower your own self, and soothe your pain, just like you do others. Keep doing this even if it feels weird at first. You will soon realize that your fear, grief, anger, or other difficult emotion does not define who you are. And when you acknowledge them, they'll show up less and less; they'll be fleeting shadows of themselves in the coming weeks. Another amazing thing happens when you open yourself up to emotions. The negativity leaves you, so you have open space to let in more awareness, curiosity, and empathy.

- **Step Four: Realize the temporary nature of your emotions**

  ♦ Emotions are impermanent. They rise and dip, arise and reside, appear and disappear. But when we are dealing with these emotions, it's hard to forget these facts in the heat of the moment.

  ♦ Give yourself permission to witness your emotions with compassion, attention, and patience. Give them the leeway to morph into something more palatable or completely leave you for good. When you are ready to embrace this process, ask yourself the following questions:

    - What is this feeling?

    - Where does it originate?

    - Is there something I need now?

    - Should I nurture it?

    - Is there something I can do for my partner?

    - What can my partner do for me?

    - How can we show loving-kindness towards each other?

  ♦ These are focused questions. It can be difficult to respond to them, but your answers can go a long way to enhance the empathy and connection within your relationship.

- **Step Five: Ask and investigate**

  ♦ Once you've calmed yourself after an impactful bout of negative emotions, take a minute to explore what just happened. Ask yourself:

    - What triggered my emotions?

    - Why am I feeling this way?

- What is the uneasiness I am experiencing, and where is it coming from?
- Did my critical mind cause it, or was it a physical reaction to something my partner said or did?

♦ We've all had days where we feel lonely and unappreciated. Instead of sulking in those feelings, step back from them and look at what brought them on. Whatever the trigger or cause, consider how it stands against your values:

- What were your expectations?
- What reactions led to anger, sadness, or anxiety?
- Is this a recurring pattern?

♦ The answers to these critical questions can take you to the root of your difficult emotions and offer insights into your emotion-laden experiences. There is no need to be in a hurry. Take yourself off of autopilot and trust your authentic self to answer these questions. This will help you detach yourself from the situation.

♦ Part of a dynamic Thought Practice is to picture what your life, hopes, and aspirations look like in the higher energies.

- Define your purpose. Gain clarity around the purpose of your visioning exercise. Let's say you are considering a career shift. Your purpose might then be to determine whether a career as XYZ would be rewarding. Maybe you're thinking about acquiring another small business or merging with another organization. You might then state your purpose as determining whether this business move would yield the personal and professional rewards you're looking for.

- Imagine your perfect scenario. Picture yourself moving from your current condition to where you would like to be. When you do a visioning exercise, close your eyes to the present. Start to see a new scenario that slowly comes into vivid detail. Come up with expansive mental and emotional snapshots of what this beautiful future looks like. Use this opportunity to envision what you look like in the future. See the movie of your life as you write the script.

- Ask yourself the right questions. Look inward for answers. Bring out that pen and notebook to write your responses for these and related questions:

  - What is my vision for my life?

  - How do I envision my career?

  - What kind of person do I aspire to be?

  - What do others think of me? Is this how I want others to perceive me?

  - What legacy am I going to leave my loved ones?

  - What does my vision for the future look, sound, taste, and feel like when I manifest it?

  - How and where can I grow and expand to step into this vision?

  - Do I need to let go of something's beliefs or emotions to be the clear instrument for this vision?

- Popular media has made visioning sound like the stuff of mythology or mysticism. The reality is that there are studies and research papers behind the practice proving that it works. Visioning is a viable way to achieve a future goal, aim, or state that you desire. The result of Thought Practice can be further strengthened with visioning as it galvanizes the higher energies.

This gives you the push you need to overcome the obstacles in your path as you reach out to your goals. Dream it, see it, and achieve it with visioning.

THE CHOICE IS YOURS

"Those who have failed to work toward the truth have missed the purpose of living."
—Buddha

AS YOU INTEGRATE THOUGHT Practice into your life, you will likely find yourself startled at how profound and simple it is. Thought Practice is both profoundly simple and practically difficult. Just because something is simple doesn't mean it is easy to do. Permit yourself to live in paradoxical thinking, realizing much of life is part of the same continuum rather than polarizing opposites. Embracing paradoxical thinking is essential to self-cultivation and our growth. Transformation is impossible without a change of thinking. Without changing your mind, change is impossible. However, from the vantage point of changing your thoughts, lasting life change is not only possible but probable. There are three specific areas of Thought Practice that, when applied to your thinking and charged with emotions, will be a superhighway for transformation in your life. They are the superfoods of your mental nutrition. They are **love, kindness, and gratitude.**

LOVE

Loving thoughts and actions often involve a paradox. You will recall a paradox is a statement that is seemingly contradictory and yet is perhaps true. Sometimes, profound paradoxes seem absurd on the surface. For example, you must believe strongly in your free will and ability to choose your thoughts while simultaneously surrendering to the energy and laws of the universe. You choose loving thoughts, which may result in having to remove another person from your life. Allow yourself to hold opposing thoughts without canceling one another out. Find ways to live in the mystery. By choosing to harmonize our Thought Practice with the consciousness of love, we come to know our authentic self. And in coming to realize ourselves authentically, we also open the door to understanding others in the light of love. Understanding others in the light of love is essential because it drastically reduces our propensity to judge.

The absence of judgment and the ability to forgive will bring new serenity to your life.

Whether you think of it as labeling or an objective opinion, it is still a judgment. Notice when you think of others as evil, lazy, dishonest, inconsiderate, stupid, ugly, fat, etc. Then change your thinking. Stop those judgments and think a thought of love towards that person and FEEL it. The quickest killer of love and peace in your own heart is judgment. A wonderful way to start flexing this muscle of your mind is to begin seeing everyone as a good person who is in a different place on their path of maturity. Heightened awareness goes a long way to living in love and eliminating judgmentalism from our thinking.

When you begin to think judgmentally, stop and question the root of the judgment. Perhaps it's a reflection of something inside you, which you don't like about yourself. As Carl Jung put it, "Everything that irks us about others can lead us to an understanding of ourselves." Could you be judging from a righteous moral position? For example, "This person lied to me, and lying isn't healthy or living from the higher energies." Loving that person may mean letting it go. Loving that person may mean having a conversation with them, such as, "It feels like you're not telling me the truth. I love you, and there is no need to lie to me. I hope going forward, you can be brave enough to trust me to tell me the truth." Maybe it is a personal bias; "Man, is that guy fat. He shouldn't be eating a hamburger and large fry!" You can replace this with any non-judgmental thought. Any thought at all. The truth is you don't know why he is fat. Maybe he used to weigh 600 pounds and is now 350 pounds. Although YOU think he's fat, he may feel skinny and sexy.

The absence of judgment and the ability to forgive will bring new serenity to your life. All of this is analogous to buying a new coat. You need a new jacket to keep you warm. You search and find one that you like. It feels comfortable but a little awkward. If, because of that uncomfortable feeling, you put it in the closet and do not wear it every day, it will always feel awkward. However, if you wear it every day and plow through the awkward feelings, at some point, it becomes like a second skin. You won't even notice the transition when it happens, but one day you will put it on and think how perfect of a fit it is. The awkward feelings will be nearly forgotten.

Eliminating judgment is simply replacing negative judgmental thoughts with love. Love correlates with non-judgment. Love correlates with active kindness. Love correlates with gratitude. Love and judgment cannot exist simultaneously in the same heart and mind. Applying thoughts of love is powerful because love is highly energetic and active. It is a chicken and egg thought. The more you love, the more your Thought Practice increases; and the more your Thought Practice increases, the more you love.

Your Thought Practice and your choice to love are about you, not others. Living in a Thought Practice of love is not concerned with if someone would love you more or better or differently. We do not condemn others for withholding love. As we pour out the love within healthy boundaries—while always honoring ourselves—we will see a magical transformation take place. Peace will increase in our hearts, and love will return to us. This love is often returned from sources that are a surprise. But it will return. Love generates more love.

You cannot receive what you don't give. When it comes to the higher energies of love, kindness, and gratitude, you cannot entirely give or receive them until you embody them. Transform your thoughts and transform your life. In the context of the higher energies, you cannot receive what you do not give.

Think and be love, and you will receive greater and greater love. Think thoughts of love and give love to others wherever they are in their journey, expecting nothing in return. Do not criticize or condemn. Do not love expecting it to return to you in a specific way. Love, just to love. Then, be prepared to receive. This is one of the paradoxes of love. As you give, you will receive and be a cheerful receiver. If you are unable to receive or are not a gracious receiver, you turn off the faucet that controls the flow of love. Love is a two-way street, so as you love, be prepared to receive love. There is a balance and cadence to giving and receiving love. We shouldn't violate the laws of the universe by refusing to receive as well. This is so important to Thought Practice because we manifest into our lives what we believe and think about. Stopping the flow of love by not receiving tells the universe you are good and do not need anymore. So the universe listens.

Real love, the kind birthed through consistent Thought Practice, is selfless, pure, and free of fear. It pours itself out without demanding any return. Do not fly past that idea. Without ANY return. It is a giving and being thankful to give love. It does not expect anything in return. As you experiment with this, notice how often there is a "tit for tat" expectation of return. But with real love, there is no *quid pro quo*. Love's joy is in the giving of itself. Love is God-manifested and the most vigorous magnetic energy in the universe. Pure unselfish love draws itself to itself. It does not need to seek or demand.

In your Thought Practice, begin to see love as cooperation and not a competition. Free yourself of the expectations of return. Sit back and enjoy the wonder as the universe provides you with love in unexpected ways. It takes time and consistency to live higher and higher levels of love. When it becomes a visceral, cellular level of living for you, you will come to see life living in cooperation and compliment. You will notice the aspects of your life falling into place naturally and at the right time. Even though it is not always on your timeline, it is perfectly timed. As your Thought Practice unfolds and increases in power and energy, you will see what real love is when you close the circuit of its energy. You will emanate a powerful love and attract its equivalent.

Begin to see love as cooperation and not a competition. Free yourself of the expectations of return.

As you modify your thinking, your world will undergo pleasantly dramatic changes. For example, you realize you are responsible for your reactions in any given moment, and your reactions begin with thoughts. Your thoughts will have changed, so your reactions will change as you understand that others do not have power over you. As you practice letting go of thoughts of what's lacking, you will find your love expanding. You don't need another thing to be happy. Everything is provided for you as you need it at the right time. Be in the moment, and free yourself to strive for something more. Choose to live the life you have now while changing your thoughts to attract the life you want. When love is the focus of your Thought Practice, you are content in the now. You don't need to be concerned about saying the right thing; you just will. An indicator of your Thought Practice growing and maturing is you lose fears and grow in love. You will see fear diminish and love expand.

Ushering in this powerful energy of love into your Thought Practice is sometimes challenging to do, but it is simple. Don't act loving—be love. Be authentic in all your interactions and love everyone. Everyone means everyone. Not just those you like and enjoy and who make you feel good about yourself. Not only those who live by the same rules and codes as you. Everyone means everyone, period.

And let's be honest—this can be quite difficult with specific people. Loving everyone is far easier than loving particular people. Loving humanity can be easy, while loving individuals can be difficult. Many of us come to Thought Practice because we struggle with loving ourselves, which makes loving others nearly impossible. Some of the indicators that show we need to work on loving others include:

- Choosing judgmentalism instead of compassion
- The ongoing inner dialogue of criticism
- Insensitivity, disrespect, and anger towards others

The way we clean up these indicators is through the energy of love and our Thought Practice. Change your standard response to thoughts of love. When you have critical thoughts towards yourself or another, stop them, and replace them with love. No exceptions.

When you realize the power of your Thought Practice and the magnetic energy of your mind, your desire may be to find an easier way—a quick way to reprogram your subconscious with the higher energies of love, kindness, and gratitude. Simple intellectual awareness of the truth will not bring results. However, energetic Thought Practice where you feel the love, kindness, and gratitude will reprogram your subconscious. But it does take time and consistency. When you were a child, you could not speed up the process of becoming an adult by overeating or sleeping more. The process is what the process is. Any attempt to circumvent the natural process ends in turmoil. Fyodor Dostoyevsky said at the end of an arduous decade-long journey in a Russian Gulag, *"The chief thing is to love."*

Love is the chief thing in life. It is the glue that holds everything together. It is the very substance of your higher self. All three supercharged energies of Thought Practice are very closely related and intertwined. Love expresses itself as kindness, which gives birth to gratitude. Kindness finds itself acting as love and being grateful. Gratitude becomes kindness and eventually love. No matter the combination, all three create and support the others.

KINDNESS

When asked to explain the essence of his teaching, the Dali Lama reportedly replied, *"Be kind."* This advice is so straightforward and simple that we can all relate to it. But in terms of our Thought Practice, what does it mean? If we take it to mean that we should try to act with kindness, isn't it just another moral dictate to change our behavior? Bringing kindness into our Thought Practice means abandoning our hard-hearted judgments about ourselves. When you come to your Thought Practice with the mistaken belief that anything outside of living the higher energies can make you feel good, you will no doubt fall into the unkindness of self-judgment where difficulties inevitably arise. What does kindness mean in the context of our Thought Practice?

Most of us are initially called to our Thought Practice by a desire to change our life. Certainly, in the early part of our practice, it is all about change. If we act kindly without changing our thoughts, we will inevitably slide back to our old actions and be disingenuous in our kind acts towards others. Transformation comes not just when we act kindly, but when we first think kindly. The kind acts will come as a natural outpouring of thinking and being kind. If we think of genuine kindness, kind acts will be a natural expression.

Kindness, as a superhighway of energy, is a natural expression of love and higher energy thoughts. When we are not thinking of the higher energies of love and kindness, we stifle the magnetism of higher energy and activate the power of low energy thoughts. The more we choose our thoughts of higher energy in our Thought Practice, the easier it becomes. The more we allow the ego to keep us in the lazy thinking of low energy, the harder it is to think high energy attractive thoughts. So, when you are unkind, you block kindness in your own life. Live in the awareness that kind thoughts strengthen, and unkind thoughts weaken.

Simple kindness to oneself is the most potent transformational force in your Thought Practice. Genuine kindness increases your power without any cost to you. Genuine kindness does not play favorites, has no exceptions, and does not expect a reward. The effects of kindness are pervasive and subtle. Love and kindness will dissolve negativity, not by attacking it but by bathing it in higher frequencies. This is analogous to how light dissolves darkness by its mere presence. When you experience permeating thoughts of love and kindness, you naturally become grateful.

GRATITUDE

The third energy that has tremendous power in our Thought Practice is to live a life of gratitude—genuine, feel it in your toes, gratitude. Practice living with gratitude every day. Be grateful for everything. As the Buddha said, "There are no friends or enemies, only teachers." Gratitude has an energy that goes far deeper than the gratitude itself. It dives deep into the reality of your being. Gratitude is understood as an outpouring of appreciation for something we received.

The energy of gratitude is closely related to the power of attraction. As Darren Cole, a friend of mine, once said, "Our vibe attracts our tribe." There is no limit to the love, manifestation, and peace we can express and attract. Living with thoughts and emotions of gratitude costs you nothing and attracts everything.

As your Thought Practice grows and matures, you will develop a deepening sense of gratitude. You will begin to see life through the eyes of the beauty of living in gratitude. The feeling of appreciation is a form of love and is a connection to the Divine.

As you practice and focus on the goodness of life around you, you will receive energy. Gratitude is a powerful attractor in your life. As your Thought Practice grows, the giving of appreciation will be a source of strength and nourishment in your daily life. Remember that everything and everyone who came into your life had a reason for being there and a lesson for you to learn. For example, write down everyone who you dismissed from your life. Maybe you ended your relationship with them, or

> **Living in this state of gratitude creates magnetism, and a magnet draws things to itself.**

you put an emotional stopper in your heart for them. Next to their name, write down what those relationships taught you. Make sure as you collect and record those lessons that you do so in a spirit of positivity. A negative learned experience is an attractor of negative energy, so stay positive. Living in this state of gratitude creates magnetism, and a magnet draws things to itself. By living in a state of genuine gratitude for all you have, you will start the flow of more good into your life. Living in a state of pure gratitude will bring the influx of more good into your life. Living in a state of genuine gratitude for the challenges in your life will start the flow of more good into your life.

Like everything else in Thought Practice, gratitude begins with your thinking. It's your choice to have a happy and peaceful mind or a stressful and anxious mind. It's all your choice based on the thoughts you choose. So why not choose a grateful mind? It is similar to the law of karma, which, in its basic form, suggests how you live will be returned to you in kind. A life of thievery leads to loss. A life of kindness will be returned to you in kind. We receive what we give. Remember, it is like a boomerang. Our thoughts, words, and deeds return to us with uncanny accuracy. This is the law of karma.

Karma in Sanskrit means *"comeback."* Whatever we sow, we reap. Karma is a law of the universe, and as such, it has authenticity, and we have authenticity. However, obedience precedes authority. The law opens when we obey the law. The law of electricity must be obeyed before it becomes a man's servant. When handled ignorantly, it becomes a deadly foe. The laws of the mind are identical. Our subconscious mind is simply power without direction, and it carries out orders without questioning. As you are reprogramming your subconscious mind, make sure to choose thoughts of gratitude. If something happens and you can't find a way to genuinely look at it with loving, kind gratitude, keep looking until you can. That is the lesson for you.

When love, kindness, and gratitude become intertwined in your life so that they are more often present than absent, they produce a depth of peace that virtually eliminates stress and anxiety. One of the fruits and tell-tale signs that they are present in your life is a natural progression of love, kindness, and gratitude in your heart and mind. It is your choice to have a mind full of stress and anxiety or full of the higher energies. You cannot have both, and the choice is yours. Only yours.

The Buddha taught two truths about this part of our life experience.

- He said that if you understand how your mind and energies work, you will have a happy life. The crux of our Thought Practice is that we get to know the higher energies on a visceral level. This knowing happens in a way that causes us to feel less frightened and anxious while simultaneously experiencing peace and happiness.

- Within you, you have the absolute ability to increase the frequencies of your energies and enhance your life experience. By living in the higher thoughts and energies of love, kindness, and gratitude, you will move away from the lower energies that keep you grounded in anxiety and stress.

CHAPTER 10 EXERCISES

These chapter exercises are designed to help you apply the principles of TRANFORMATIONAL THINKING in meaningful and transformative ways for you. They are not designed that one should do all the exercises for each chapter. Record the notes from the chapter, the exercise you are doing, and the results in your notebook.

1. You are only responsible for your thoughts, feelings, and the life that they help you create. But here's the deal: *you think.* No matter what the circumstances or times, your thoughts never stop coming. So why not indulge in Thought Practice and envisioning exercises? This will help you create the life that you were meant to live. Just as the lower energies and negative emotions are like junk food for your mind, higher energies of love, kindness, and gratitude are the mental superfoods. Are you ready to feed your mind what it needs to stay healthy?

    • Make it a daily exercise to say out loud three good things that you are grateful for. This is a simple yet powerful exercise to do with your kids as you express gratitude as a family. But it's also just as effective when you do this exercise alone.

    • Keep a gratitude journal. As I mentioned earlier, this is a highly effective way to become conscious of your higher frequency of thankfulness. Write in it every day, noting down all the things you were thankful for that day. Then, anytime you feel particularly down or defeated, go through these pages in solitude.

The gratitude journal will make you realize why it's so good to be you. Relive the moments as your face lights up because of the good memories.

- Every day thank your partner. When spouses and partners express gratitude for one another, it creates a potent feedback loop of understanding and trust, where both do their best to meet the others' needs and have their own desires fulfilled.

- Don't forget to thank yourself while you are at it. Gratefulness doesn't always have to be fixated on the nice things that others have done for you. You could thank yourself for being healthy, happy and trouble-free.

- Send out three gratitude messages every week. The chances are that you have at least that people in your life who have done something for you, treated you nicely, or simply made you smile. Tell them you appreciate them.

- It can be challenging to find the silver lining when things are tough. Remind yourself of all the times that things have gone well. Give gratitude.

- Do one or two acts of service every day. It does not have to be grandiose. Let someone else get into the lane in front of you when driving; pay for someone's coffee; or talk to a colleague. The smallest act of empathy can trigger thankfulness, setting in motion a circle of positivity as others pay it forward.

2. A strict or judgmental mindset can stress your professional and personal relationships and put your dynamic Thought Process in jeopardy. It can be difficult to change the way you meditate on life, but it isn't impossible. Here are some exercises to help you along the way:

   - Stop and breathe any time you have a judgmental thought coming on. Yes, it is automatic, but it is possible to learn how to put the brakes on them, which is a valuable skill. Acknowledge the self-criticism going on in your thoughts, hear it out, and then tell yourself to stop.

- Challenge your judgmental thoughts. Once you have identified a thought that's making you feel bad about yourself or others, it's time to figure out why it's in your head. For example, if you catch yourself judging a person by what they eat, wear, or how their children behave, the chances are that you were making a lot of assumptions about their lives. Now challenge those assumptions to shut down those thoughts for good.

- Show off a bit of understanding. Once you have examined your assumptions and suppositions, it is time to practice compassion. Try to find reasons why they behave, look, talk, and seem the way they do. If you see a messy child, don't just automatically blame it on bad parents. A better reason for that could be that it's hard to raise children and not everything goes right every day. Maybe they just had a bad day.

- Identify what makes other people so unique. Everyone has their strengths. So, try to find things you like about people as you avoid making quick judgments and appreciate others instead. For example, when interacting with a colleague who annoys you, remind yourself of their strengths. Perhaps they are always kind and willing to lend a listening ear. Try to focus on the positive traits of others. The more you focus on the positive, the more you will see it.

- YOU are the only person who's responsible for your thoughts and what they attract to your life. No matter what's going on in your mind, it has a price. Only with Thought Practice can you ensure that you don't end up paying too high of a price. There is no way around this. If you tried to lay off the responsibility of your thoughts, life might feel less demanding for now, but there will be more pain and suffering in the long run.

- Stop blaming others. An essential step in taking responsibility for your thoughts is to accept your fault in creating them. It is no use blaming others for your situation and misfortunes. Bad relationships, challenging childhood, socio-economic issues, and all other sufferings can be an inevitable part of life, but what will blaming others get you? No matter how hard you try to blame someone for your complicated life, will it really be a justification for what's happening to you? Own all of your issues; that's the first step to rising above them.

- Stop making excuses because it doesn't give you an opportunity to learn from your past mistakes. It also fuels cognitive bias. After all, it can never be your fault, right? It never was. This lack of personal accountability can stop your growth dead in its tracks. You can get stuck forever in a cycle of negativity, sulking, and complaints without ever moving forward. The only way to silence that negativity is by accepting your own faults and taking responsibility for your thoughts and actions.

- Find out how other people impact you. If you feel like a victim all of the time, take some time to stop and think of times when perhaps people were kind to you and impacted your outlook on life. For example, if someone is rude to you or makes a snarky remark, the chances are that they are saying more about themselves than they are about you. Their negativity is often a reflection of their self-worth. But we often fail to think logically in these circumstances and start feeling attacked. There is no point at all in taking other people's vices personally. But don't forget when you are judgmental about a person, it says more about you than them.

- Take the time to love yourself. The lack of self-responsibility is like a rampant disease these days. People have self-esteem issues that often compel them to blame others for their mistakes. This constant victim mentality breeds negativity. Do not be a victim. Instead, give your self-esteem a proper boost by taking responsibility for your actions. It's time to heal and grow, improve your life, and live it to the fullest. When you love yourself, it's difficult to be judgmental. Here is what else you can do:

  ♦ Pick your thoughts wisely.

  ♦ Explore the higher energies even if you do not feel very positive.

  ♦ Take care of your sleeping patterns.

  ♦ Eat healthy for a better body and mind.

  ♦ Take the time and space to appreciate spirituality.

  ♦ Exercise regularly.

  ♦ Thank yourself and others because it's a good thing to do.

  ♦ Reflect and meditate.

- Love yourself; make it your default state of mind. Be mindful of the actions and habits you indulge in. You have the biggest responsibility to yourself, so take care of yourself and choose yourself every day. Loving yourself should be a priority.

3. Determine what you will do and then do it. This act encompasses the very essence of taking responsibility. Make it a promise to yourself. Part of evolving is taking responsibility for your thoughts and flexing those mind muscles for successful Thought Practice. It is possible to increase your credibility with these principles:

  - Only make a promise if you are 100% sure of delivering on it. Your "yes" is a contract that you must abide by.

- Create a schedule. Now every time you make a promise, put it on the calendar.

- Do not make excuses for yourself. Sometimes life does get out of control. But if you must break a commitment, do not give random justifications for it. Own it, say you are sorry, and make things right in the future.

- Tell the truth. It won't be easy but then it will pay off in the long run.

PERFECT IMPERFECTION

"One of the basic rules of the universe is that nothing is perfect. Perfection simply doesn't exist…Without imperfection, neither you nor I would exist"
—Stephen Hawking

WE ARE OBSESSED WITH perfection or our opinion of perfection as a society. We diet and abuse our bodies to attain some mythical look that is achieved only through Photoshop. We would rather have the appearance of a perfect family rather than capture a teachable, intimate moment with a child misbehaving at Target. In reality, what seems to be imperfect has perfection in the blemishes. What may seem to be frustrating or broken contains profound spiritual truths and lessons supporting it. There is perfection unfolding in the imperfection.

As your Thought Practice grows, choose to see the imperfections in your life as perfect, just as they are—even if your ego cannot understand it. Whether something is imperfect or perfect, an obstacle or an opportunity is all determined by your thoughts. It is all determined by how you view the circumstances.

I recently experienced this while walking. Once or twice a day, I do a meditative walk through the vineyards near my home. I began my walk, and each time I began to rest into the mediation, thoughts of a financial need surfaced. My ego was fighting hard to protect me by thinking and worrying about this need. The sun was out, and it was a cool, 70-degree

Perfect Imperfection | 183

morning. The day was bright and happy. Throughout the entire walk, I battled with my ego. I was cold, bummed that the weather was not better, and saw nothing but hundreds of acres of weird-looking bushes. My ego got the better of me that day for sure.

It happens to all of us no matter how long you've been at Thought Practice, but it does dissipate, and these battles now occur in my mind perhaps once a year. The next morning, I began my walk at the same time. The sun was out, and it was a cool, 70-degree morning. The day was bright and happy. I looked up at the beautiful sky with a fluffy white cloud and said thank you. Smiling, I said, *"Thank you for providing for this need, and the solution is already on its way and will arrive in the time I need it. Thank you that I don't have to worry about it."* Then I went on to give thanks for all the times I could recall where God and the Universe provided for me as far back as I could remember. I gave thanks and celebrated my Thought Practice and how it had brought abundance and peace into my life. By the time I knew it, my hour walk was over. Arriving back at my house, I went inside to begin my writing for the day. An hour later, I received a text from a coaching client who owed me money; he was paying it in full that day. The amount was exactly to the dollar of my financial need.

What changed? Two things:

1. I stopped allowing my thoughts to drive me and regained control and chose my thoughts; and,

2. I changed how I viewed the circumstances and transferred that view into energy.

One of the universal laws is that in God, there is only perfection. He is complete. In appreciating the perfection of imperfection in your life, give thanks. You have already received what you need. It's in the ether and on its way to you. Make active preparation for receiving it into your life on the material plane. With confidence, tell God what you need: *"God, give me a definite lead, reveal to me the solution to this need. Bring it to me."* Not as a demand where you are telling your servant what to do, but as a child of the King going to your Dad with bold clarity because you know he wants to bless and provide.

Remember that doubt and fear are tools of the ego to protect us and kill the energy of your Thought Practice. They destroy peace and prosperity. Our focus is critical in our Thought Practice. In High School and College, I used to snow ski. There were times I would see a tree, and if I thought, *"I don't want to hit that tree,"* and allowed fear and doubt to reign, do you know what happened? It was like a tether line from that tree to me, pulling me towards it. Instead, what I learned to do was ignore the tree and focus on where I wanted to go. I would focus on the clear path in front of me that I would not see if I focused my energy on the tree. Focusing on what I wanted and where I wanted to go, smiling at the joy of the journey, I made it down the mountain every time. After several times of practicing this, it became natural, and I began to put my mental focus on where I wanted to go. The more I did this, and the better my skiing Thought Practice became, the faster I arrived at where I intended to go. It's counter-intuitive to the ego mind, but the secret is to look away from what you're afraid of and towards what you intend. It is up to you.

It is the individual consciousness that begins the transformation process in partnership with the universal laws. If we are not satisfied with our present life condition, our consciousness can bring about change. We create our desired life by living in partnership with the universal laws and Thought Practice. As our consciousness is enriched through both truths, our life grows healthier. Our mental life grows healthier. Our emotional life grows healthier. Our physical life grows healthier. Our home life grows healthier. Our financial life grows healthier. All of these expand as our subconscious and the conscious mind is imbued with the universal laws of truth.

When you embrace the freedom to be you—100% authentically you—you will have the ability to transform your life. If you know the power of your thoughts, align with the universal laws, and are intuitively led by your thoughts and words, you start actions in unseen forces that can reshape your life. It is important to choose the right thoughts and the right words. Carefully choose the affirmations you speak into the universe. Say these affirmations with your heart and soul. When charged with belief and emotional energy, they catapult energy into the universe that manifests in your physical life. Ask God the following: "Open the way for my immediate supply and needs, bring to me that which I need in an avalanche of abundant blessing. Give me a definite lead and tell me what actions to take and if there is anything I should stop doing."

Remember that giving opens the way to receiving. To create activity in your finances, you should give out of gratitude. You should present these gifts with genuine joy, love, and cheerfulness. Pay your bills with joy. Send forth your financial expectations and your finances fearlessly and always with a blessing. This freedom and attitude make you a master of your money. It is yours to obey, and your thoughts, spoken words, and actions open vast reservoirs of abundance.

> **Remember that giving opens the way to receiving.**

Many people live a life of poverty and scarcity because they are anchored to their past. When we are anchored to our past and history, we give others a certain control over us. They expect us to be something we were or were perceived to be in our past. We have all disillusioned people in the past. We then take on guilt because we let them down or didn't meet their expectations. Of all the enlightened and peaceful souls I have met, one of the common traits is they are not tied to their past.

Through their Thought Practice, they look only in the rearview mirror to learn lessons, and then they move on. It's tough to live in peace if you are in the past because peace is in the present. They don't allow how they were in the past or how things used to be to define them or their lives today. Your imperfections and failures are as much a blessing from God as the success. And they teach you a lot more. You are free from your past. It is your choice to live in the constraints of the past or the freedom of the present. Only yours.

You are perfectly imperfect now—as you are. That being true, your ego will still try and convince you that you are not okay. Your ego will try and convince you that you would be okay if or when you:

- Lose some weight.
- Have more money in your bank account.
- Achieve a specific career opportunity, etc.

The siren song of the ego is never-ending and never true. Your ego will try and convince you to listen to the lower energy thoughts. Remember, you are building new habits in your Thought Practice. It takes time as there will initially be a temptation to return to the ego-driven ways of your mental training in the past. Your past conditioning trained you to believe you could only have joy and peace if life were going the way you wanted it to. Stress, anxiety, fear, and other low energy feelings are experienced in your mind by processing and evaluating your life from a perspective of not having. When you experience these kinds of thoughts, you must remind yourself not to accept this false picture. Replace this illusion with thoughts of attraction and what you want.

Choose not to indulge your ego in dwelling on the process of struggle to get answers. There is a significant transformation that takes place as you wrestle and do the work of your Thought Practice that no one can do for you. You are more than capable right now of keeping your energy field uncontaminated from the lower energies of judgment, anger, resentment, and fear. As Johann Wolfgang von Goethe observed, "When you treat a person as they appear, you limit them. However, if you treat them as they could be, you make them what they should be."

A vibrant and healthy Thought Practice is coming home to oneself—your objective is applying the wisdom and laws in the face of the disparate universe of anxiety, stress, and fear. Healthy thoughts create space for peace, purpose, and happiness. In your Thought Practice, there will come a moment when you wake up. It is like suddenly going from black and white to a full 4k HD television. POW!

Thought Practice is training your mind. It's the most amazing tool you have available to create the life you want. But you must use it. In addition to choosing your thoughts, you can increase your thinking capacity by choosing to be mindful and present. Living in mindful appreciation for your imperfections will free your heart and mind, creating joy and peace. Begin by being mindful of your moments. Whether you are walking, cooking, cleaning, working, showering, or anything else, be present in THAT moment. Choose to notice and appreciate what you are experiencing. You can do this anytime, in any place, and in any situation. As your practice grows, you will find this simple exercise will help you focus and live with less distraction. This will help enormously as you continue to be mindful and choose your thoughts and energies.

Throughout my life, I have enjoyed riding motorcycles. Dirt bikes offer thrills and freedom. Street bikes are exhilarating. However, when I ride, I am very much in the moment. Mindful. Present. I am paying attention to my driving, the road conditions, other vehicles, and everything else in the experience. My mind must be concentrating, focused, and mindful. Otherwise, the experience could be deadly. I cannot afford to be distracted by anxiety, stress, or other thoughts. It is a form of meditation for me to the task at hand. It's so easy not to carry this to other tasks. For example, when driving in my car, I can immediately go off into far off places in my mind. I am not forced to be mindful of the task of driving. I am distracted, dangerous.

Letting go and living in a state of mindful presence can be as simple as awareness. It prevents the thieves of joy, which are the past and the future. To break free and transcend distraction, you remind yourself of the difference between your ego and your higher self. ego's voice seeks to dominate and control with thoughts of your imperfections. Thoughts of comparison. Thoughts of lack. Thoughts of worry. Comparing leads to despairing. Getting rid of the low energy attachments of the ego is a shattering of false beliefs. The only power it has is convincing you that those thoughts are real and that your imperfections are imperfections.

Begin by practicing appreciating your imperfections with statements that transform them. Replace the ego phrases of your imperfections with the same attitude and appreciation you bring to other things—like a sunset, a flower, looking into the eyes of a loved one, a piece of art, anything for which you have a deep appreciation.

As you learn to embrace your perfect imperfections, it will become apparent to you what areas you will learn to appreciate. It will also become evident which ones are areas for your growth and maturation as a soul. Resistance can be our teacher. When we resist circumstances, we carry them with us. When we accept the circumstances, we let them go. If we try and run from them, they chase us. Eventually, we get exhausted, while the area we resist never tires in its pursuit. Agree that the imperfection is good and choose not to be disturbed by it. By embracing the imperfection and not resisting it, its power falls away peacefully. If you are experiencing disharmony in the circumstances, it means they are borne out of something inside you that lacks harmony with the higher energies of love, kindness, and peace.

This means imperfections are good, and we should embrace them. We are undisturbed by them. We do not allow them to move us from peace. Once we genuinely believe this truth, everything changes. We have a wiser relationship with ourselves and the events of our lives. If a situation is painful and we cannot change it, we can be confident that our pain will not last forever, and there are lessons for us. Powerful lessons. The impermanence of any experience doesn't diminish it; it enhances it if we are present. The good news is nothing lasts forever. The bad news is nothing lasts forever. It's all perspective, and when you change the way you look at things, the things you look at change.

Living in perfect imperfection within your Thought Practice leads to your purpose. You will begin to live a life on purpose. What does the divine flow of higher energies and living on purpose mean in a practical sense? This is not about vocation or how you make a living. It is about living in your purpose. Sometimes that leads to a vocation but not always. Begin your day by asking God to lead you on your purpose. THEN mindfully look for those leadings throughout the day.

All of this comes naturally and without being forced by us when we live in higher energies. The harmony of Divine love through our Thought Practice includes happiness, love, peace, and purpose, which makes life this amazingly smooth and transformative experience. When you have consistently flexed your mind's muscle and begin to see the transformation of your life, the positive changes begin to snowball. It becomes an avalanche of blessing. Perfect self-expression and purpose will never be hard. It will come out naturally. It becomes so easy that your Thought Practice begins to feel like playtime. As you connect deeper and more meaningfully with the Divine, you will come to see how God takes immense pleasure in lavishing you with abundance.

Abundance comes as you embrace the perfectly imperfect of your life—embracing those imperfections and coming to the point of truly appreciating and loving them. Embracing these brings us back to gratitude. One step to living in this abundance is to make affirmations immediately when you wake up—every morning when you wake up. These can be statements, affirmations of gratitude, or requests for leadings such as:

- Show me what you want me to do today.
- Bring into my life someone today who needs me.
- I am grateful for sleep.
- Thank You, Thank You, Thank You.

Anything that affirms the higher energies of love, peace, kindness, non-judgment, grace, and purpose works. The last one is mine.

Abundance comes as you embrace the perfectly imperfect of your life—-embracing those imperfections and coming to the point of truly appreciating and loving them.

I generally wake up happy. That is a choice. I used to wake up foggy. About twenty years ago, I decided I was going to wake up happy. I started changing my foggy brain with little thoughts of happiness upon waking. After a season, it became natural to me. As my Thought Practice matured and my mental, emotional, and spiritual health grew from dysfunctional to functional, my morning affirmation changed. I do not know how or when, but for as long as I can recall, I wake up and say, "Thank You, Thank You, Thank You." My affirmation is genuine and authentic. Heartfelt thanks. For what? It changes every morning. For instance, I am always thankful for my bed. I have a great bed, which is a loving expression of care for my body. For over three years, I have expressed gratitude for my feet.

My feet were a mess. I had genetic non-diabetes neuropathy and arthritis. That means I could not feel the bottoms of my feet when I walked, and the bones felt like I was walking on broken glass. It became so bad that a friend asked me why I walked like a 90-year-old man. Every step was excruciating. I was in a situation where there was no medical attention or care. I was on my own. So, each day, I began a focused mediation of healing on my feet. I rubbed them and thanked them. This may sound strange to new Thought Practice ears, and it should—it was weird to me when I had the idea. Every day I meditated several times throughout the day. I apologized for abusing them with poor nutrition. I thanked them for all the years of walking and running and playing. I came to a place of love and appreciation for my feet. Four years later, my feet were in amazing shape. I still have neuropathy and arthritis, but I walk nearly five miles every day. I can exercise. I practice great foot care, as well. But 90% of the healing happened without medical attention.

Make your morning affirmation a habit, and you will see amazing miracles brought into your life. Make sure your affirmation is satisfying, convincing, and from your heart. Thoughts and words have power. So, you better believe them when you say them. It's a practical way to start your day with your Thought Practice and open the pathways of Divine love into your life. It helps with practicing grace towards yourself and others throughout the day. The morning affirmation helps prevent inner conflict by setting the tone for the day. You will begin to live with joy, peace, and purpose that is usually reserved for mystics and children. Remember, it is impossible for hope and despair, judgment and love, or any low and high energy to exist in the same heart at the same time. There is only space in your heart for low energy or higher energy. Period.

Embracing the perfection of your imperfections brings peace and purpose to your life. When you suspend your ego and choose high energy purposeful thoughts, you will find your purpose. This is done thousands of times throughout the day and becomes how you live, so there is no effort put into it. It is a wonderful way to live. It's like bathing in joy as you accept and appreciate your imperfections. It's a simple way to live on purpose and in the river of Thought Practice. Time disappears as you are in communion with the highest aspects of yourself. You wake with a deeper sense of purpose and meaning to your life.

Joy is a way of processing the world from the perspective of what you have and what is right, not what you are missing. Joy and peace will be perfectly yours in your imperfections as you give thanks for all that you are and are becoming.

CHAPTER 11 EXERCISES

These chapter exercises are designed to help you apply the principles of TRANFORMATIONAL THINKING in meaningful and transformative ways for you. They are not designed that one should do all the exercises for each chapter. Record the notes from the chapter, the exercise you are doing, and the results in your notebook.

1. It's interesting how we humans are designed to follow patterns. This also means we tend to repeat our past—including the mistakes. We're creatures of habit and following patterns of behavior is in our nature. Sometimes, these habits are hard to break, while at other times, we are simply deluding ourselves. We like to believe that something has worked for us in the past, whereas it may not have at all. We continue with our old communication style, thinking it is an effective way to communicate with our partners when our partners are confused about what is going on inside of our heads. We are more aware of our histories than anyone else, and you're the ultimate expert on the subject of "You." So even though you may seek the assistance of a therapist or a psychologist to guide you, eventually, the only person who can really make a change is you. And as difficult as it may seem right now, breaking from your past while keeping with the lessons you learned from it is not impossible. We will share some practical ways to help you make your past patterns work for you while also helping you lose the chain of repetition.

- Take your masks off. The first thing you need to do is identify yourself—the authentic self to implement a change. You need to remove the layers you have put on to project that you are a different person than you are. Identifying with your authentic self is the first step you need to take to proceed. There is no harm in starting small. Don't be someone you're not; rather, strive every minute to become a better version of yourself, even if it means making minor changes to your life.

- Learn from your own past experiences. You can still implement the lessons you have learned from your experiences without repeating them. In fact, this is the most direct way of learning through your personal history. For instance, if your sarcastic way of communication does not work with your partner and has created problems before, then try and figure out why you're still using the same sarcastic tone. With a bit of change in your attitude, you can solve the problem. And although it requires an effort and a lot of patience, there's no harm in trying over and over again, especially if the result makes you happy. Every time you make a positive change in your life, realize it, remark upon it, and appreciate yourself. The key is to be more mindful of what you say and how you express it. Use your own personal history to gain the general guidelines that will help you bring positive changes in your life.

Learn from the imperfect circumstances. It is not natural to always have life's circumstances line up in your favor. However, if you are using this as an excuse to hold back, I consider it a copout. When a sentence starts with statements like "If only I had this…I never had the opportunity…You don't understand my situation," I stop listening. It is a simple blame game, where people tend to blame their circumstances for their failure. Many people grew up with lots of money and all the possible opportunities to make a successful life of their own but end up leading very average and far from perfect. The best way to face the circumstances you believe are holding you back is to change your mindset towards them. If you are stuck in a challenging situation, use it as motivation. Life will always present you with two choices—either become bitter or become better. When you change your perspective towards circumstances, the circumstances change for you.

> **Life will always present you with two choices—either become bitter or become better.**

2. Once you control your Thoughts, you can use them in your best interest and do what you will with them. The power of shaping your life lies within your thoughts. If you are wondering how to tame the uncertain thoughts, the solution also lies with you. You need to stop resisting the flow of thoughts, regardless of how oppressive they are, and eventually, they will take a back seat in your mind. However, if you continue to value them and invest your time and energy, the intensity of those thoughts will continue to grow. These principles will help you redirect your focus and thoughts towards the higher energies of love, kindness, non-judgment, receptivity, abundance, fulfillment, and honesty. Don't let lazy thinking take over your mind. Make an effort to replace these negative energies with positive, higher energy thoughts. The more you practice this, the lower the voice of lazy thinking will become until it is a mere vapor that evaporates.

3. Get rid of all the *'if when'* and *"if only"* thinking and excuses from your mind. This is just another way for lazy thoughts to take over your brain. Don't let that happen. Act as soon as it pops up in your head. Pause and look for the lessons that your soul is attempting

to call your attention to. By eliminating these excuses, you will empower your mind and allow it to wander in higher energies.

It can be challenging for anyone to be stuck in a problematic situation where nothing is working right. Well, there are many others like you in the same situation. This happens because we fail to appreciate ourselves. Lack of appreciation is what leads to a lack of motivation and belief. Regardless of the problem you're dealing with, don't forget you're fighting it and still standing firm—and those reasons are also enough to appreciate.

Instead of seeking validation from others, earn your own trust and self-respect.

- **Believe in yourself.** That is when you will truly be able to appreciate yourself. The best way to do this is to immerse yourself into higher energies as to who you are and how you want your life to be. Instead of seeking validation from others, earn your own trust and self-respect. If you're not able to respect yourself, others will follow. Take time to appreciate the little things. Let's start with appreciating your body, mind, and personality this week. Every person has some unique attributes—time to highlight them and be appreciative of them. Perhaps, you have a physical issue with your feet, or your work requires you to stand all day long. Spend a few minutes every day telling your feet how you appreciate them by massaging them and sending the energy of love and gratitude. Value yourself with higher energies.

- **And I will repeat: Learn from your mistakes.** If you use your failures as an opportunity to learn, they will not be failures anymore. They become your guide to lead a better life. However, not using life's lessons as an opportunity to learn can keep you from making progress.

- **Don't let others' perceptions or actions control you.** If you let other people take so much control of your emotions, it will keep you from moving forward. Whether you are running a business or working in a company, it is natural to come across people who always try to put you down and discourage you. Know your worth and be ready to take others on.

THE ART OF SELF-CULTIVATION

*"Cultivation of the mind is as necessary as
food to the body."*
—Marcus Tullius Cicero

THOUGHT PRACTICE IS SOMETHING that each of us can only do for ourselves. We can learn from others, receive encouragement, and be held accountable. However, it is ultimately a discipline and freedom each of us can only do for ourselves. Thought Practice is something we can feel connected with, know, and trust. It's an inner awareness that we explicitly believe and yet, at the same time, cannot honestly describe with words. Self-cultivation with Thought Practice begins with a determination to flex the muscles of your mind and reprogram your subconscious.

When we know and embrace our powers and abilities in the working of our minds, it's easy to be tempted to look for a quick and easy fix. We want a fad diet to impress the subconscious mind with life-changing practices. Thought Practice is an earned discipline and not a quick fix. Any quick fix would rob us of developing life-changing skills and the cultivation of our natural, healthy selves. This programming of our subconscious happens

> **Thought Practice is an earned discipline and not a quick fix.**

whether we choose the thoughts or let thoughts choose us. So why not be in the driver's seat of your life? Here is how this works.

Years ago, I had a friend who often said, "I don't like being married to my wife. I love her, and I'm in love with her, but she is hard to live with, and I don't like being married." He said something like this every time we got together. He was likely saying those things to others as well. His tone was never confidential but much more casual. One day, his wife told him she had been having an affair and was in love with the man and wanted a divorce. He was hurt and angry when he told me. I told him, "The divorce is exactly what you brought into your life with how you have programmed your thoughts. You created this with your thoughts, then your words, then your actions. It was a natural progression."

The most common unintended subconscious programming is in the areas of relationships and money. When a man or woman stops caring, when they stop dressing to attract their spouse, or when they stop connecting, they allow themselves to slip into the white noise of daily life. They will naturally have indifferent thoughts that perpetuate indifferent actions. When partners cease to think and speak concerning one another and instead choose to be critical, they create tension and unhappiness. On the other hand, choosing your thoughts, words, and actions so that your partner is always attractive to you will ensure the relationship stays alive and vibrant. It ALL starts with your thoughts. It is the same with money. No one can attract money if they act like they do not want it.

I was speaking with a coaching client recently. She is a starving artist and said to me, "I don't care if I make money, I just want to do my art." I told her that her thoughts and attitudes toward money were keeping her poor. Her attitude toward money was creating separation with finances and creating a lack and need. I challenged her to begin thinking and believing that she wanted and was entitled to financial success and security. Manifested finances must be in harmony with our thoughts and Thought Practices. Money is important because it provides freedom—these thoughts about money aren't about greed. Money, like everything else, must be in harmony with the higher energies. But money does need to be kept in circulation as a tool to bless others. Hoarding like a miser will stop the flow as it is a low energy of lack and insecurity. When you let go by giving genuine joy and gratitude, you invite more money to come to you.

Like everything with Thought Practice, self-cultivation is up to us. And unfortunately, most of what goes wrong in our lives is a result of our shipwreck. We create or invite it. There are two categories of thoughts that cause loss: lack of appreciation and fear. Lack of appreciation creates thoughts and actions of rejection. Fear creates thoughts and actions that create a loss. These old patterns need to cease. Otherwise, you are giving energy to what you do not want, which brings more of what you do not want into your life. Why would anyone do that? And yet, so many of us have done and continue to do so. We do so because our subconscious has been programmed this way by our ego and experiences.

One of the things that separates those who live the life they want from those who don't is the unwavering knowing that they will achieve success. Such a belief requires a healthy Thought Practice. Such knowing starts with a thought, like everything in the world. Everything begins with a thought. Remember, thoughts are things, and they have energy. A thought immediately launches magnetically into the ether. These thoughts begin to translate themselves to manifest into the physical. Everything that we have started with a thought and desire. Thought takes the first lap of its journey, from the abstract to the concrete. Then on into the workshop of the mind where plans for its transformation are created and manifested in reality.

Self-cultivation is a natural part of your Thought Practice. Self-Cultivation is defined as the development of your own mind and abilities through your healing efforts and work. It is like self-care. All three are intertwined. Your self-care will shine through self-cultivation as you refrain from judgment of yourself and others. You will gain strength as you reject the judgments and abusive words that others put on you. Remind yourself that you don't have to be better than anyone else. You don't have to "win," and others don't have to "lose." Begin to live your essential nature of love, peace, kindness, and joy. Relinquish your tendency to be offended and defensive when someone has a different opinion or perspective. Feed the thoughts of your natural nature rather than allowing your mind to be seduced by the ego. When you genuinely change your thoughts and the way you look at life, the world begins to look very different.

The self-cultivation of Thought Practice is only attractive to those who are already wise enough to know how foolish they've been. By now, you have probably seen that you have gotten some doubt and pushback from your ego. That is normal. Your ego has been in control for a long time and does not want to cede power. However, if you stick with your Thought Practice, things start to move. I know when I concentrate on manifesting something, coincidences happen to facilitate that vision. In my reality, these events occur at the same time.

Remember, your subconscious receives and files impressions regardless of their nature. So, voluntarily plant seeds in your subconscious mind of the plan, thought, or purpose you want to manifest in your life. Your subconscious acts predominantly on the dominating thoughts which have emotional energy attached to them. Your subconscious mind works day and night. It never stops working. Remember that thoughts are things and have magnetic energy attached to them. That magnetic energy pulls towards you what you think about.

Your subconscious mind will not remain idle or empty. If you fail to choose what thoughts to plant in your subconscious mind, your ego will gladly accept that role. Your ego will plant thoughts of neglect, fear, poverty, lack, and any negative limiting thought it can. As a part of your Thought Practice, you will have to choose to master the impulse to feed the ego's seeds and instead nourish your mind with the thoughts you want in your life. Remember, every material thing started with a thought and thought energy.

> **If you fail to choose what thoughts to plant in your subconscious mind, your ego will gladly accept that role. Your ego will plant thoughts of neglect, fear, poverty, lack, and any negative limiting thought it has.**

Our thoughts are to our minds as food is to our bodies. If you feast on junk food, you will likely not have a body that serves you well. You will more than likely struggle with body image issues. If, however, you eat nutritiously, feeding your body the fuels it needs to meet your physical goals, you will have a healthier body. Similarly, positive and negative thoughts affect your mind. Your thoughts bear fruit in your life. Keep planting seeds of worry, stress, anxiety, and fear, and you will grow those fruits in your life. It is your responsibility to make sure that positive thoughts constitute the dominating influence of your mind. This is where habits are so important and can serve you well. The more you flex the muscle of your mind and choose your thoughts, the more likely it is to become a habit. Eventually, the habit is so strong that the lazy thinking cannot enter—there's no room for them. As you practice allowing and living in the path of the flow, success is not something you go after—it's simply what you are. Abundance is no longer a fantasy but something you live in. It flows unimpeded into your life and through your life to others.

Look at the misbeliefs you have held. They must be eliminated or transformed into what you want. Whatever you desire to become or attract to yourself, make that internal shift from "it probably won't happen," to "it's on its way!" THEN begin actively looking for evidence—even tiny evidence—that what you desire is indeed on its way. You get what you think about, whether you want it or not. All these thoughts play a part in self-cultivation. There are four key actions you can take that will increases the effectiveness of your self-care through self-cultivation:

- Persistence
- Visualization
- Experience
- Practice

PERSISTENCE

Without persistence, you are done before you start. With persistence, you will win and change your thoughts and, therefore, change your life. There is no substitute for persistence. People who have developed the habit of persistence do not fail. No matter how many times they fall, they get up, so they eventually DO arrive where they wanted to go. They discover that every "*failure*" brings with it the seed of an equivalent advantage, lesson, and opportunity. Persistence is a state of mind.

Remain in a persistent state of awareness of the energy of your thoughts, and you will embody love, peace, honesty, kindness, and abundance. This is the alignment that will bring you into balance and restore harmony in your life. Reprogramming your subconscious autopilot is not difficult, but it does take time and consistency. The more you do it and practice it, the more it will become a healthy habit and start to pay dividends in your life. That is when things get exciting! As Winston Churchill said, "Never give in, never, never, never, never give up or quit."

VISUALIZATION

A visualization is a powerful tool in your self-cultivation arsenal. It can help you in reprogramming your thoughts, your Thought Practice, and your meditation. It is easy and natural to do as an expression of your soul dreaming. It's your soul whispering to you above the clamor and posturing of your ego. Visualization is also in harmony with the magnetic laws of the universe. Keep in mind, you will receive what you see yourself receiving. The form may look slightly different, but if it's a vision that is in line with the higher energies of love, honesty, kindness, and compassion, you will receive it. For clarity to make sure we are on the same page, let's look at what visualization is for a moment.

Visualization is a mental activity led by our choice of consciousness. It's choosing to daydream and see your life as you want it and believe that it is YOUR life you are viewing. Smile when you take the stage. A beam from your happy place as you embrace that friend you envision spending time with.

In my youth, I had an opportunity to speak in front of a few hundred other high school students at the church I attended. I had never given a talk before and did not know what to do. I spent weeks writing and envisioning the words as I spoke them on stage. I saw myself taking the stage and moving around it during various points of the talk. I could see the audience laughing at jokes I'd made. I could see the entire talk happening in my mind. The talk went great. I was asked to speak again and public speaking has been a part of my life and livelihood ever since.

When I look back on that first talk, it couldn't have gone any other way. I spent hours preparing, hours visioning what the forty minutes on stage would look like. I lived that speech perhaps a hundred times before I gave it.

Every thought you have can be calculated to determine if it's strengthening or weakening your living in the higher energies. There are no neutral thoughts. All thoughts have energy. We attract to us what we emanate. The energy of our thoughts is like an energetic magnetic tractor beam pulling those things toward us. Therefore, you must be conscious of your thoughts and choose your thoughts with purpose and passion. Every thought you have impacts you.

The energy of our thoughts is like an energetic magnetic tractor beam pulling those things toward us.

William Shakespeare once said, "Our doubts are traitors, and make us lose the good we oft might win by fearing to attempt." One of the keys to manifestation is realigning your inner world and your outer world, so they are both in harmony with the higher energies of love, non-judgment, peace, joy, happiness, kindness, etc. This way, your thoughts and the laws of the universe work for you rather than against you. Choose thoughts of what you want rather than what you don't want. Inventors don't think about how NOT to make something. They think only of ways to make it and allow the closed doors to lead them to the right open doors.

As you do your Thought Practice and visualization, it is imperative that you keep love at the forefront of your consciousness. Living in the energy of love protects your energy field and heart from contamination. Anything that you experience, which is not love, is an agent of the ego and will keep you shackled to your problems. For example, sometimes it is most loving to yourself to remove someone from your life. It may feel unloving, but if they are unhealthy for you, removing them IS part of self-care and loving yourself. When you allow toxic people into your life, you will find your Thought Practice struggling and feelings of love embattled with the ego's thoughts. So, envision the types of people you want in your life and maintain clear boundaries of who you will allow into your life.

One simple way you can begin to practice visualization is when you wake up in the morning. It will only take ten minutes, and you can do it in bed, in the shower, or sitting down. However, you want. Envision the day before you, what will happen, how it will go. Smile and send the energy out as if you are watching a movie of the day you are about to live. Then, when you are alone during the day, begin to envision what you want your life to look like five years down the road. As you visualize your life, your work, your relationships, end the time by asking God to show you what He wants you to do and what the next steps are.

Ask with an expectant heart as a child would ask their loving Daddy for a hug. Keep asking throughout the day. Ask for clarity, and as clarity comes and you visualize what your life will look like in five years, there are no doubts it IS going to happen. This is unleashing the energy of the universe, which begins sending that vision to you. Those are two straight-forward ways to implement visualization exercises. Once you make them a part of your day, you will begin to notice experience backing up your vision and speaking to you.

EXPERIENCE

No one can do your Thought Practice for you. Nor can you be transformed through the experience of others. Transformation begins when the application meets direct experience. Invariably before the transformative power of experience occurs, you will see "signs of land." Before explorers like Columbus reached their destination, they saw birds and twigs floating, which showed them that land was near. So it is with experience. But often, new Thought Practice practitioners mistake the signs as the experience itself and are then disappointed.

> **Transformation begins when the application meets direct experience.**

Wayne Dyer, one of my heroes and mentors, used to conduct an experience during his talks. He would invite a person on stage who had never tasted a mango. Then he would invite four or five people who had tasted a mango to come on stage and asked them each to describe the flavor of the mango to the first person. When they finished, the person had a few ideas about how a mango tastes and understood some of the concepts and words about a mango's flavor. The individual's understanding of a mango's flavor was all imparted by other people's experience, understanding, and interpretation through the filter of THEIR perspective. However, everything changed for that person when they tasted a fresh, chilled piece of the fruit. Their experience changed it all. It is the same for all of us in the transformative power of our Thought Practice.

Throughout my life, I heard how good God was and that we could trust Him. But there was always an "if," or "but," or "when" attached, which implied the need for perfection. Combined with my childhood trauma, I most certainly did not trust God to care about me or be anything other than a cruel disciplinarian. My lack of trust in God, and anyone other than myself, had been a critical factor in my decisions—the decisions that shipwrecked my life.

I was discussing this concept of trust with a dear friend in the wilderness of a state park in Northern California. As we sat by the lake enjoying outstanding cigars, he did his best to explain to me how to trust God. We had been discussing this off and on for years. I had to relieve myself and walked deep into the woods to find a tree to water. As I walked deeper and deeper into the woods, I prayed, "God, I'm terrified, and I want to trust You, but I don't. PLEASE show me a sign that I can trust You." I found the perfect tree secluded away from the view of the lake.

As I arrived at its base, I looked to the ground to make sure my boots were in the clear, and there buried with just a tiny portion exposed above the surface, was a plain, green glass marble. That was significant to me because when I had moments where others earned my trust, I put a marble in a jar. It was a symbol that I keep on my writing desk. Finding the object I had used to symbolize trust for years in the middle of a gigantic state park was a significant sign. That I had picked that particular spot to pee just after praying that prayer was the perfect alignment of circumstance, conversation, being ready, and the physical moving through the ether to manifest. I put the marble in my pocket.

As I emerged from the forest, my friend asked, "What?" He could tell something happened. I held up the marble to show him, and he said, "Man, I have never seen someone God loves more who just hasn't gotten it yet." Later that week, I was at a Catholic cemetery in Portland, Oregon, which has always been a place of peace for me. A dear friend and mentor called and asked if she could join me; she wanted to discuss my lack of trust in God.

Weird. I had not told her about the marble I had found in Northern California. She shared from a place of love and wanted me to be free of the slavery of mistrust. She was not trying to convince me. It was more like one soul loving another and wanting them to be free. After an hour or so, I excused myself for a moment to use the restroom. As I was walking back behind the caretaker's shed, I prayed again. "I want to trust you but don't know how," when something caught my peripheral vision. About four feet away was a pile of soda can pull tabs—a huge pile. At the time, there was a rumor floating around that if you mailed them into the American Kidney Association, they would provide a minute of dialysis for free to a needy patient.

I got on my hands and knees and started filling my pockets. It was a good thing I was wearing cargo shorts; the pile kept going as I dug them out. At the bottom, there was something buried that looked like a shard of broken green glass from an old beer bottle. I began to dig carefully around it so as not to cut myself but also grab as many pull tabs as I could. As I investigated, I uncovered a large, green glass marble the size of a golf ball. It matched the one I found a few days earlier perfectly. I showed my friend both marbles and explained the circumstances and meaning. She laughed and said, "How much more do you need? That is about as clear as heavenly messages get!" The next day as I lay in bed, something changed, and I crossed the experiential threshold and trusted God. And I have trusted Him ever since. A short time later, I found myself in completely uncharted territory as I took responsibility for imploding my life.

I'd been in prison for less than a week. I was stressed and depressed. I had already had an altercation. I did not know how the place worked or how to navigate it. Spiritually, I was in a good place. I was taking responsibility for the abuse and trauma of my childhood and all of my choices as an adult. I had a long way to go, but I was heading in the right direction. It was early—5:50 AM—and black dark outside.

I was navigating through the prison and woods to find the woodshop for a job interview. The fog that morning was so thick I could only see a couple of steps ahead of me. It hugged the ground like a protective blanket. I was getting stressed about not knowing where I was going or how to get there. I only had shoddy verbal directions from another inmate. I was told to go past the out of bounds signs. There were several turns on the path I had to take. I was trying to keep those clear in my mind, take direction on a path I'd never seen, and I had very few points of reference to navigate by. I was stressed and getting frustrated. I looked up at the predawn sky and said aloud, "I need some help here. I don't know where I'm going or how to get there." Not expecting an answer, I was surprised at the voice that rose within me.

"Your future is on a need-to-know basis, and right now, you only need to know the next step or two and trust that I have you on the right path." I froze in place and looked around to see if someone was speaking to me. The voice was real and palpable. I was told to stay on the path to the right. At every fork, stay to the right. I came to a turn in the path and felt a nudge to keep going straight and not take the path to the right. Fifty steps later, another Y in the path, I felt a nudge to stay to the right this time. I walked along a creek that was raging with little rapids as the water flowed hard from the recent rains. Maybe 75 yards down the path, I was faced with three options. One to the left, one straight ahead, and one to the right. I must have looked like a crazy person as I exasperatedly asked, "Which one do I take?"

My head hung in exhaustion. There was a green glass marble in front of me on the middle path identical to the one I found in Northern California. Laying there in a dusty path was shiny clean green glass marble. I took that path, and it led me straight to the woodshop.

My experience with the Divine, as demonstrated through the three marbles and the foggy dirt path, was transformational for me. I could not come to a place of trust through other's experiences and interpretations. I had to taste it for myself. Trust may not be the issue in your faith journey. Perhaps it is resentment, envy, anger, jealousy, or hate. Regardless of the specifics, once you transcend intellectual understanding to experiencing, you will likely heal from those issues. None of this is good or bad; it all just is. Your path is your path, and my path is my path. I don't expect you to understand it fully; it's my path, not yours.

As you experience your Thought Practice and its effect on your heart, mind, and body, you will see the transforming power of higher energies on the world around you. By sending love, compassion, honesty, and kindness to confront the problems in your daily life, you will begin to see them dematerialize. It all merely takes practice.

PRACTICE

Practically speaking, Thought Practice takes practice. It is like searching for happiness. There is no way to happiness—happiness is the way. And so it is with living your Thought Practice. It's not something you arrive at; it's how you live your life. A healthy Thought Practice is a key to healthy self-cultivation. It's not something you find; it's how you live your life bringing the thoughts you want to everything you do. Be aware of anything that's directing you towards activities that feed the higher energies of love, peace, kindness, gratitude, and honesty, and avoid those of the lower energies.

Pay attention as synchronicity and serendipity collude to bring new higher energy opportunities to your world. Avoid justifying your fear of change and come to a place where you made friends with the change in your life. Recognize the higher energies coursing through you and go with the flow. Give up the ego's need to be in charge. Return your practice to the most foundations elements of higher energies, such as:

- Love
- Kindness
- Peace
- Abundance
- Attraction
- Gratitude

Realign your energies and thoughts so that there is no room for the ego. Make sure there is also no room for focusing on lower energy thoughts. Thoughts are things and magnetically charged. What you think about is what you attract. Period. The magnet doesn't differentiate between fear or faith and brings to you what you think about. Choose to focus your thoughts on abundance rather than lack. Choose thoughts of compassion rather than judgment. Choose to think about love and kindness rather than anger and retribution. It is all your choice. The choice is yours and only yours. Choose. Choose. Choose. This is way beyond thinking positive thoughts. It is a reprogramming of your subconscious mind to live naturally in alignment with the higher energetical laws of the universe. Positive thinking is just that, thinking positively. Nothing wrong with that. We are talking about reprogramming the hard drive of your mind so that you naturally think in line with the laws of responsibility, respect, kindness, truth, love, and receptivity. Choosing your thoughts means stopping low energy thoughts in their tracks and proactively choosing higher energy thoughts. It takes time, focus, and practice as we reprogram a mind that has been conditioned and bruised by life. Choosing your thoughts is the cornerstone of Thought Practice.

As you choose your thoughts, you will become increasingly aware of specific patterns of thought. These are areas of default which your mind naturally regresses to—one of the most common is to be mindful of our thoughts of judgment towards others.

Many of us who tend to think of ourselves as non-judgmental live with subtle and pervasive ways of judging others in our thought life. We judge others with thoughts that could be triggered by their clothing, tone of voice, how they act, the way we see them parent, or thousands of other prompts. When we judge others, it says nothing about that person and a tremendous amount about ourselves. Carl Jung observed, "The areas that frustrate you or irk you in others is a window to the areas of your own life that need work."

When you have thoughts of judgmentalism towards another person, STOP, and replace those thoughts with the choice to be kind, compassionate, and understanding towards them. You should send that person thoughts of love and then act in those ways towards them. Start to pay attention to how many times you catch yourself in thoughts of a judgment of yourself and others each day. You may well find yourself shocked. Judgmentalism not only diminishes the judger far more than the judged, it stops higher energies dead in their tracks. It virtually brings higher energies to a grinding halt.

The issue of judgmentalism brings up one of the clearest practical tools that will transform your Thought Practice and is vital to your self-cultivation. Every time we hold thoughts of judgmentalism, we miss an opportunity to apply the Double Bind. I was first exposed to the concept by my therapist, Harry. Harry is no non-sense, straight-thinking, kind, and enlightened man. He does not suffer those foolish enough not to take their therapy seriously. Of all of the truths he passed on, the Double Bind was the most transformational. It is a simple principle. When you are confronted with two or more choices, which have potential payoffs and consequences, you have encountered a Double Bind. A Double Bind, as defined in the dictionary, is a psychological predicament when a person receives conflicting messages simultaneously that create potential consequences with any decision. It's a contradictory double imperative. As Einstein said: "No problem can be solved from the same level of consciousness that created it."

For example, you are late for an appointment, and a traffic light turns yellow. If you run the light, you risk a ticket or even an accident. If you stop at the light, you run the risk of being late for your appointment. What do you do? You have a microsecond to decide. How do you know the right and best decision? It is simple. The correct choice is the one you don't want to do. As I applied this principle, I began stopping at yellow lights. I noticed my stress diminished, and it didn't really affect my travel time.

So, whatever the scenario, it is about seeing the setup of the problem and understanding the nature of the dynamic. This is how you empower yourself to make a decision. It is one thing to be undecided about which path to choose. It is quite another thing to be unaware of the contradiction at play. The worst thing is being stuck in a place of confusion while not recognizing the source of the confusion.

Only through a deeper awareness of yourself and the nature of your situation can you empower yourself to break free. Liberation flows from understanding. And understanding comes from having the courage to look deeper, listen, and take new actions.

The Double Bind comes into our Thought Practice at the foundational level when we choose to judge and flog ourselves or others. We can pursue and feed the thoughts birthed by our ego, which stops the flow of higher energies surging through us, OR we can choose thoughts of compassion, kindness, and love. These increase the magnetic flow of higher energies creating joy, prosperity, and peace in our lives. Like all of Thought Practice, the choice is yours and only yours. As you start to apply the Double Bind, you will likely notice the prevalence of its use in your life. You will see how easy it is to make its use habitual. Practicing the Double Bind and making it a part of your Thought Practice can be one of the more powerfully transformative aspects, resulting in a dramatic reduction of stress and an increase in peace.

As you grow in your Thought Practice, there is another tool that can increase the flow of higher energies into your life. As you lay in bed, put your book or magazine down and focus your mind on one of two areas. The first is to ask your subconscious questions. For example, I had a general idea for this book clear in my mind. As I prepared for sleep, I simply repeated the phrase, "Reveal to me the path and outline for this book." After three days, I woke up at 3:30 in the morning with the entire outline crystal clear in my mind. I got up and put it to paper. Ask your subconscious questions, stay with the same one until you have answers. The second action you can take is to visualize a future aspect of your life as if it has already happened. Visualize every detail.

A friend of mine did this with a house he wanted to purchase. He did not have the financial means to buy any home, let alone his dream home. Every night for over five years, he visualized the house, the yard, each room, the street view—everything. One day a realtor friend of his called to let him know he had a house to show. As they drove over and approached the house, he found himself looking at his visualization in real life. It was the exact home he had been holding onto in his mind. Sixty days later, he was moved in and living in his dream home. Your meditative focus activates autosuggestion in your subconscious, and two actions occur:

- Your thoughts send these messages across the ether and magnetically draw those visions into your life; and,

- You activate your subconscious and conscious choices that help you create what you are envisioning.

The way to self-cultivation and Thought Practice is through self-cultivation and Thought Practice. This is similar to reminding yourself that there is no way to happiness, but rather, happiness is the way to happiness. Practice changing your thoughts in everyday situations, and you'll know contentment in a deeper sense. When your actions toward yourself and others are pure and selfless, everything settles into its own perfect place—peacefully.

CHAPTER 12 EXERCISES

These chapter exercises are designed to help you apply the principles of TRANFORMATIONAL THINKING in meaningful and transformative ways for you. They are not designed that one should do all the exercises for each chapter. Record the notes from the chapter, the exercise you are doing, and the results in your notebook.

Implementing the different principles of Thought Practice into our daily lives is essential. With time, the way we think and live will become a habit, and therefore we will not have to put in much effort and discipline in doing so. This complete change cannot happen without you making an effort. In this process, you are the key. It is up to you how you apply higher energy thoughts in different areas of life. Here are a few tips that will cover most of our habits.

1. **Your Body**

   - Body image is how we see ourselves and how attractive we feel of ourselves. We human beings are always so conscious about our bodies. We are in constant worry about our weight, our skin texture, our hair, or the size of a particular body part. When a person has a positive image about his or her body, it simply depicts that they have understood their self-worth and that they are aware their self-worth does not depend on how they look. To have a positive body image includes:

- ◆ Accepting and appreciating your body. It means loving the way it looks and what it is capable of.
- ◆ Understanding beauty on a broad concept.
- ◆ Having a stable body image.
- ◆ Possessing positivity from within.

- A person who has a negative body image is unsatisfied with his body no matter how attractive they are. The person will:

  - ◆ Compare themselves to others and feel insecure.
  - ◆ Be ashamed or embarrassed about the way their body appears.
  - ◆ Lack confidence.
  - ◆ Be uncomfortable in their body.
  - ◆ Look for faults in their body.

- Here are tips to feel more positive about your body:

  - ◆ Be around people who have a positive outlook on things.
  - ◆ Try to talk positively to yourself. Say something like, "I have strong arms" instead of "I have flabby arms."
  - ◆ Try to dress in a way that complements your body and is comfortable.
  - ◆ Never compare yourself with others.
  - ◆ Always keep in mind that beauty is not only about how you look.
  - ◆ Appreciate the abilities of your body, such as laughing, dancing, and being creative.
  - ◆ Learn to ignore media messages and images that make you feel like you should be any different than you are.
  - ◆ Write down what you like about yourself.

♦ Look at yourself as a person and not just a body part.

♦ Try to pamper your body; get a massage or a haircut.

♦ Try to adopt a new hobby instead of always thinking about your body.

♦ Try to adopt a healthy lifestyle and healthy eating habits.

♦ Remove any lazy low thoughts and replace them with positive thoughts sustained in the higher energies.

2. **Your Finances**

- It is important that you think about where your life currently is and where you want it to be in the future. The basic principle of Thought Practice is to believe that it works. You need to start with the inconsequential things first. To understand and feel how Thought Practice works, you need to start with the minor things that are possible. If you are doubtful, try with something simple. This step is important to master Thought Practice. Small things can include parking in the right spot, finding a $10 bill, or hearing from an old friend. These small gestures are best to begin with because it is easy to believe in them. Once you see results, it will strengthen your belief in the power of living along with the higher energies of the universe. Here is a 4-step process to change your dreams from being a desire to reality:

  ♦ Make your Decisions

    - One of the most crucial steps of living a dynamic Thought Practice is deciding what you want. This will require a clear vision of what you desire. Whether you want to attract something minor or whether you are looking for a huge fix in your life, you need to be very clear about what you want. While imagining a "new" thing in your life, you need to imagine it using all of your senses. Sit in a quiet place and imagine your life after you have attracted this new thing. Whether it is something as simple as finding $10 or meeting your true love on the street, you need to accept and feel this new thing as every part of your existence. Think about what this new thing feels like, smells like, sounds like, and even how it tastes.

- Think of it as being as real as possible in your mind. In addition to thinking about getting this new thing, also think about how it will affect your life after you achieve it. Think about the changes it will bring to your life.

- Your subconscious mind cannot really differentiate reality from imagination. So, when you engage your mind in imagination, your brain pushes your body to move forward. Every part of your body, including the muscles, blood flow, heart, and lungs, all work together to achieve what you are imagining. All you need to do is open yourself up to the possibilities and prepare your body to get whatever it is attracting. This may sound pretty simple and straightforward, but this is the first step to working along with the energies of the universe.

♦ Practice Living among the Higher Energies

- If you do not put your mind to believe in the things you deserve, you will not be able to get it. Your subconscious fears and doubts send clear messages. If any part of your body tells you that you do not deserve what you are imagining, then that part of you is fighting against your desire. For example, think of a radio signal. As you scan through radio channels, different stations fight to catch a signal. Two separate stations compete, and you will end up hearing part of one song and parts of another. You will notice that you cannot get a clear signal of either channel. Similarly, when you doubt yourself and your desires, your thoughts and feelings interrupt and compete with your desires. This step is crucial because it keeps you aware of your thoughts and your feelings. The best way to fight those fears and doubts is to be aware of them and replace them with positive, higher energies.

♦ Open Yourself to the Universe and its Generosities

- Understanding and acknowledging your fears and doubts is important. But after you have acknowledged them, it is even more important to replace them with positive thoughts, appreciation, and gratitude. These positive thoughts can change your views and perspectives and open up a new possibility that will be great for you. Here is a comparison to help you see the positive side:

- Firstly, think about the bad things happening in your life right now. Can you see any connection to your fears, your doubts, and any old habits that led those things into your life today? Recognize those fears and how they have infested themselves in your life. But that certainly does not mean that bad things happened in your life because of you. It simply means that the universe has reacted to the signal you sent out via your Thought Practice. You need to understand the system, and eventually, your awareness will guide you through.

- The second step is to think about all the great things in your life. Think about how good dreams and imaginations have brought good things to you. This is where you reinforce your mind. When you believe that something can happen, it does. In this case, you should understand how the laws of the universe are a part of your life. They have always been. The only difference is that you are aware of it now. This step is important due to the connections, the awareness, and the gratitude. Picking every little thing in your life and tracing it back to a thought is not healthy. Instead, you need to make connections where you currently are, and in the state of mind that led you there. Once you notice that the laws of the Universe have worked without you even knowing, it will change your understanding. All you need to do is work with your awareness of the laws and understand how they work and impact your life. Then you can align yourself with them.

3. **Persistence**

- Persistence is another key piece to the puzzle of Thought Practice. There is no straightforward formula of how long it takes for things to manifest in your life. Each of us has our own hurdles to overcome, and therefore it will take time to see any visible results. The key in this process is patience and persistence. When you come to a stage where doubts or fears start to take over, refer back to Step 2. If you have lost your intentions, repeat Step 1. And if your belief has gone low in the higher energies, go back to Step 3.

- Be grateful and appreciative of everything every day. Be positive and just recall all the connections that you have made. Take time out every day to review the exercises mentioned above and prepare your mind and body to receive this gift. Thought Practice is a law that will work with or without your permission. Your understanding of how it works in your life will attract more of the things that you desire.

THE POWER OF WORDS

"The limits of my words mean the limits of my world."
—Ludwig Wittgenstein

OUR SPEECH REFLECTS OUR thoughts. If we speak in ways that create harmony, we help others grow and become. Living in awareness of our words helps prevent us from creating discord and pain for others. Our words are powerful and have a formative influence on our lives, the lives of others, and how we interact with everything on our journey. Our words send out energies and then become self-fulfilling prophecies. Think back to your childhood for a moment. There is likely some baggage you carry because of someone's unkind and unthoughtful comments towards you.

A friend of mine, William, carried such a burden for sixteen years. In the second grade, he courageously tried out for a school play. His impressionable little boy's heart was thrilled when he got a lead role. Just before opening night, during one of the last rehearsals, a co-lead of his turned to him and said, "You stink!" William immediately took a shower when he got home. Every day for the next sixteen years, he took multiple showers, used cologne and antiperspirant throughout the day. At their five years high school reunion, she came up to William and said, "I'm so sorry about saying you stunk when we were kids. I noticed you never did another play and always felt bad about that. You were not a bad actor. I was mean, and I am sorry." For sixteen years, he thought he smelled bad, but she thought he was a bad actor. Words are things. Thoughts are things.

They create, and they destroy. When you change the way you look at life, life changes. Your words change.

If you want transformation, peace, and happiness in your life, your Thought Practice and your words must match. As you contemplate the power of your words and the effect your speech has on your life and the lives of others, don't expect an instant miracle. These universal truths take time. It could be a few seconds or much longer. It depends on how you have spoken in the past and the damage you have done. You may have repairs that need to be made. The laws of the universe are laws—you can choose to live them to your benefit or ignore them to your detriment. They can be used to free or enslave, and the choice is yours. Only yours.

Many people have brought turmoil into their life through their words. The person who causally says to their friend over and over how money isn't important to them, and then they wonder why they don't have enough and are perpetually in a state of lack and need. The law works regardless of the words. As long as the thoughts and words align with the higher energies and laws of the universe, they are magnetically drawn into your life. When they arrive, they may look different than your preconceived notion, but they will arrive. Words of lack can be transformed into words of plenty by stopping to use them and replacing them with the right words of attraction. False words, harsh speech, and idle chatter all create a disharmony and break in the energy field.

A lot of the idle words and energies that we lazily dispense come out of our perspective. Perspective is primarily created through experience, ego, and not taking charge of our thoughts. Naturally, most of us consider our perspective accurate and often don't pause to consider where it could be askew. Doesn't everyone see the world the way we do? You can check the level of your ego's hold on your perspective to consider your thoughts when others disagree with you. If you see those people as idiots, jerks, or any "ism," you likely have an ego-driven perspective that clouds your experience. Most people assume their view is accurate without question.

Several years ago when I was a younger man, I was standing outside the office with a good friend of mine. We were looking at these gorgeous deep, bright, green trees with intense red blossoms on them. They lined the entire atrium corridor of the complex. I made an innocent statement about how beautiful the blooms were. My friend laughed and said, "There aren't any flowers on those trees!" His tone was dripping with condescension. At first, I thought he was joking because bright red blossoms were beaming against the vibrant green of the leaves. I pointed them out, and the result was a growing and heated debate. He was getting heated as he stammered at what a jerk I was because there were no blossoms on those brown trees. Wait. What? Brown trees? The trees were green. Now I figured he must be messing with me as some joke that failed to make me laugh. Then it hit me. I asked, "Are you color blind?"

He was! He then went on to say that he thought everyone knew he was. It was then that I realized two people could see the same situation in completely different ways. I understood that our ways of seeing are conditioned by the contrasting lenses of experience that we each wear. This affects our perceptions. I learned a valuable lesson that day. I understand that my sense of perception colors my opinions. This realization gives me a gentle understanding in conversations with others. Taking into consideration the lens of the other person allows me to experience them from a place of higher energies rather than the defense of the ego.

As your Thought Practice develops and matures, you will come to understand the power of words. You will see that transformation takes place in your own heart and mind and how others respond to you. This is why open-minded thinking is vital to your transformative thoughts. Closed minds do not inspire others. Closed minds don't inspire faith, courage, or belief. With an open mind and carefully chosen words, you will notice that most lazy words come back to one or more of these five concepts:

- **Being offended:** Most people are truly not offended; they just don't like what the other person said. There is a chasm of difference between not liking someone's opinion and truly being offended. When people are offended by everything, practically speaking they are offended by nothing. It becomes white noise.

- **A need to be superior:** choose to see others as important as yourself.

- **A need to be right:** let go of your need to be right. When you have a choice of being right or being kind, choose kindness.

- **Identifying yourself based on your accomplishments or what you do:** embrace who you are rather than what you do.

- **Worshiping your reputation:** let go of what others think of you. Just let it go.

> **Taking into consideration the lens of the other person allows me to experience them from a place of higher energies rather than the defense of the ego.**

Keep in mind that your subconscious mind takes input in the spirit of faith; that is true. Once those orders are repeated enough and presented over and over, they bear fruit in your life as thoughts and actions. Part of your success in Thought Practice is the repetition of affirmation of the orders you program into your subconscious. Any thought impulse that is repeatedly passed on to the subconscious mind is ultimately accepted and acted upon by your mind. The final fruit is manifesting into the physical in your life. When you feel the power of words deep in your soul and determine to make the right speech a part of how you do life, you will see your Thought Practice grow by leaps and bounds. A sense of peace will permeate your life and soul. You will use words in your own life and the lives of others with love, tact, and purpose.

THE POWER OF THE WORD

A person who knows the power of their words becomes especially careful about their conversations. You only need to watch the reaction to your words to know that they do not return void. Through your words, people make way for themselves or create a blockage for themselves. Like when I was a little boy, I had a rabbit's foot. Someone told me it was lucky, and I believed them. And it was lucky! Whenever I carried it in my pocket, good things happened. I now know that it was the subconscious energy attracting those things to me. Once we understand how this all works, we are responsible because once we know, we can't unknow. Remember: thoughts are things. Thoughts are words, and words have power. Thoughts and words are powerful. When your words are combined with purpose, kindness, honesty, and love, they are translated into manifestations in your life. Words can be used to bless or curse. The choice, as always, is yours and only yours. It is entirely up to you in your life, and the way you choose to use words will either bless or block your Thought Practice and experience.

When you are connected to the Divine through a vibrant and consistent Thought Practice, everyone you meet is affected by your energy. As you become the higher energies of love, kindness, purpose, and peace, you will see yourself causing ripples in others' lives by your presence. This new way of seeing will enable people in your presence to feel comforted and peaceful and to indirectly be loving accomplices to your connection to the Divine.

If you watch the reaction of your words, you will know they do not come back empty. Words impact others. Through our spoken words, we continually bring circumstances into our lives. In my case, I know it took a long time and consistent effort to get the false beliefs and phrases I said to myself hundreds of times a day out of my head. I had to change my words to change my thoughts.

Words matter. When I began to replace those false beliefs with words of truth focused on the higher energies of honesty, love, acceptance, kindness, and purpose, life changed. Through your Thought Practice, you will come to notice that your words have attractive energy that is magnetic like your thoughts. Whatever you speak, you attract. To strategically harness the power of your words, you must maintain words of truth in the higher energies of honesty, kindness, love, peace, attraction, abundance, and love. You will also want to strategically stay away from the lower energies of jealousy, anger, greed, and dishonesty. Remember, the ether carries our thought energies and words in a fashion similar to WIFI's principles. You don't see the WIFI. Although you can't feel it or touch it, it is there. And, when the signal disappears, you know it's not working.

How this works is quite simple—it takes place through living the higher energies in your thoughts, words, and deeds while eliminating the lower energies. There is no neutral. Our words have power. The words we speak are powerful and active. They carry the energy and are never idle. Our words are so powerful that they can manifest their meaning and influence over our own lives as well as the lives of others.

SPEAK INTO BEING

How, what, and why we think the thoughts we do is in large part to our conditioning. Our conditioning creates our beliefs. That's a large part of how the subconscious is programmed and runs on autopilot. These generate an ego-protected sense of a false life protected by shields and masks. Thought Practice is about proactively changing those conditions and beliefs. Our conditioning doesn't disappear; we reprogram it through Thought Practice and choosing our thoughts based on the higher energies. Instead of running out of the lower energies of ego, we get to a point where our autopilot runs on the higher energies. That is why our words are vital.

When we speak, we are sending out powerful energies. We can talk things into manifesting into our lives. We bring them to the physical plane of reality through our thoughts and words. Remember: thoughts are things. You cannot deny part of the truth and embrace truth. Truth is truth, and any alteration bastardizes it into an ineffective crutch. When your mind is focused on higher energies, the energy is palpable around you—it ignites reactions and feelings in others. If you believe thoughts are things and have energy, you cannot deny that words are things and have energy. Words have strength and power all their own, which is one reason it is essential to think before you speak.

You can attract and draw things into manifestation through your Thought Practice and speaking them into being. Energy is magnetic and brings things to you. The next steps will suddenly spring to your mind, encouraging you to take action. The right person will appear in your life, apparently out of nowhere. Coincidences, synchronicity, and serendipity all align in perfect manifestation. It is essential to remain vigilant in your thoughts and words. Eliminate from your thinking thoughts of lack, limitation, or labels. Do not entertain even the seed of possibility that it won't manifest into your life. Thought Practice is the gradual dissipation of ignorance and the gradual increase of awareness. Your understanding grows as you spiritually awaken. That awakening brings about a change in perspective. As you transform, you will come to a core belief that beautiful thoughts build a beautiful soul. Eventually, it becomes second nature for you to see opportunity and peace in every situation, no matter how difficult.

If our words are ugly, we will attract ugliness into our life. Words start with thoughts, and thoughts are things. Thoughts lead to emotions, which lead to words, which lead to manifestation in our lives. Choose your thoughts and what you want to focus on carefully. Speak with grace, truth, kindness, and compassion, seeking ONLY the other person's benefit. Your words will become transformative in your life and the lives of others. Think about what you think and say what you say because you are operating within the universe's laws. You will see your world expand, and possibilities you hadn't possibly dreamed of will come into your life and the lives of those around you.

When your words focus on the higher energies, your presence paves the way for others to feel better about themselves. You likely have people in your life whose presence makes you feel good. Their energy is loving, kind, compassionate, and honest. You also probably have had others in your life whose words and energy are toxic and draining. They cause a stressful reaction inside you that you experience physically. Low energy people are toxic and leave folks feeling insignificant and dismissed. As your Thought Practice matures, people will sense your care and compassion and want what you have. You will cease using conversations to get others to massage your ego and focus on genuinely caring for them. How you speak to others begins with your thoughts and how you talk to yourself.

SELF TALK

Self-talk is one of the most vital aspects of Thought Practice. It is crucial to your growth and maturation into living in peace and purpose. Words carry magnetized energy just like thoughts do. If you use the higher energies, it will be like a bullet train for your life. If you focus on the lower energies in your self-talk, it is like a traffic jam during rush hour in your life. Self-talk is powerful, and its importance cannot be overstressed. You cannot connect to the higher energies of love, peace, kindness, honesty, and contentment by using the low energy self-talk of judgment, hostility, and anxiety. They are incompatible and cannot exist in the same mind at the same time.

> **Self-talk is one of the most vital aspects of Thought Practice**

The importance you place on your words is in direct relation to how you view yourself. If you see yourself as stupid, your self-talk will reflect that with lower energy statements. If you view yourself as worthy of love, your self-talk will reflect that resulting in magnetically higher energies. Thoughts and self-talk are not neutral. They are either lower or more highly energetically charged. The conditioning that created low energy self-talk is just that, conditioning.

This means if it was conditioned through circumstances to be low energy self-talk, it can be reconditioned into higher energy self-talk. Your core belief comes out in words to yourself—then in words towards others. To change those types of words in your mind, you will have to reprogram yourself through your Thought Practice.

However, Thought Practice—harnessing the higher energies and creating a life of peace, purpose, and prosperity—only works when you are in alignment and harmony with the laws of the universe. If your thoughts and words conflict with the higher energies, you will leave a brokenness trail within yourself.

That leads to creating a legacy of damage in the lives of those around you. Once you correct your thinking and align with the fact that God loves you and is crazy about you, He is not offended by your humanity. He created it. Once you truly believe that God is good and the universe is a warm, friendly, and abundant place, then the transformation begins through your Thought Practice. Your thoughts and words are imbued with power and energy that transforms.

If you are serious about changing your life, and if you're weary from living in the lower energies of anxiety, stress, and worry, you must align your desires with your self-talk. Your self-talk mirrors your thoughts. If your low energy self-talk conflicts with your high energy desires, your self-talk will win. Your desires will ultimately manifest in your life if you match your desires, thoughts, and self-talk in harmony. When your thoughts and self-talk are aligned with the higher energies, there is virtually nothing stopping you from achieving your desires. However, if your thoughts and self-talk are misaligned, low energy focused, you will meet obstacles. This creates more low energies like stress and anxiety in your life.

All of us use our self-talk to create the world we choose. Unfortunately, most of us are not aware of this connection, so we create a world we didn't want and don't enjoy. Fear, doubt, and self-flogging are killers. Shakespeare declared, "Our doubts are traitors and make us lose the good we oft might find by fearing to attempt." Aligning your inner world of thoughts and self-talk with the higher energies of the universe magnetically pull your desires into reality.

You create them with your thoughts and self-talk. Your self-talk mirrors your thoughts. Your thoughts create your reality. By removing the obstacles and focusing on what you want rather than do not want in your life, you clear the universal freeway for those things to make their way to you. Remember that every thought has an energy that is either lower or higher. There are no neutral energies.

Take responsibility for all aspects and circumstances of your life without accompanying guilt, shame, or excuse. Once you take responsibility, you can then take control. You are no longer a victim or at the whims of circumstance. Changing your thoughts and your self-talk takes practice, consistency, and time, but it is transformative. Your self-talk is crucial to transformation. Start talking to yourself like you would someone you love, adore, and are excited to have in your life. Practice self-talk that expresses unconditional love for yourself. Accept and forgive yourself. If you need to clear the air, make amends, or apologize to yourself or another, do so. This is not a covering but rather a rebuilding of yourself. Speaking to yourself with love and respect is simple and powerful. It is easy to do. Be kind to yourself and only speak words of truth from the higher energies into your mind. If words of lower energy sneak into your thoughts, immediately stop them and replace them with ones of higher energetic truth.

One of Thought Practice's biggest gifts is finding out that you can like and love yourself, speak nicely, and create a life of internal peace and prosperity. You can be free of anxiety and live in anticipation of the blessings flowing into your life. Your words play an integral part in the process. Thoughts matter, and your words matter.

> **Start talking to yourself like you would someone you love, adore, and are excited to have in your life.**

CHAPTER 13 EXERCISES

These chapter exercises are designed to help you apply the principles of TRANFORMATIONAL THINKING in meaningful and transformative ways for you. They are not designed that one should do all the exercises for each chapter. Record the notes from the chapter, the exercise you are doing, and the results in your notebook.

1. We have all experienced the power of words in a way that we cannot forget. Even today, we still remember how those words hurt us. So how can a few words have a significant impact on your life? Words are powerful, and when you experienced that power yourself, only then do you begin to understand it. You can use the power of words to comfort others or hurt them. It all depends on how you use them. Your character is built by the way you utilize this power. This is why the way you talk and how others speak impact your Thought Practice and how it transforms your life. Here are tips on how to use the power of words in the right way:

   - **Speak with Honesty.** Words have the power to either break to make. When words are true, they have the power to change our world. Trust is built on honesty. People want to know that they can trust you to tell them the truth. You may come across situations where lying can save a life. However, in most cases, a reputation of telling a lie will take away your power to connecting with those people. Without truth behind your words, it will have no meaning and sound just like noise.

- **Avoid Exaggerating.** Using sentences like "You never…" or "You always…" to belittle others just sends a negative message about them across. As a result, this will conceal the actual message that you are trying to send across.

- **Do Not Perpetuate Double Standards.** Double standards are when you have different rules for different people of the same ability and in the same situation. For example, assigning two people of the same ability to do two different jobs in the same given time. However, one person gets two easy jobs, and the other person gets two difficult jobs to be completed within the same timeframe. This is imposing a double standard. This creates an atmosphere of injustice.

- **Avoid Manipulating Others with Your Words.** Marketing is not about using words to pressure to manipulate people into buying what you are selling. Also, it is not about competing with other marketers to see who can make use of their words effectively. If you are building a relationship with someone to get something from him, he will sense it. And even if you do persuade that person to buy something from you, it will do nothing but leave a negative impact on them. They will never forget someone who misused their words and lead them to spend.

- **Think Before Speaking.** A daily practice of mindfulness teaches you to be more acutely aware of your thoughts and feelings. In relationships, this can help you can identify whether someone's words or actions have manipulated you in any way. If you determine they are attempting to manipulate you, there is no need to strike back with harsh words. You can simply take a step back and retain your power and use your well-chosen words to bring balance to the conversation. When you use the power of words in this manner, you are putting the good of the relationship ahead of any desire to retaliate.

- **Use your Words to Help Others.** Karma says that we must pay for every unkind word we say. Every time we use the power of words negatively against someone, we will have to experience the same pain that we have once caused. Next time you say something negative, think about that. Instead of turning their words against them, it is best to realize that victory is not worth the pain you will cause. Use your power to build them up instead of tearing them down.

2. When you look back on your words, what does it show about your Thought Practice? What are you leaving behind for others with your words? Open your mind and choose words carefully. You will notice that the laziest words come back to the following five concepts:

   - **Being offended.** You should stop being offended. Most people genuinely do not get offended. They just do not like what the other person has said.

   - **A need to be on top.** You should choose to see others as important, the way you see yourself.

   - **A need to always be right.** You should let go of the idea of being right all the time. When you have a choice of being right or being kind, choose kindness.

   - **Identifying yourself based on what you have achieved.** Accept yourself just the way you are instead of what you do.

   - **Worshipping your reputation.** Let go of what others think of you.

3. J.K. Rowling beautifully said, "Words are the most inexhaustible source of magic we can have." What we say has power. Below are selected examples of how you can use this power to your advantage and speak your dreams into existence. This is just another way to work with the law of attraction while using your Thought

Practice. So how is this done? All you need to do is speak about the things you want to happen. Eventually, they happen! When we pay attention to something for an extended period of time, it always takes up some form or another. Here are some tips that you may find helpful:

- **Speak with Positivity.** When you speak, speak with hope, enthusiasm, and knowledge. When you speak about dreams and your desires, you should talk about them with passion. You need to trust in your heart that the Universe hears you and that it will deliver. As you practice, this gets easier. As you witness the possibilities, the more confidence you gain in the creation process.

- **Pay Attention to Your Words.** Getting good at speaking your dreams into existence requires practice and discipline. We are the kind of people who complain about what we do not want instead of praising what we do want. Here is how to deal with it. Every time you want to complain about something, try being grateful for something. For example, when you think, "I hate it when my husband doesn't listen," turn it into, "I love it when my husband listens." If it is impossible to turn your complaint into something you are thankful for, then just move on to something else. Try to talk about something that makes you feel good about talking. Feeling is the key to manifesting.

- **Just put it out there.** When sharing your hopes and your dreams with people, the universe is also listening. It works to make your dreams come true. People love to help others. If they are unable to do it themselves, they will lead you to someone who can. All you need to do is throw it out there and see what happens. The worst-case scenario is that nothing will happen immediately. The best-case scenario, however, is that you will get the help you need. You will find someone who knows someone, and you will eventually get the break you have always wanted. Whatever it is, it can only be possible when you put it out there.

LIVING FLEXIBLY

*"Whatever is flexible and flowing will tend to grow.
Whatever is rigid will wither and die."*
—Tao Te Ching

IN GENERAL, OUR MINDS get caught up in the tangles of our external world. Consequently, we react in habitual, programmed manners toward that outside stimuli. When we are preoccupied with the outer world of the ego, we neglect our minds with lazy thinking. We then live in a constant state of reaction until we proactively take control of our life through our Thought Practice. We learn to be attentive and present to our minds, hearts, and experiences throughout our daily lives. Most of us came to Thought Practice because we felt a need to change our life. Perhaps, we were fed up with being fed up; weary of being weary; or stressed from all the stress. Regardless, we wanted to change. In the early part of your practice, you will spend time and energy trying to improve and evolve. That is part of the practice. Our dissatisfaction is a gift in that it is motivation helping us discover what it means for us individually to be awake and present. This is where living flexibly is so essential to our Thought Practice.

Along with living in the present, we are bringing our attention to the moment. We all are faced with a choice. We can choose to allow our minds to spin off into areas that incite anxiety, worry, and stress. Or we can be here, choosing our thoughts, and remaining present in whatever the moment offers. For some people living in the moment and being present can sound contradictory to living flexibly. Living flexibly is about living without attachment. It is about remaining open to what God and life have for you. It is living life on life's terms.

Some of the most troubling beliefs that give us fits in a new journey of Thought Practice belong to our attachments. Attachments make it challenging to live flexibly. They can be hard to identify. You can determine areas of your attachment by looking at which beliefs that have become cemented in your mind that you feel you must defend. It is the belief that we can never be happy without this specific person, thing, or belief.

Living flexibly without attachments begins with seeing these beliefs with clarity, precision, and honesty. As we examine our potential attachments, we will see that they are an anchor to both unhappiness and a lack of peace. It's because we are attached that we are unhappy. We think that this person, belief, or thing will make us happy, protect us, or bring us relief. Our ego naturally senses stability in the familiar, even if what is familiar makes us miserable. Through our practice, we can see that these beliefs and attachments are false, and we no longer need to use them to identify ourselves.

Our Thought Practice redefines how we define ourselves. We forge a new foundation in health and alignment. We can find attachment anywhere:

- In our achievements
- Our identities based on how others see us
- By a relationship (Husband, Wife, Mother, Father, etc.)
- Our occupation
- Where we live
- What car we drive

Take, for example, living in an attachment to a particular person where you believe you need them to be in your life. Perhaps you believe they need to be a certain way for you to be happy. But that's not the meaning of love. The happiness we find in love is not based on need. The extent to which we are attached to the fulfillment of needs means we really cannot love that person. Giving up the belief that love will make us happy frees us to love and find a connection. The love and relationship then ADD to our fulfillment rather than being their source.

Think about people, things, or beliefs that you may have an attachment to. Hold them in your mind. Consider that they present to you a substitute life that narrows your way of living. These confines are rooted in our need to be comfortable and to hold onto what is familiar and feel safe. Some of this stems from the pain of unhealed wounds; while some may simply be fear or a desire to cling to safety. Unfortunately, living in attachment prevents us from truly living with an open and peaceful heart.

> **Attachment is based on an illusion that something external can relieve our pain and bring us peace.**

Attachment often seems like the way to happiness, but it prevents happiness and peace. Attachment is based on an illusion that something external can relieve our pain and bring us peace. However, when we are willing to expose ourselves to the pain we've been avoiding, the grasp of the attachment fades. The path to peace becomes clear as we live flexibly and unattached. Relinquishing our attachments is much easier said than done.

Most attachments are rooted in fear and insecurity. Their roots run subtle and profound as the ego seeks to protect us against our fears. Slowly as we identify our attachments through our Thought Practice, they lose their hold. The result is freedom. When we see ourselves without our filters, judgments, and fear-based desires, we learn to appreciate living in the higher energies of love, peace, and purpose. When we can see through our fears, the result is love. When we live unattached, life becomes more comfortable and natural—we live in the flow.

To illustrate living flexibly, consider water. Yes! The wet stuff you drink every day. Water is mysterious and spiritual for many people. Water is supple and flexible compared to the terrain it carves through. Water works its way through barriers, naturally cutting its way through rock by patience and consistency. Imagine showing up to your relationships as yourself. Living in authenticity and the higher energies, you harmoniously influence others in ways you previously wouldn't have imagined. Previously, when you were attached, you would have sought to force, coerce, argue, and defend your point of view; you can now enjoy the natural flow. Water is flexible.

Imagine showing up to your relationships as yourself.

Living flexibly means you live like water. When you reach into a river and try to squeeze water tightly in your hand, you end up losing what you wish to hold. Water is elusive until you stop clenching and learn to relax and let it be what it is. Overcoming the attached part of your life by yielding feels counterintuitive. We inherently feel like we need to do something. We feel like we need to act. When we are persistently gentle and unattached, we see the resistance in life melt away. It sloughs off like water off a duck's back.

When you live flexibly, you act almost without effort because you are honoring yourself and living in the higher energies. By letting go of your inner drive to push ahead, achieve, and force, you will see that, ironically, you do better than when you acted out of ego. Ken Blanchard says the ego is E.G.O. or "Edging God Out."

In your work and relationships, you become more tolerant in your drive to achieve and create by softening your attitude and behavior. You will see others more attached to you. Living flexibly does not mean a lack of planning or laziness. It does not mean you cease to have ambition or goals. It does mean you listen to the still small voice within that speaks clearly when you are engaged in a consistent and healthy Thought Practice. Living flexibly and without attachment does mean that when we planned on going straight, and there is a detour that leads you to take a turn, you take it. It is important to have goals while being supple and flexible as you work towards those goals. The goals do not change, but the path to achieve that goal very well may change course. When you look back, you will see God led you on a path that was more enjoyable, more fulfilling, and less stressful.

There are three stages to living flexibly that most people go through:

1. The first is through wanting to change something in your life. It's when the problems in your life become overwhelming enough that you want to change. As you learn to live flexibly, apply your Thought Practice, and live the higher energies, you will gain perspective. One day you will look back on those obstacles and see that they were gifts disguised as problems.

2. The second is to live in the present moment. In a time of difficulty, you ask yourself, "What do I have to learn from this experience right now?" I know there's a gift hidden for me in the misfortune. When they realize they do not know, people can find their way. In other words, effective Thought Practice guides us to our true nature.

3. The third is by getting out of your way. In other words, effective Thought Practice guides others to their true nature.

The realization here is that you are invited to consider that your job is to help others know that they don't know. If they think their beliefs are 100% accurate and complete, they will never heal. That's because they are relying on ego as their foundation. One who is in harmony with the Divine knows that the ego is a false master. Remember, water is flexible. Everything water accomplishes is through its strength and flexibility.

A key element in your Thought Practice is to live like water and get in the flow of life and gently allow yourself to proceed with the current. As you listen to your soul, you will begin to hear whispers of your attachments. These voices will speak through lust, fear, doubt, regret, greed, and others. Learning to live flexibly and free of attachment is key to your Thought Practice growing and your life changing. Attachment is a narrow way of living. It is rooted in our need to be comfortable and our ego's need to protect. As humans, we naturally strive to avoid uncertainty, the pain of wounds, and discomfort. Unfortunately, living this way prevents us from growing and maturing into a life lived in the higher energies.

We all have developed attachments to the people or things we believe bring us happiness. The belief fuels our efforts to attain or maintain this relationship with someone or something. If we succeed, we feel happy, but because we become anxious about losing what we gained, happiness is like a vapor. As soon as we lose the object or the person no longer gives us the *high* they initially did, we become dissatisfied. The feelings return, and we look for another substitute. If we want to be free of attachments, we must first be aware of our attachments. We must see it with clarity, responsibility, and honesty. Next, we must see that this belief is false, but it also clogs and blocks the sources of happiness in our lives. It's because we are living in the lower energies of attachment that we are unhappy.

It's easy to see how we can be attached to other people. People we love and who love us and make us feel good. Therefore, they tend to be attached to our happiness. They make us feel good, and we equate those feelings with happiness. We come to believe that our emotional well-being is inextricably linked to having what we believe will make us happy. However, holding beliefs of attachment guarantees that we won't ultimately find true and lasting happiness. In other words, we have to choose between happiness and attachment. Do we want to be attached or do we want to be happy? The answer is evident. If we look at how most people live, they would rather be attached then do the hard work to be happy.

The path of Thought Practice takes us to a place where we can see through and experience our attachments. Once we see how we are attached, we can then lose them and live in freedom. We step out of our fears and into love. To help facilitate the process of identifying and addressing your attachments, begin by asking yourself a couple of questions:

- What is something or someone I feel like I need to be content?
- Do I have beliefs that can also be or lead to attachment?

Living without attachment creates flexibility in our life that allows us to bend and move as life unfolds and opens more doors for higher energy to come into our life.

LIVING BY BENDING

One of the keys to living unattached is by becoming flexible and living by bending. You must live flexibly in your spirit and firmly in your Thought Practice. We lose our attachments to people and things but also need to let go of the past. If we remain chained to our past, we miss the present and cannot embrace our future. One of the gifts of living unattached is that we find peace.

You must live flexibly in your spirit and firmly in your Thought Practice.

Peace is not the absence of conflict or turmoil in our lives. To be alive is to have issues arise. There will always be people with unenlightened souls attempting to tear us down or cause conflict to enrich their lives. There will always be circumstances that are not what we would have invited into our lives. For years, I flew out of Portland, Oregon, nearly every week for work. Most of the year, Portland is overcast and raining. One day, I was driving to the airport, and the rain was pelting so hard that the freeway became a small river of standing water. The wind blew hard enough that I had to accommodate for it while steering my vehicle. I thought to myself, "How can an airplane take off in this?"

When I entered the airport, I noticed the familiar din and energy of business travel and those who worked there. No one was rushing around concerned about the harsh weather. We boarded as usual, and as I took my seat, you could see the rain hitting the aircraft in a violent assault. The plane shook a bit more than usual as we took off. We flew up through what seemed like endless, dense clouds. They were thick, greyish black, and ominous. And then it happened. We broke through and were flying above the clouds in crisp blue skies. The sun was shining. Bright, happy, and peaceful. You see, the peace existed above the storm. The peace and the storm coexisted. From the perspective of the ground, all I could see was the storm. From the perspective of the sky, I could see the storm would soon pass, and peace was ever-present.

Part of our Thought Practice is perspective. Perspective, peace, and flexible living go hand-in-hand. A vibrant Thought Practice does not force life to be on our terms but accepts life on life's terms. Flexible living allows things to work themselves out, and it produce results naturally. So, when life unfolds as you intended, you can live in exciting peace. When life doesn't unfold as you intended, you can live in exciting peace because God is closing a door that is not THE right door for you. Either way, you are peaceful. Flexible living allows you to escape the slavery of others' opinions of you. When we are ego driven, we tend to lap up the praise of others like a thirsty puppy. We are never satisfied because enough is not enough. Others' opinions of you are critical; however, flexible living frees you from the tyranny of trying to woo and win their approval. As your Thought Practice matures, you will learn to abandon your ego. The ego identifies with the world of things, possessions, and achievements and reenters the priceless peace of living in the higher energies through your thoughts. This is the heart of flexible living.

> A vibrant Thought Practice does not force life to be on our terms but accepts life on life's terms.

Having lived in the Pacific Northwest for years, I have come to appreciate the region's rainforest-like beauty. There are millions of pine trees throughout the area. These trees can grow to immense heights, yet their root system is shallow—usually, only going two to three feet deep. In the winter, there can be tremendous storms that come through the area. High winds, snow, and rain are common. As a little boy, I would watch out my window on stormy nights and see the trees that surrounded our house swaying at the top in what seemed to be an impossible bending to the winds. I thought for sure they would come crashing down onto the house. They are very flexible and soft at the top of the tree—they bend to the wind rather than be broken by it. But the key to their long-term survival is their root system. I wondered how thin, shallow roots could hold up such a big tree. The pine trees have a tap root and reach their grounding roots out and intertwine with the trees around them. Together, these giants can withstand nearly any storm. Their root system provides support by linking with others who are on the same path. Their root system is tapped into their universal life force of the earth. The foundation of the trees is strong, yet the tops remaining flexible.

I invite you to reconsider what strength looks like in your life. As a part of your Thought Practice, consider strength as being firm in your roots, linked with other souls on a similar path, and flexible when it comes to the defense of ego. Pine trees are strong and flexible. They are linked. The trees remain grounded to their source.

It is the same for us. Be strong by living flexibly. As you relate to others, listen more. Allow your views and opinions to be challenged. Bend and grow when necessary. This is strength and health. Rigid, dogmatic digging in is a weakness and shows the ego is in the driver's seat, not your spirit and true self. The more you think in rigid ways, the less you will grow and live in the higher energies. When you live flexibly, you remain strong and indestructible. Like water, flow where there is opening rather than attempting to force and dominate. Soften your hard edges by living more tolerantly of contrary opinions. Interfere less and replace telling with listening.

When others offer you their opinion, think of their firm hard edges as areas where they may need healing. Try responding with a genuine, "Thank you for sharing your thoughts. That gives me some things to think about." Send others the higher energies such as love, kindness, compassion, understanding, and respect by feeling it when you speak with them. Send it to them with your thoughts and feelings. This action creates an energy that is like a superfood. Living flexible will increase your mental and spiritual limberness.

CHAPTER 14 EXERCISES

These chapter exercises are designed to help you apply the principles of TRANFORMATIONAL THINKING in meaningful and transformative ways for you. They are not designed that one should do all the exercises for each chapter. Record the notes from the chapter, the exercise you are doing, and the results in your notebook.

1. A crucial aspect of dynamic Thought Practice is prioritizing your thoughts while living in the higher energies and not holding onto expectations. A lousy thinking process and expectations are the real causes of anxiety, depression, worry, and stress. If you genuinely want to live a flexible life, it is imperative to let go of expectations and live with the flow. Look for opportunities and make the most out of them as they emerge into your life. To live a flexible life, it is vital to keep your expectations low and just go with the flow. It's an outstanding skill that you need to deal with the inevitable changes and challenges life brings. Enfolding this great skill will help you keep a more open approach towards the new challenges, circumstances, and situations in life.

2. As important as it is to keep control over your Thought Practice, it is imperative to know when to stop thinking. Our advice would be to practice Thought Stopping. That's one of the best ways to gain control over thoughts that keep recurring in your mind and cost you your peace. The key is to become mindful of these thoughts and try to dismiss them right away. Practice saying 'Stop'

to yourself or envision a red stop sign when something pops up in your head. The more you're mindful of it and practice it, the more you can control it. Another interesting trick is to put a rubber band around your wrist and every time you find yourself trapped in a loop of negative thoughts, give yourself a snap!

3. Document what you feel and expect. Clearly, it is impractical to live without expectations at all. The best way to deal with it is to write down your thoughts and deal with them more rationally. Write down:

- The expectations that keep popping into your mind.
- A higher energy solution as you deliberately disconnect yourself from that expectation.
- Things you just cannot let go of concerning your expectation.
- A statement in accordance with the higher energies of trust that should replace the expectation.

   NOTE: If you expect your husband to give you a passionate kiss as soon as he lays eyes on you after a long week of work, you will be thoroughly disappointed if he just gives you a peck on the cheek as he continues to discuss his schedule. Naturally, since the expectation wasn't fulfilled, you will be triggered and instead feel emotionally distant from your spouse. Now, instead of being so specific about your expectation, if you replace it with general thoughts of love, care, and appreciation for him, even a happy greeting with a light peck on your cheek will make your day.

4. While there's nothing wrong in saying "No" when you have to, it is important to be mindful of when you need to say it. Some people are in such a habit of denying things that the word "No"

comes out before they analyze the question. This may work in areas where you need to prioritize yourself, but this can be troublesome in personal relationships. It is unnecessary and limiting to permanently dismiss the idea or disregard your loved ones and their requests. Take time to respond. When something is asked of you, take a deep breath, hold it for a few seconds, slowly exhale and take this sweet time to analyze the situation and how you should respond to it. Not only will it make you look much more confident about your response, but this technique will also improve your mental flexibility. When you're in control of what you think and how you respond, it helps reduce your worries, remove the stress, and improve your relationship.

5. Change is inevitable. And the more you're adaptive to altering your routine, the better you'll be at building cognitive flexibility. It is never too late to adopt new habits, change your routine, and start doing the same things differently. For example, if you take the same subway or the same route to work every day, it could be both fun and exciting to tweak that a little. Consider taking a bus or just change your route for a different experience. Similarly, if you usually hit the gym to stay fit, alter it up by going to the park for a jog in the fresh air or taking a bike ride. It is all about building and strengthening the new neural pathways, and you'd be surprised how things as simple as changing your commute or using a different hand to brush your teeth can make a difference.

6. Live in the moment. As the Millennials like to say—YOLO—which means *You Only Live Once*. Why waste your precious life by trapping yourself in the thoughts of the future or regrets of the past. Why not live in the moment, enjoy every bit of it, and make the most out of it. It is weird how our brains work sometimes. While sipping on a cup of coffee, we often think about how they serve better coffee somewhere else or how while eating food, we're already worrying about what we will eat the next day. This

habit takes away the pleasure and experience that the present has to offer you. Instead, luxuriate or relish in whatever you're doing today—right now! It brings immense pleasure when you try to focus on the present. If you're eating a delicious pastry right now, you will only experience the flavors exploding on your tongue at the moment. Later, you can only think about it and feel bad, and that's because most negative thoughts concerns either the worries of the future or past experiences. As Mark Twain put it, "I have known a great many troubles, but most of them never happened." If we surround ourselves with negative thoughts, it becomes hard to enjoy whatever is happening in the present. The hallmark of anxiety and depression is catastrophizing—thinking or worrying over something that hasn't happened yet or may not happen at all. You hardly ever worry about a situation you're in because you're busy looking for a solution or mourning over it. Worrying happens when you're thinking about the future, making scenarios in your head about all of the *"what if's"* that could occur. If you want to notice the difference between practicing this positivity in your life, start today. Savor the present and be grateful for what you have today—in this very moment.

7. Other than expectations, another critical thing that we need to let go of is attachments. This helps us forge a new foundation in alignment, stability, and health. Attachment means we are finding meaning and significance in that thing, status, or person rather than in our own healing. It's important to let go of the attachments we find in:

- Our achievements
- Our occupation
- Our salary
- Our identities based on how others perceive us

- The car we drive

- The house we live in

- Our relationships (husband, wife, mother, father, child, etc.)

> NOTE: Being attached to things, successes, or even people make us dependent on them. We start to believe that our life is incomplete without them, and we need to have those people or those things to survive. Eventually, it starts defining us as a person. If you feel too attached to someone or something, think about it and hold them in your mind. Think about it as a substitute in life that narrows down the way you live. We need to get rid of these confines to become more comfortable with who we are. Some of these attachments stem from the pain of unhealed wounds, while others may simply come from fear of failure or a desire to find peace.

8. Next, you need to consider attachment to things. For instance, imagine having a house where everything is either beautiful, essential, or both. It is filled with things that you like and prefer. Just imagining it can give you a sense of fulfillment and pleasure. When you start cluttering your space with unnecessary items just because you feel a sense of attachment to it, you are preparing to stress yourself. Don't hesitate to set the bar really high. When you're decluttering or buying new things for your space, ask yourself if you *really* need it. Sometimes we spend money on something or hoarding items because we feel a particular attachment or likeness towards them. Soon, it becomes monotonous and doesn't spark the same excitement anymore. That's when you realize you just cluttered your space with unnecessary items. Keep things that make you and your house look comfortable and feel like a million dollars.

9. Stemming from the previous points, reflect on your attachment to people. When it comes to relationships, everyone wants to be happy, satisfied, and not to be hurt. Once you're able to find that perfect relationship where all the emotions are perfectly balanced, it is natural to start feeling too dependent on one person for all emotional needs. Just the idea of losing that person you're extremely attached to can become highly stressful. Being in a happy relationship doesn't make one person the owner of the other. You're still two individuals with your own lives. It is a common misconception that your perfect partner now belongs to you and is responsible for your happiness. It becomes pressurizing for the partners, and soon the ideal relationship starts to become toxic. While honesty and devotion are priceless in a relationship, freedom is crucial, too. Give your partner space to breathe and be who they are instead of owning and controlling them. When you become too attached to a person, you give them the power to destroy you and make you miserable. The way you feel should only depend on you and not the people who are close to you.

- **Start by becoming your own best friend.** Some people attach themselves to other individuals to gain a sense of worth. Again, it is similar to giving someone else control of your life. If they someday find you worthless, you will end up feeling the same. Your worth does not need anyone else's validation. You're worth it whether someone tells you that or not. Don't let other people make you feel a certain way about yourself. Be your own friend and tell yourself, "I am so totally worth it!"

- **There is nothing wrong with being alone.** I can't emphasize the importance of some quality *me time*. I believe everyone deserves to enjoy their own company and just be themselves. If you want to be happy and learn to depend on yourself for all of your emotions, it is important to be alone sometimes. That is the best way to understand the person you are.

- **Do not limit yourself to certain relationships.** Never lose your options or limit yourself to a handful of people or relationships when you can interact with many people and live a much more fulfilling life. Limiting yourself to few people will make you dependent on them. And if you have more people to share your life with, you will be happy to know you're open to making new connections.

- **Stop explaining or justifying your choices.** Life goes on—with or without the people you once considered your lifelines. You may feel a little different, miserable, or even incomplete if you lose a meaningful relationship, but nothing really stops. It is only a matter of time, and everything will start falling into place once again. The only way to feel less pain and let go quickly is to believe you're strong enough to carry on. It is important to realize that your life doesn't depend on anyone else.

- **Do not suffocate or be suffocated.** Relationships are like sand. The tighter you try to hold it, the faster it slips between your fingers. When you're in a relationship, it doesn't make you someone's other half. You're still an individual—a separate, whole person. And while there is nothing wrong with keeping people close to your heart, squeezing too tightly will suffocate them.

10. Attachment is a significant aspect of one's life, whether related to other people or things. It is critical to put in a lot of deliberate effort and mental work into determining where your attachments lie. When you put in this effort, you realize your self-worth and you become stronger. It also makes you capable of maintaining healthy relationships in the long run. As you learn to live flexibly, apply your Thought Practice positively, and live in the higher energies, it will become easier for you to gain perspective.

- One day, you will look back and smile when those hardships and obstacles appear as gifts disguised as problems.

- You will gain perspective about all the goodness of living in the present. Even if you experience problems, you will prefer looking on the brighter side and considering it an experience to learn from. Right when you think you're lost, you will find a way. Effective Thought Practice guides us to our true nature.

- Additionally, get out of your own way. Don't sabotage the process because Thought Practice will guide you to your true, most authentic, best version of yourself.

11. Here are a few essential questions that you can ask yourself to facilitate identifying and addressing your attachments:

- Is there a thing or a person that I feel I need to be content or complete?

- Do I have erroneous beliefs that can lead to unhealthy attachments?

12. If other people offer you advice or opinions, take it positively and respond firmly, like, "Thank you for sharing your thoughts. That gives me some things to think about. I will surely ponder over it."

- Do not hesitate to share your higher energies with other people. Energies like kindness, love, compassion, respect, and understanding should be shared with everyone. Pass it on with your words, feelings, and thoughts. This action will create positive energy that works like a superfood for living flexibly, and it will continue to elevate your mental and spiritual limberness.

IT IS ALREADY HERE

*"Act as if everything you desire is already here...treat
yourself as if you already are what you'd like to become."*
—Wayne Dyer

HOW MUCH OF THE day are you aware of? How much of the day do you have
an essential awareness of what life is presenting? Or, like so many others,
are you lost in a waking sleep? Is your day spent blindly drifting from
one form of comfort to another to you avoid the anxiety of discomfort
in facing your naked soul? How much of your life is spent fortifying a
particular self-image? How much is spent pleasing others or trying to gain
their approval instead of living authentically? These are critical questions
that each of us must ask and answer if we want to lose the chains and
shackles of self-oppression.

After I began what I came to call Thought Practice, I spent a few hours
with three enlightened souls. Marie, Wayne, and John all had practiced
mindfulness, active presence, and their Thought Practice for years. At
this particular meeting, it became clear they did not know one another
well. The conversation found each of them present and without ego. The
impression I gathered was they were all lifelong intimate friends, but
they weren't. They discussed the intimacies of life with ease. The higher
energies were now natural to them.

Making Thought Practice real in your life is much more difficult than
having a simple intellectual understanding. The greatest hurdle to waking

up is that we do not realize how asleep we are. It takes more than dabbling for a short while to understand how difficult Thought Practice is. However, magic happens when you ultimately cross that line, and it becomes natural and second nature for you. Remember: thoughts are things. Powerful things. Real things.

> **When you combine your thoughts with a definite purpose, persistence, passion, and a burning desire, you will create the life you intend.**

When you combine your thoughts with a definite purpose, persistence, passion, and a burning desire, you will create the life you intend. Part of combining these principles in your Thought Practice is knowing that it is already here. So just to make sure we are on the same page, let's get an accurate and practical picture of what it means to live as if "it's already here." To do that, let's go back to where many of us lived before our Thought Practice.

Do you try and maintain a sense of control to avoid feeling the fear of chaos? Do you try to maintain that control to avoid the feelings of rejection? Do you try and gain acceptance and approval? Do you seek busyness or pleasure to avoid the deep holes that need healing inside your heart? All of these are coping strategies of the ego. They have one thing in common—they keep us encased in an artificial life where we don't truly live.

The essence of Thought Practice is cultivating awakening. This process has two essential components. The first is cultivating and clarifying the mental process and energies of Thought Practice. The second is experiencing by entering the awareness of the physical reality of the present moment.

The process of clarification entails seeing through our substitute life. This is identifying our deeply held thoughts and most basic identities.

The point is to see that these beliefs have become solidified—as if it's always been this way, and this is the right way to live. So, we accept it as truth. We also must see how our subconscious behavioral strategies have become conditioned so that they also seem to be true. As we see these thoughts and procedures clearly, we also must deal with the emotional pain that initially gave rise to them—the pain embedded in our core. We do this through the process of experiencing it and bringing awareness to the moment.

Experiencing our lives transforms them because it eventually empowers our Thought Practice. Our Thought Practice then helps us experience our lives more fully. As we connect with the physical reality of the moment, we realize experientially that our thoughts, judgments, emotions, identities, and experiences are all separate yet bound together in the concept we call "*me.*" When we enter the present moment without our judgments, hurts, wounds, and preconceived opinions, we can experience life differently. As we stop identifying with the narrow sense of "*me,*" we begin to identify with the broader sense of self-awareness in the higher energies.

As we find the reality of life through our Thought Practice, we will continue to have bouts of ego dissatisfaction. This reality cannot be described with words, yet it's genuine. All we can say is that it's who we are and continue to attend to those wounds. It calls us to go deeper and deeper into uncovering our substitute life's falsehoods. This includes holding onto the core beliefs of the ego that have defined our identity. Slowly we heal, become, and then we emerge into the life we've always wanted.

Thought Practice is not a straight line. It's a mixture of struggle and integration, confusion and clarity, seeing no progress, and diving deeper. Seeing through the veil of our deeply held beliefs, dismantling the sense of self we've known, facing our worst fears, healing our deepest wounds, and opening into the unknown all lead us in a natural, gradual healing process until one day we emerge. Coming to understand this means seeing through idealized pictures of how to think we are supposed to be. We must let it go. Then, we must develop compassion for ourselves as we walk the path of awakening.

Realizing it is already here involves a Thought Practice that projects and brings the future into manifestation in the physical. To do that, we must live without attachments and in the higher energies. It is a tenuous balance. On the one hand, you have the possibility of hopes and goals and the desire to pursue them with vigor. On the other hand, you let go of controlling the path to those goals. Acting this way involves a clear purpose and passion, accompanied by a determination to produce the desired result. Living in the higher energies while pursuing your passions requires vigilance against the ego's desire to inject itself.

Remember how the ego convinces us to consult our false self and cling to the ego's protection? This is not evil, but rather the learned ways we have adopted by allowing the ego to guide us. As you learn to live in the realization that it's already here, there are three common pitfalls people can fall into that stop the flow of manifestation into your life.

- **Boasting.** An inclination to draw attention to yourself and misrepresent your accomplishments so that others might view you positively.
- **Distorting.** Stating facts as you would have liked them to have occurred. These little white lies or petty exaggerations become a way of life.
- **Deceiving.** Leading others down a path to save face or prevent embarrassment. Making up a scenario to convince yourself and others of your innocence in wrongdoing.

When you commit to an active and consistent Thought Practice by living in the higher energies of love, kindness, honesty, abundance, attraction, and peace, you create a silent knowledge that builds into your life. You become a vessel to bless others.

Living as if it is already here means remaining receptive to what you intended to manifest, as well as what the universe wants to bring to fruition in your life. It's living in a state of ready receptivity for guidance to express your manifestations. It's living in receptivity to give the higher energies back to the world you live in. This is especially important during a season when everything seems to indicate you are not accomplishing your desires. In those moments, refuse to give doubt a foothold in your life and choose to remain receptive. Being receptive involves letting go as well as a willingness to let go, remove the ego from leadership, and live in the higher energies.

The good news about letting go is we come to realize the impermanence of circumstances and possessions. Things form on the mythical horizon, pass by as experiences, and disappear into the rearview mirror of life. For most of us, life is a series of ongoing adjustments in search of comfort. By choosing or allowing that to be our focus, we miss out on real life. Life is an endless stream of experiences that bring us lessons and opportunities to love. Each can helps us mature, grow, and live in peace and enlightenment. It results in a spiritual

Life is an endless stream of experiences that bring us lessons and opportunities to love.

maturity that expands our Thought Practice even deeper. The choice of living this way through your Thought Practice is wholly yours and yours alone.

The quality and quantity of your thoughts determine the amount of resistance you encounter. Thoughts that generate what you don't want are resistant. Any thought that places a barrier between what you want and what you have in your life and your ability to attract it into your life is resistance. Remember—thoughts are things. Thoughts have energy. Thoughts are magnetic. As Shakespeare once said, "Our doubts are our betrayers." Our thoughts are like a magnetic tractor beam that pulls what you want in your life through the ether and into your life.

Living as if it is already here involves giving forth what you want to attract. Once you've formed a picture in your mind of the people and opportunities that you intend to show up in your life, and you know how you want them to treat you, you must BE what you want. For example, you can't have a desire to attract a mate who is confident, generous, positive, non-judgmental, and gentle and then expect that desire to be manifested if you are acting in non-confident, stingy, negative, judgmental, and harsh ways. This is why most people don't attract the right people into their life. They want what they are not.

Remember—it takes NO more effort to go for it in life and demand abundance than it does to accept depression and lack. Allow God to speak through your hopes and dreams and use faith blended with your thoughts to create the energy that programs your subconscious mind. Your thought energy backed by a strong desire tends to transmute itself into its physical equivalent.

We all become what we are because of our dominating thoughts. Period. Every deeply seated desire has the effort of causing us to seek outward expression through which that desire may be created in reality. We make our life through our thoughts and the programming of our subconscious by those thoughts.

It's a fact that what we believe is what we have repeated to ourselves and tinged with energy. Whether that statement or thought is true or false, accurate or inaccurate, is irrelevant. You will believe it to be true. Everyone is what they are because of the dominating thoughts which they permit to occupy their mind. Thoughts that are mixed with any feelings and emotions constitute a magnetic force that attracts from the vibrations of the ether other similar and related energies towards that person. A thought magnetized with emotion is like a seed that will germinate and ultimately bear fruit when planted in fertile soil and nurtured properly. Eventually, that one seed creates millions of others like it in its fruit. Remember, the subconscious mind doesn't distinguish between constructive and destructive thought. It works with what we feed it through our Thought Practice. Like the wind that can carry a ship east and another west, your thoughts will pull you up or push you down according to how you set your sails of thought.

Living as if it's already here doesn't mean you can wish something into existence. Remember, there is no such thing as something for nothing. A price must always be paid. There are no free lunches. The ability to reach and influence your subconscious mind has its price, and you must pay that price. You cannot cheat or take shortcuts.

The price of the ability to influence your subconscious mind is persistence in applying the principles of Thought Practice and living in the higher energies. To get results, you must flex these muscles until their application becomes a fixed habit. Fortune gravitates towards those whose minds have been prepared to attract it just as water gravitates towards the ocean.

Living as if it is already here also involves the glue of persistence. Persistence is essential in the procedure of transmuting desire into physical manifestation. Persistence is not a sexy thought. It is usually not motivating or emotionally encouraging. However, it is the backbone of any growth. Too many people give up when they put in the effort and don't immediately see the specific results they want.

We have been conditioned for instant gratification. Enlightenment and peaceful maturity do not happen instantly. Like a tree that grows from a seed or wine that requires aging and fermentation, growth needs seasons and the right nourishment to bear fruit. One of those nourishing factors is our persistence. Far more people lack the strength of persistence than do not. If you lack persistence, don't panic. You can develop it. Persistence is a state of mind and a developed habit. It's made much easier if you know your purpose and goal. Knowing why you are doing what you are doing and what you want to receive from your Thought Practice will help grow your muscle of persistence.

When you dig in your heels to remain persistent, you should keep in mind that every thought you have either strengthens or weakens you. You attract what you emanate. It is vital to your Thought Practice to become conscious of your thoughts—every thought you have impacts you. Every thought you have is either strengthening or weakening your ability to stay connected to the Divine and the energy of the universe. If you want a lack of funds and a normal life, by all means, do not adopt a vibrant, targeted Thought Practice. Settle and allow lazy thinking to dominate your energy. You will attract ordinary people who are mired in lazy thinking. Surrounding yourself with these like-minded souls will create more worry and anxiety in your life as your thoughts bear fruit. If you genuinely want to live in peace, purpose, and love, then you must take your thoughts seriously and ensure they are synchronized with the higher energies of the universe. You are aligning with the very energy of God, and He is anything but ordinary.

Remember, there is a difference between a rut and a routine. Routines can add fuel to your growth as you develop good habits. Ruts in our road of life lead nowhere and make the journey rougher. Shift your focus upward out of the rut of the ordinary and into the routine of the extraordinary.

You will attract to your life what you think and feel inside. For example, if you think you are not worthy of respect or do not respect yourself, you will attract disrespect. If you respect yourself and feel respect for yourself, you will draw others toward you who respect you.

There is a wonderful scripture in *A Course in Miracles* that reads, "Infinite patience produces immediate results." This means that the right people will show up on their Divinely ordained schedules. The universe reveals as we need and not according to our schedule. The immediate result you will experience from infinite patience is deep and lasting peace. You will know that God WILL do his part, and you are doing yours through your Thought Practice.

When you choose to live in the higher energies of love, kindness, compassion, non-judgment, acceptance, and abundance, you will live in the powerful magnetic energies of the universe. Research has shown that acts of kindness directed toward another improves our lives. It stimulates the production of serotonin in both the recipient and the donor. Even more remarkable is that the person observing the act of kindness has similar beneficial results. Likewise, when you are unkind, you're blocking the face of kindness. You're not just moving away from the higher energies, but you're inviting the low, destructive energies into your life. No matter your faith or what you call God, be aware that unkind thoughts weaken—and kind thoughts strengthen—your connection. Period.

Interestingly, it's the very expression of our unkindness that leads us to have more inner work. The expression of lower energy thoughts, emotions, and actions is almost always based on the erroneous assumption that someone or something—outside ourselves—is to blame for our unkindness. To dwell in blame prevents us from taking responsibility for ourselves.

If we look honestly at ourselves, we will see the extent of our lack of ownership and responsibility for our thoughts and actions. In the 12-step program, we take a ruthless and fearless moral inventory. The idea is to observe our actions and take ownership of those that were in the lower energies that caused others harm. First, we see them for their judgments, resentments, preferences, control, etc. The willingness to look at and attend to our lower energy, thoughts, and actions like unkindness is what untimely heals and transforms them into the higher energies. It's easy to be kind and display actions of the higher energies when you are in a good mood or when things are going your way. However, when life starts to go in a direction you dislike, then living in the higher energies and being kind is a sign of maturity and growth.

All energy is attracted to you through your thoughts. Those thoughts will attract like energies into your life if they are aligned with the higher energies and rooted in love. You have the power—only you. Do not think that because your thoughts are key to attracting the life you want, you have been given a prescription of idleness, lack of hard work, or lack of clear goals. You cannot embody any of those things. But your Thought Practice will create what you want, serendipitously producing peace and purpose while removing anxiety and worry from your life.

No one can do this for you. But God will do it with you. You impose on the universe what you desire, and you calmly and knowingly proceed to act on that picture as if it already exists. Align yourself and partner with God so he can work through you and produce the results. Abandon all fear and go about your life as if knowing that what is necessary will manifest and soon come into view. Stay alert for circumstances that indicate the first sprouting of the seed that you have planted. Nourish it as it grows into materialization.

"Living as if" is an important muscle to flex in your Thought Practice. It's natural to ask, "What if it doesn't materialize as I picture it?" It's the way of the ego to try and force things when they aren't going as we want. It would be pointless and destructive to get down on our hands and knees and start tugging at new vegetable shoots as they sprout in the spring, hoping to get them to bear fruit more quickly. They need to grow at their own pace and in the right season. They will flourish at precisely the right time. If your picture does not manifest in the period that you have designated, relax. Retreat to your knowing that it is already in place in the spiritual realm. You may also be attempting to misuse your power by placing restrictions and contingencies on the universe. Your trust in the power of attraction and receptivity is necessary.

Begin living as if what you would like to attract is already in your life. If you want to create healing, formulate the picture in your mind and radiate out the energy as if the healing is here now. Be cheerful and trusting in your knowledge. Begin acting in a new, healthy manner. The universe will give you minimal clues and encouragement to your new thoughts and actions. Proceeding to act in your inner picture speeds up the process if you want to materialize more prosperity and start thinking of prosperous thoughts. Choose thoughts and actions of abundance on faith that the abundance is already yours. It's on the way to manifesting. Live in conscious gratitude for all the abundance that has already come your way. Look for ways to be grateful and flex your muscle of gratitude. Gratitude begets more gratitude from the universe.

God is abundant. He has no boundaries and is everywhere at once. He is endlessly abundant and lavish. His abundance never stops, and He wants to bless us. Through your Thought Practice, you can establish a relationship with the God's abundance and lovingkindness. For example, if you change your thoughts and actions surrounding kindness, imagine yourself being kind, people acting kindly towards you, and thinking kind thoughts.

After a season of flexing this muscle, it will become natural and part of your everyday life. Beautiful thoughts build a beautiful life. Seeking the beauty of the higher energies in the worst of situations is not naïve—it's self-leadership. If you focus on what's ugly, you attract more ugliness into your thoughts and life. By choosing your thoughts in the worst situations, you can process anything with the energy of appreciation and growth and create an opportunity that moves far past the situation. Your Thought Practice is powerful. Your thoughts start the machinery of the universe into operation. Your subconscious mind is key to this, and this is where suggestion and repetition are important. Repetition of affirmations leads to belief, and once faith becomes a deep conviction, things begin to happen. You create your own life of prosperity and peace. No one must change for you to experience prosperity. Only you can change your life.

Beautiful thoughts build a beautiful life.

Hold fast to the vision of the life you want.

Mediate on your prosperity. Hold pictures in your mind of what your prosperity looks like. Refuse to let those pictures fade. Despite circumstances you have created in your life, hold fast to the vision of the life you want. Stated another way, "Create the life you love!" Your mediations will begin to give you an inner guide to follow as you create your future in your thoughts. Use this practice to manifest what you want to experience in your life in the physical plane.

Remember, live as if it's already here. Getting into the swing of your Thought Practice is no easy thing for the average person. You are fighting against years of lazy programming. But it can be done.

It's simple but can also be difficult, as is the process of building any new healthy habit. Doubts initially come from our subconscious. A big demonstration of the universe working energetically is usually followed by tormenting thoughts. This is a time when you must make your affirmations of truth repeatedly and rejoice and give thanks for what you have received. The universe responds to gratitude. Every good and perfect gift is already yours—it's just waiting for your recognition and acceptance.

When you act as if dominant forces, faculties, and talents come alive and you discover yourself to be a greater person than you may have dreamed of, extend your awareness of the energy of the universe beyond the world of form and material manifestation. The energy is both in the physical and non-physical worlds. So although Thought Practice can be difficult at first, it is also easy and attainable.

All that is required is realigning ourselves and activating our Thought Practice. You are reprogramming your subconscious, and that will require discipline, vigilance, and consistency. The discipline to persevere will foster the ability to focus and be patient as you harmonize your thoughts, feelings, and beliefs into one energetic work. As you begin to act "as if," you will see love emerge more and more in your daily life. You will grow in awareness of your Thought Practice as a power that reconnects you to the Divine Source of all energy. You will discover that it is a seamless way to live in the higher energies rather than something your ego must accomplish. Everything necessary for you seems almost effortlessly available. You can then open yourself up to the possibilities of you and God collaborating to produce a fulfilling life.

Living as if it's already here means you are open to receiving the help you desire and need. Trust in the principles of the higher energies. Look for and be willing to accept the guidance that comes your way because it will. Stay in harmony with the higher energies of honesty, love, non-judgment, kindness, and attraction. Eliminate from your thoughts any doubts. If left undisturbed and nurtured in your mind, an alignment with the higher energies will bear fruit and manifest in your life. Living as if it's already here reinforces the belief that all you desire, you have already received. And do know you will have your desires filled. Treat yourself as if you already are what you would like to become. Think and live as if it's already here.

CHAPTER 15 EXERCISES

These chapter exercises are designed to help you apply the principles of TRANFORMATIONAL THINKING in meaningful and transformative ways for you. They are not designed that one should do all the exercises for each chapter. Record the notes from the chapter, the exercise you are doing, and the results in your notebook.

1. It is often said that the comfort zone can actually become uncomfortable. And there could be a little truth in that. Often, we look for comfort to divert ourselves from the chronic wounds we carry. We look for comfort in alcohol, sex, food, romance, shopping, and other similar experiences. Just like every individual is different, the way they look for comfort is distinct, too. When we settle ourselves into lazy thinking, comfort becomes our coping mechanism to deal with bad experiences and wounds. But to find out what's truly comforting for your soul, try and answer the following questions.

    • What are some real coping mechanisms to avoid facing your naked soul?

    • Is the fear of chaos becoming too dominant? And how are you planning to maintain a sense of control to avoid that feeling?

    • Is there a coping mechanism to avoid the feeling of rejection or the sense of not fitting in?

- Do you try too hard to gain acceptance and approval from other people?

- Do you try to stay busy or seek pleasure to disregard the bad experiences and deep holes that need healing inside your heart?

The answers you get are the coping strategies associated with our ego. These strategies keep us encased in an artificial life where we do not truly belong.

2. It is important to remember that a rut and a routine are not the same things. Routine is an excellent way to fuel your growth as you continue to develop great habits. On the other hand, a rut takes you nowhere and instead makes the journey more challenging. To make things work, shift your focus from the rut of the ordinary towards the routine of the extraordinary. This will start changing the way you think and feel inside. You attract and become what you think. So, if you do not respect yourself or think that you're not worthy of respect, you will automatically attract disrespect. While it's not easy to change the way you think, putting in consistent effort to think positively can be a game-changer. It even impacts your personal growth and makes an immense difference to your emotional, physical, and spiritual wellbeing. A slight alteration to your mindset can change your life for good. Here I will share with you some tips and activities that you can implement to create a routine for success and transform your life through Thought Practice:

   - The Double Bind: Don't feel like hitting the gym today? Push yourself and go anyway! Do not want to continue practicing the piano? Encourage yourself and play. The results of keeping up with your commitments are very promising. It helps build confidence and changes your mindset so you can continue to grow. Of course, doing what you do not want to do may not be fun, but showing up and fulfilling your commitments allow you to take care of bigger goals in life.

- Hold onto the anchor. Everyone needs an anchor in their lives. That's one thing that keeps you grounded and positive when your thoughts start wavering. Whether you believe in God, share a spiritual connection with the Supreme power, or have a relationship in your life that keeps you grounded, make that your anchor. The purpose of doing so is to keep yourself positive when your thoughts or external factors are putting you down. It is about staying strong by having trust and faith in that one thing that still works for you when everything else becomes useless. To change your mindset, this is what you need the most.

- Do not be scared to ask *"Why."* To change your thought process, you must look deeper into what's causing a reaction.

- Find out why little things bother you or trigger your emotions.

- Find out why you become uneasy when eating alone at a restaurant.

- Why do you feel happy after buying something you have always wanted?

- We are always ready to question external factors. But we are hardly ever prepared to question ourselves. Once you start questioning, however, you will learn a lot about yourself. As we begin to explore and answer these questions, it is easier to see how these external factors aren't the reasons we experience emotions such as happiness, guilt, sadness, or joy. These emotions are connected to our values.

3. Now, start a conversation with yourself and analyze your values based on your answers:

- For instance, maybe you're irritated because someone else took the parking spot you've been waiting for. <u>Reaction:</u> you have a lot of things to do, and you don't have time to look for another parking space.

- <u>Reflection:</u> The time restriction that you're experiencing can cause unnecessary stress. If you prioritize your schedule, you may not feel overwhelmed.

- For instance, you are feeling uncomfortable eating alone in a restaurant. <u>Reaction:</u> You may feel uneasy for fear of being judged by people who may think you are a loner.

- <u>Reflection:</u> You care about what people think of you, including strangers, and it could affect your emotional wellbeing. Please don't be so insecure about yourself, especially regarding others' perception of you. If dining out alone brings you joy and helps you step out of your comfort zone, go for it.

- For instance, you are feeling happy about buying a dress that you've been eyeing for a long time. <u>Reaction:</u> You feel happy about your purchase because it brings you confidence.

- <u>Reflection:</u> Confidence is essential to boost your self-morale. It determines how you look and feel about yourself when stepping out in public. But you can experience the same fulfillment and confidence without splurging on things. If it is just about feeling great about yourself, you can do that with a bit of boost in confidence. You can look and feel your best in your pajamas, loosely tied hair, and your glasses on.

Having such straightforward yet mindful conversations with yourself is a surefire method to change your mindset. Reflecting on how you feel about a given situation and reanalyzing the whole scenario can help you understand your strong and weak points.

4. Let's get rid of *"buts"* once and for all. This is the word we often turn to when looking for an excuse for a situation we're stuck in. Unfortunately, we tend to use it much more than we should. For example: "I want to become healthier and lose that extra weight, but my schedule is so tight that I hardly get any time to prepare my meals or hit the gym." "I so want to upgrade my car, but my cash is tied up with the other debt." "I can't wait to set up my own business, but I don't have time or finances to commit to it." Sounds pretty familiar, no? Now eliminate the "but" and imagine how easy your life will become if you didn't let the external factors matter so much. This is a powerful way to alter your thinking and make an effort to get rid of the roadblocks that keep tapping unnecessary *buts* in your life. Don't forget, changing the way your mind works is a work in progress, and it gets rewarding as you continue to put in the effort. It is about analyzing your self-worth on a deeper level and taking the first step to make those changes permanent.

5. Another commonly used word that often puts us in a confusing situation is *"if."* No matter what you are about to commence, the *"what if"* can ruin it all. What if it does not turn out the way I want it to? What if I never reach there? It is a way of the ego to force things when they aren't going as we want. This is where visualization comes into play. It is regarded as an inner transformation that takes us to the outer results of the real world. Do not let the power of imagination take control of how you want the situation to turn out. If you invent doubts before starting something, you may end up in the wrong place. A significant aspect of Thought Practice is to stay positive, and that requires eliminating all the *"if's."*

6. Visualizing is powerful. While it can give you a sense of safety and control if you stay positive, it can also lead to stress and fear if you visualize negative events. Our brain works in a funny way.

Sometimes, it starts thinking and visualizing things that we do not want to happen, and it can cause stress. Taking control over what you visualize is an excellent way to rewire your brain and build empowering and helpful habits. For the sake of Thought Practice, take action as soon as you notice negative visuals popping in your head. If you experience anxiety, worry, or stress, make an effort to replace those thoughts with more positive visuals—something that brings you a sense of happiness or confidence, for example.

7. Enhancing your perception to avoid worry and anxiety is another excellent step you can take. Put the power of visualization in your favor and use it to improve your perceptive observation and awareness skills. This is of great value as it helps you become more aware of your situation and the people around you. Additionally, it improves your memory to recall happy events easily and feel great about them once again. Here are some interesting tips to make visualization work for you:

   • **Step 1:** Calm your mind and sit in a peaceful, quiet place. Spend a few minutes observing your surroundings.

   • **Step 2:** Now, close your eyes and try to visualize everything you just observed in as much detail as you can. Don't miss out on the fine details because that's precisely what it is all about. Recall the texture, colors, and variety of the things you just saw in your surroundings. If you're finding it difficult to recall all the details in the first few minutes, repeat the process until you improve and can memorize better.

This simple process will enhance your ability to visualize and utilize its power. Not only will it help you become more aware of your surroundings, but it will also sharpen your mind to visualize your experiences with all the fine details.

LIVING IN THE FLOW

"[Living in the flow] is making the best of what we do have, instead of begrudging what we don't, has a way of creating all that we'll ever need."
—Charles Glassman

YOUR MIND IS LIKE a computer. Every thought that you choose to flow through it and every image you create is inscribed on your brain. You choose what you think about it. Everything in your life started as a thought, as part of your imagination. Imagining is the act of creating mental images of what has never been and what could and will be. One of your most valuable assets, is your power to imagine. It's such a powerful tool in your Thought Practice that if you are misusing it or not using it, you will want to consider some significant changes if you're going to live a fulfilling life. Have you ever paused and thought about your ability and power to imagine?

> **One of your most valuable assets is your power to imagine.**

Picture a tropical beach, perhaps Maui. See the color of the water and the waves keeping rhythm with the earth. The sun is glistening off the water. How the sand feels on your feet, the sun warming your body. Can you picture it? Spend a few moments there. What about a park full of green grass, vibrant trees, well-groomed shrubs, and flowers? Feel the grass and the texture on the blanket you lay on. The sounds of families.

Can you picture it? Spend a few moments there. Imagination is powerful in your Thought Practice to bring intentions into reality. It aids in your meditation, presence, and magnetism of thought. God values our power to imagine. He knows why He created this power within us and how He intended us to use it. The purpose of imagination is to play and create. It is powerful in our Thought Practice and holds all the components in a gentle, mental hug.

None of the components of Thought Practice are steps to be followed in sequence. They all play a part in the transformation of our lives. They are analogous to the intertwining strands of a cable that require all the strands' contribution for maximum strength. With a certain degree of process, all the components can be present simultaneously, each supporting the other. Similarly, the more Thought Practice becomes intertwined into your life, the more it will attract and transform. Too many of us have bought into the lie that behind our choices and goals are peace and purpose. Our actions determine natural consequences for sure. The consequential results depend on the actions, the energy behind those actions, and the extent they are within the higher energies of the universe.

Within the higher energies of love, kindness, honesty, and non-judgment, Thought Practice leads to liberation. Living in the flow of higher energies and your Thought Practice does not just mean spiritual progress. It is emancipation for the tyranny of the ego. Freedom. Peace. Purpose. LIFE! Living in the flow means taking ownership and responsibility for your life, thoughts, emotions, actions, and circumstances. You are the owner and beneficiary of your actions. You choose the thoughts that produce feelings and actions. Based on the underlying motive, our actions may be wholesome or unwholesome, good or bad, edifying or destructive. This is imparting a belief system onto your thoughts and actions. Regardless of your personal worldview, all of this is quite simple. If it is based on the higher energies, it will be blessed. If it's based on the lower energies of the ego, it won't. An easy way to tell is if the thoughts and actions are based on fear, anxiety, or greed, they are of the ego. If they are rooted in love, kindness, and honesty, they are aligned with the universal laws.

One of the essential features of Thought Practice is the capacity to produce results corresponding to the ethical quality of the action. An immanent universal law holds influence over our actions, which brings about the blessing or curse of these actions depending on their roots and energy. Whenever we perform a deliberate action, the thought leaves an imprint on our energy continuum. It remains there until it stirs up potency and is released as conditions become favorable for its manifestation. The trigger of effect brings the natural magnetic equivalent into manifestation in our life.

If the thought is ego-based or higher energy-based, it will bring the equivalent pain or pleasure, decline or progress, disorder or peace. These energies can also ripen over the years through millions of microscopic thoughts and intangible actions. When they bear fruit, there is no stopping them until they have fully manifested. This is true, regardless of the root of the thoughts and beliefs. Healthy, higher energy thoughts bring peace, purpose, love, and fulfillment. In comparison, lower energy ego thoughts bring turmoil, heartache, pain, and suffering.

Living in the flow begins with embracing an attitude of openness and then maturing in your active Thought Practice. This redirects the lazy energy that has dictated your life thus far. Through the right view, we understand that cruel, harsh, and spiteful thoughts are harmful to not just us but also others. They wreak havoc with our hearts as we live their karmic consequences. Wholesome higher energy thinking that is consciously and skillfully developed becomes automatic, then magnetically pulls peace and purpose into our life, creating abundance.

Living in the flow is embracing the attitude of openness as well as welcoming the higher energies. It's living in those energies even when you don't feel it. Wholesome higher energy thinking is undertaken consciously and then skillfully developed and made to become automatic in our lives. We stop thinking along the lines of selfishness and what we can get for ourselves. As our Thought Practice grows, living in the flow, we intuitively abandon thoughts of cruelty, ill will, anger, envy, greed, and lack. These intoxicants of the ego disappear from our life, only showing back up as indicators of an area that we need healing in and have work to do. They then become our guides instead of our way of life. When we choose higher energy thoughts that are acted on and carried out in our speech, we receive peace and prosperity for ourselves and others. The result of a growing and maturing Thought Practice is serene contentment supported by peace and abundance, which will then become your new normal.

A good way to check if you are living in the flow of your Thought Practice is to review your speech. Higher energy words begin with abandoning all harsh, low energy speech to self and others. It means we quit telling lies, exaggerating, and gossiping. Higher energy speech means that we cultivate and practice speaking kindly about others and bringing about their good qualities. It means not talking about their shortcomings except with kind honesty and tact. It is practicing well-timed, honest, kind, loving, tactful speech so we can speak to others' lives rather than speak at their life.

It means we quit telling lies, exaggerating, and gossiping.

The more you feed and nourish the higher energies in your mind, the more they will grow in strength and consistency and also emerge naturally in your speech. At some point, you will turn a corner, and there will be no space in your thoughts for lower energy speech of lies, exaggeration, and gossip. It then becomes easier and more natural the more consistently you choose the higher energies which grow to bear fruit in your life. This all becomes easier and more natural with consistent application, which also requires awareness. Without awareness of what is going on in your mind, the higher energies wouldn't be able to take root and grow as they are meant to do.

In one sense, living in the flow is an awareness of what you are doing and experiencing in your mind from moment to moment. This is so that you will abandon any low energy ego thoughts and have the skill to be aware. The effect is a purification of your mind from ego impurities and its tendencies. Having a transformative Thought Practice is a lot more than awareness. We come to a place of understanding our mind through direct observation and seeing how choosing our thoughts affects every area of our life. We come to discover that living in the higher energies provides us everything for which we have hoped.

None of this is about the conventional western notion of morality. The English word "morality" and its derivatives suggest a sense of obligation and constraint that is quite foreign to our souls. The higher energies of Thought Practice are based on being in harmony rather than the notion of obedience. Living in the higher energies leads to peace and spiritual, intellectual, relational, and karmic fulfillment. At the psychological level, living in the higher energies brings harmony to the mind and protection from the stress and anxiety of guilt and remorse over our actions.

You may recall the old schoolyard rebuke many of us learned as children: "sticks and stones may break my bones, but names will never hurt me." In my opinion, this old English proverb is not true. Words can break lives, create enemies, start wars, and leave scars. AND words can give wisdom, heal divisions, and create peace. It's always been this way—words do matter. Words and communication are critical hallmarks that distinguish the difference between humans and other species. From this, we can appreciate the need to make this capacity for words a means to love and bless others with higher energies rather than a sign of degradation.

If you want to transform your life and live in peace and purpose, you will have to guard your words. You should be especially careful what you say and how you say it. Of course, you must eliminate all abusive and derogatory speech from your life. Using negative low energy words to wound others is even worse than attacking them with weapons. It is harmful, and it magnetically brings those things back into your own life. Years ago, before I was healthy, one of my intimates called herself an admonisher. She was stating that her role in the lives of people she loved was to admonish them. She even claimed that it was a spiritual gift. This created many issues for her and ultimately ended some dear relationships. Admonishing speech assumes some dangerous perceptions as accurate. The admonisher believes that their worldview and opinion is right, and others should ascribe to it. Admonishing is rarely received constructively by the receiver and, therefore, causes more damage than positive change. It often leaves the receiver wounded and resentful. Admonishing is a mark of low energy because the individual has not used the higher energies and skills to coach up the other person. Many times, the admonisher was never invited to speak into the receiver's life. If you struggle with a tendency to admonish, I would like to encourage you in a couple of areas.

The desire to admonish flows out of pain, fears, and a need to control. Typically, the admonisher was admonished repetitively as a child, and it's natural for them. They often admonish gentle people who will not fight back and offer only quiet acceptance to end the conversation. When you feel the need to admonish, let it go and ask yourself why you feel this need at this time. You should examine your depths of heart and motivation. Then, if you come to a place where you genuinely are trying to help another soul, you should find a way to do so that they can use and will accept. Thoughts and words are magnetic and charged. They are not neutral, so ask, "Why am I doing this and will my words bring about positive or negative results?"

Another couple of low energy speech patterns that should be avoided at all costs are lying and drama. If you lie often, people will not believe you when you do end up telling the truth. If you continuously stir up disputes between people, you will then bring the dispute into your own life. People are intuitive and smart. They will catch on to both of these quickly. They may not be able to identify it, but they know in their gut that you can't be trusted or have the tendency to create tension.

The practice of truth-telling means conforming your actions to your words and maintaining a spirit of honesty in all your dealings. Where there is dishonesty, love and peace are destroyed. There are many ways to be dishonest with our words. Improper remarks can even be more false than untrue ones. Honeyed words that are dishonest ultimately cause more pain than honest words would have. Two-faced speech serves only to stir up drama and mistrust, and it instigates trouble on both sides of the issue.

In Thought Practice, living in the flow begins with your concentration and choices. It's moving from moral imperatives to a natural way of living. It brings the Buddhist tenants of right effort, right mindfulness, and right concentration into a seamless stream. Repeatedly, I hear Thought Practitioners stress the need for effort, diligence, and perseverance. These are so crucial that each person must work his or her deliverance from low energy ego thinking. Many people have done what they can by pointing you to the path of liberation; the rest of it involves the path of practice. The energy you invest in your Thought Practice is applied to the cultivation of your mind and its energies. The starting point is defined with a thought in your mind.

The goal here is the liberated mind and living in the higher energies. What comes in between is the ongoing effort to transform the enslaved mind into the liberated mind. Anyone who applies the principles of Thought Practice can accomplish the goals of liberation and peace. However, it requires determination and honesty.

Stuff will boil to the surface of your life as you dig in and do the work of healing. Issues swell from the depths of your wounds, which have been buried in your past. The congealed low energy garbage in our minds and hearts must be cleaned out, wounds healed, forgiveness given, and then amends made. Our new effort into the higher energies then feels natural and begins to bring much-needed peace.

When a low energy thought surfaces and clamors for our attention, redirect it into honest higher energy. For example, if you get angry reliving a wound, stop. You should redirect it into gratitude for what the person taught you and what the wounds have taught you. You should give thanks for the healing that has taken place. Perhaps, you should give thanks that they are no longer in your life and then offer them a blessing.

You should bless them with love and kindness. You have now transformed your energy and began to reprogram your thinking. Whatever you do, make sure you change your thoughts honestly. Burying or denying low energy is unhealthy, and the wounds may need to be cleaned so they no longer fester and can heal. The darkness of low energy disappears when it is brought into the light.

In a twelve-step meeting one evening, a man shared the following thoughts that radically propelled my Thought Practice to the very next level: "All you have to do if you want to change your life is change one thing. That one thing is to change everything. Get rid of all your old ideas.

That is all it takes." Then, he shared a story about his addiction being a rock he held onto for dear life. When I heard about turning over my old ideas, I realized that my old beliefs were my entire game plan for living. Everything. Every conviction. Every attitude. Every prejudice—everything means everything. Then, a thought came to mind. My ideas were so burdensome that it was like carrying around a 100-pound rock with me everywhere I went.

He explained to me this is an old recovery story and that it was MY rock. It was mine, and it was who I was. The rock was me. I was the rock. And I was, therefore, drowning in an ocean of resentment, fear, and dysfunction. Thought Practice was like a rescue ship fifty feet away while I was drowning deep in the ocean. I was holding on to the rock while trying to swim to the rescue boat. I am clinging to the rock for dear life while the rescuers are telling me to drop the rock. But this was my rock. It was mine. And they are yelling, "Drop the rock!"

I cannot drop the rock. It is all that I've ever known. It started as a pebble of hurt and resentment, and slowly throughout my life it grew to be so large that it was now destroying me. I was drowning, but I couldn't let go of the rock. This went on for some time. I was nearly drowning, catching one desperate and precious breath after another. Gasping. Going under. They were shouting to me to drop my rock and let it go. And then it happened.

I grew so weary I could not do it anymore. I could not carry the 100-pound rock around. I was exhausted. Weary in the depths of my soul. Alone. My choices were to either give up and die—or let go of the rock and change. I let it go. I dropped my rock. It sank away quickly. I was terrified. I knew that my life would never be the same, yet I feared that lasting peace and change would continue to allude me. To become the man I wanted to become, I had to drop the rock. All the grasping and holding on to my old ideas in a death grip seemed so pointless. Now, looking back years later, it seems crazy for me to have held on as I did. But I look back and give myself grace, knowing that I did not know what I didn't know.

Perhaps, you are holding onto a rock of resentment or a rock of pain, and you are stuck and unable to forgive. Maybe, your rock is an addiction to work, shopping, pornography, or substances. Regardless of what the specific rock is, once you drop it, you can swim to the lifeboat and transform your life. When you drop your rock, you will find your resistance to living in the flow of Divine love melt away. Almost imperceptibly. You will shift to an inner knowing that you are bringing the Divine back into your life, and you will leave the how and when up to God without judging, demanding, or even insisting. Your knowledge will be enough.

There is a provocative line in *A Course in Miracles* written by Helen Schulman. She mentions the Gabrielle Bernstein quote, "Those who are certain of the outcome can afford to wait and wait without anxiety." Patience and certainty go together. When you trust and know that you are connected to that universal, all-knowing intelligence, you can then live in patience and peace. You place no time constraints on your manifestation. You just go about your affairs with an inner awareness that says, "I've got all the time I need, and I am certain of the outcome, so I will allow it to show up naturally in due time."

The secret to living in the flow is in the certainty of the outcome. You cannot be certain if you are living in the lower energies as they create discord. You can be sure of the outcome if you live in the higher energies as they create peace and synchronicity. When that certainty is manifested in you in the form of trust and knowing, you can then turn your thoughts away from how you will get there to knowing you will get there.

Without anger or anxiety, you can turn your attention and Thought Practice to whatever it is that occupies your daily life and purpose. As you now live in the flow of your Thought Practice, you know the truth and you have patience that puts you at ease. The principles of higher energy living become knitted into the fabric of your life. You willingly allow God to do what He does and gently own what is yours in this Divine partnership. Your desire to manifest is already present. And your inner attention is one of well-being that you are already blessed with that which you seek.

Consequently, there is no pressure for you to make it show up impatiently. You come to see that living in your Thought Practice creates peace and patience, along with your purpose. *A Course in Miracles* also states, "Patience is natural for the person of God (living in the higher energies and flow). All they see is the certain outcome, at a time perhaps unknown to them yet, but not in doubt." Living in the certainty of the outcome and being unconcerned about the details have provided me with tremendous freedom and removed stress and anxiety from my daily life.

When you are sure about the outcome and unconcerned about the HOW or WHEN, then you have cultivated the power of infinite patience. Simultaneously, you have detached yourself from the result. When this detachment occurs, you can then go about your daily life and patiently be present. Patience is natural when you are in harmony with the Divine as you consistently engage in healthy Thought Practice.

Vigilance is essential to love in the flow of your Thought Practice. This is because the ego wants what it wants, and it wants it NOW. If it is not satisfied, it will convince you only to trust your perspective and opinions. The anxiety level will increase as you compete to meet the ego's demands. Your efforts are greeted by a greedy ego that has a new set of demands for you every new day. The cycle then continues until the ego is no longer in charge. However, as soon as you take the wheel of responsibility back from your ego, infinite patience then produces almost immediate results in your life. You become free when you relax your insistence to have it now, even though it may not have shown up as you would like in your immediate surroundings. Like an infinitely patient person living in the flow, you now know that you are already where you want to be. You know that there are no accidents and that all that appears to be missing is nothing more than just a distraction perpetrated by your ego.

Living in the flow is quite simple. If you do not take leadership of your subconscious mind, someone else will. Did you let that last sentence penetrate the depths of your mind and soul? Look at it again. If you do not, someone else will!

Whatever is true will reveal itself to you from within your being if you open your consciousness to it. That can be difficult as life is eternal but inhabits a material body. And you will take your material body with its wounds throughout the entire journey of life on earth. The truth is, if you saw God as a source of your good, you will reap infinite, eternal good, regardless of what happens in your experience. If you sow to the spirit of the higher energies, you will then reap the spiritual good, and if you sow to the ego, you will reap the ego's corruption. As humans, we can and frequently do get this messed up until we live in those higher energies. It would be like looking at a cluster of electrical lights and expecting the energy to come from the bulbs. The light is not there at all. The light is the emanation of electricity. If we limit ourselves by looking at the bulb for light, we would be disappointed as the bulb will burn out eventually, and we then would be without light. But if we are looking at the electricity, we will have light. So, it is with our Thought Practice and living in the higher energies. If we are looking to God for love, we will always have it. However, if we are looking to others to complete us, they will end up disappointing us.

When living in the flow, rest assured you have already grown so much in your Thought Practice and understanding. Circumstances that lack harmony and come into your life can be met with effective tools, understanding, and growth. This is MORE than your Thought Practice—it's the understanding that God loves you and has nothing but your best interest at heart. An expression of God's love for us is that everything which comes across our path is an opportunity for our learning, growth, and enlightenment. Inharmonious situations come from some disharmony within us. They are magnetically attracted into our life. As soon as we deal with it and learn what we need to, the situation vaporizes. If we run away from it, it will run after us until we learn what we need to learn.

LIVING PRESENTLY IN THE NOW

In letting go and living in the flow, we become a silent witness who is aware of what comes and goes. We are freeing our mind from being blindly repressing. Therefore, if we become obsessed with trivial thoughts, fears, doubts, worries, or anger, we can deal with them through our Thought Practice making them our teachers rather than our tormentors. This isn't to analyze but rather to take these low energies to their conclusion where they are exposed for what they are and then removed from the natural programmed progression of our thoughts. We watch and listen to them as conditions rather than living as their captives.

As you live in the flow and do your Thought Practice, you should deliberately catch your thoughts. You should look at the thoughts and choose them. You should notice what arises from your subconscious, examine it, and decide. Determine if it is a thought to be captured and replaced or if a wound in need of your attention. There is a chasm between being caught in lazy habitual thinking and focusing on a festering wound that requires healing for you to release those thoughts. You'll notice that you can only catch and examine thoughts after you've had them. Determining if it's lazy low energy thinking or a wound asking for attention is a choice you will have to make for yourself. Like your practice, no one can do it for you. If you are unsure, you can ask someone you can trust to be candid with you and with whom you can be brutally honest. Taking honest responsibility for our wounds rather than justifying or explaining them away is required if we want to heal.

If you think of yourself as a person who needs accomplishments to shield them, you will be a slave to your ego and its demands. You will not have time for anything that doesn't bolster your mask. If you want to be a loving, high-energy person, you will need to avoid thoughts, speech, and low energy actions. If you are going to be a loving, kind, and generous person, there will not be any room for mean, petty jealousies in your life. You will have to eliminate the lazy ego thinking of jealousy, pettiness, and snarky speech.

You stand at a crossroads in your life looking towards the future, glancing at the past. There are three choices before you. The first is to wring your hands and complain about shifting the responsibility of your life to others. This is playing the victim. There are plenty of things to blame, such as your parents, spouse, boss, or the government. The result of this is living in a constant state of "if only" and confusion; there is no peace here. The second choice is to resign yourself to the decay of your mind and then live in the ego's lazy thinking and low energy. The result of this choice is to live the life you have with all its discontent, drama, and pain. The third choice is to live your Thought Practice and change your life. The results will be peace, purpose, a lack of drama and pain, and anxiety will be a distant memory. If you reflect on this, you will see it has enormous implications. It means that you are responsible for the prosperity or decline of your thoughts and life. YOU. Only you.

You should remember that the choice is yours and only yours. Thought Practice represents an intensification of your thoughts in every state of your consciousness. By living in the higher energies, you then unify your other mental factors, ensuring that every thought, word, and action remains centered on the higher energies. Your mind will move from lazy division and deflection to unification. It is very much like taking the energy used in a light bulb or a laser. The amount of energy can be the same for both. In the case of the lightbulb, the energy is spread out. In the case of the laser, it is focused. One lights up the room, and one cuts and penetrates with precision. That's what Thought Practice does—it focuses your mind's energy into a single focus. It is enormously powerful.

Centering your mind and spirit is a wholesome concentration that collects the ordinary and then transforms them into the extraordinary. Two features of a present mind are (a) unbroken presence to the moment and (b) the tranquility and peace of your spirit. A distracted mind of lazy thinking is a deluded mind that seeks confirmation bias to justify a lack of responsibility. Overwhelmed by worries and concerns, it sees things only in fragments that are destroyed by the ripples of random thoughts and worries.

Thought Practice is not attained all at once. Like yoga, learning to play an instrument, or any skill, you will get better and more effective the more you practice and make it a part of your life. When activated, your Thought Practice picks up momentum and power. You may have noticed as you have already begun your Thought Practice that it does the work of directing your mind and heart to the higher energies. Your thoughts drive your experience like a hammer drives a nail through wood.

Sustained application and appreciation of the higher energies in your thoughts anchor your mind's energy and then bears fruit in your words and actions. You should think of it like this: The initial thought is like striking a bell, while the sustained application is like the bell's reverberations. When your practice is developed, you will notice that your life is flooded with peace, purpose, and passion. You become a magnet for abundance and transformation in the lives of others.

Centering your mind and spirit is a wholesome concentration that collects the ordinary and then transforms them into the extraordinary.

As you absorb and share the higher energies of love, kindness, honesty, non-judgment, and gratitude, you will then notice that each of these higher energies opposes a low energy hindrance such as obsessive thinking, resentment, anger, doubt, and anxiety.

As you are embarking on the transformative process of your Thought Practice, you should give yourself grace. Think of it like a child learning how to walk. She stands and lets go of the table, sways on shaky legs, and her muscles learn to act intuitively. After she has mastered standing, she takes a few tentative and wobbly steps. She falls, gets up, walks some more, and falls again. Very soon, she is running, and walking has become second nature. Her world has completely changed with this new skill that she won't even remember learning years later. It will just be how she lives.

As your Thought Practice progresses, like the toddler, you will become stronger, more adept, and agile. You will live naturally in the flow. Despite changes, your mind and spirit will remain centered and content in love and peace. You will get to see hindrances and hurts as teachers, embracing their lessons in your life. With diligence, you will become more proficient in your Thought Practice and live the life you want and crave. You will become the person you want to be. Your life will change. It is simple: once you change your thoughts, you change your life. Remember, when you evaluate yourself as being good or bad, right or wrong, that is a comparative value, diminishing your absolute value.

There is no need to evaluate yourself by a limited ego when your measurement is a natural outflow of living in the flow of the higher energies we talked about. You will know when you are and when you are not. That is enough. Your life is in your hands. The kind of life and experience you want to have is up to you. You can and should create the life you've always wanted. Your future self will thank you very much for it!

CHAPTER 16 EXERCISES

These chapter exercises are designed to help you apply the principles of TRANFORMATIONAL THINKING in meaningful and transformative ways for you. They are not designed that one should do all the exercises for each chapter. Record the notes from the chapter, the exercise you are doing, and the results in your notebook.

1. Since Thought Process enriches the higher energies of love, honesty, kindness, and non-judgment, it also leads to liberation. Living in the flow of higher energies and carrying on with your Thought Practice doesn't mean just spiritual progress. It is emancipation from the tyranny of the ego. It involves personal transformation which brings freedom, peace, purpose, and life! Living your life in a flow means taking ownership and responsibility for your life, emotions, thoughts, actions, and circumstances. You are in control of what action you choose and how you take such action.

2. The most effective way to find out if you're living in the flow of your Thought Practice is to review your speech. The difference will be visible through the words you choose. When living in the flow of higher energies, you tend to abandon all harsh, low-energy speech while communicating with others and yourself. It means we abandon lies, exaggerating, using cuss words, and even gossiping. Higher energy speech encourages us to speak kindly and use kind words. It means mentioning the good qualities of people instead of highlighting their shortcomings. However, with honesty,

you can tell people if they lag at some point. Higher energies and living in the flow is practicing well-timed, kind, honest, and polite speech. You will be surprised to experience the change it brings to your Thought Practice and your overall growth. And while all of this may not happen overnight, one step at a time can surely take you closer to your goal. After some time, you can note your progress and the changes that have resulted from your diligence. Put everything down in a notebook and be as specific about the details as you can. The clearer you are with your experience, the more progress you will make towards growth.

3. Just like a toddler learning to walk, when your Thought Practice progresses, you will become stronger, more agile, and more adept. You will be excited to live naturally in the flow. Despite the changes, your mind and spirit will remain centered and content in love and peace. And even though you will come across hindrances and hurts, they will become positive and bring a lesson with them. With diligence, you will become proficient in your Thought Practice and live the life you want and deserve. You will become the person you want to be, whose charm works like a magnet. With your mindset, your whole life will change, too. To provide strategic attention in your Thought Practice, ask yourself the following questions and write down the answers in a journal.

- What areas of Thought Practice are natural and easy for you to do?

- Which components are more challenging for you, and why?

4. Thought Practice is an ongoing process that does not end. It's a continuous form of learning that helps us grow and develop habits that promise a good life in return. These new habits reprogram our subconscious. They become our way of life. Others will prove stubborn and take more time and attention to transform. It is exciting when you reach the tipping point, and you become more

about the higher energies when it comes to leading your daily life. To encourage your continued growth and effort, use this book as a how-to guide for living a mindful life. Here are some more actions that will help you achieve that goal:

- When you go through this book a second time, try the exercises at the end of each chapter that you skipped the first time. Or see how your answers are different the second time you read the book compared to the first. Use a separate journal to record your answers and insights.

- Please do not turn the pages for the sake of it. The purpose of this book is to help you implement meaningful changes in your Thought Practice and overall life. Take your time and read each chapter one at a time and connect with it. You will notice areas that stand out, which were not meaningful in a prior read. You will also notice areas where they have become so ingrained in your life that you skip over them because you got it. It is yours!

CHAPTER 17

FAQS: RETRAIN YOUR BRAIN

"Let us make our future now, and let us make our
dreams tomorrow's reality."
—Malala Yousafzai

1. **Are addiction and additive thinking interchangeable terms?**
   <u>Addiction</u> is a disorder/disease characterized by a persistent and intense urge to engage in certain behaviors despite substantial harm and other negative consequences. A sign of addiction is choosing the object (drugs, alcohol, sex, gambling, food, work, etc.) at the expense of relationships, health, career, financial security, delayed gratification, and almost everything else. Repetitive use of the object of addiction often alters the chemicals in the brain in ways that perpetuate cravings and weakens self-control. <u>Addictive thinking</u> is living with addiction characteristics without a specific avenue, such as drugs, sex, or alcohol. A well-trained therapist can be priceless for those seeking help with addiction and addictive thinking.

2. **What are the warning signs of an addiction and of addictive thinking?**
   Denial is one of the classic signs of addiction and addictive thinking. It is essential to identify the warning signs and address the problem by healing the wounds that have caused these patterns. Once you're clear that you or someone you love has an addiction or addictive thinking, professional help is available. Here are some of the common signs of an addiction:

- Urge to use the object of addiction regularly
- Needing more of the object over time to achieve similar effects
- Justifying its use and your focus
- Disregarding financial status when it comes to the object
- Social and work life impacted due by object use
- Continuation of use despite the knowledge of consequences
- Unsuccessful attempts to stop the use on your own
- Decreased attendance and performance in workplace/ school setting
- Frequently engaging in conflicts (fights, illegal activity)
- Hiding or in denial of certain behaviors
- Changes to eating/sleeping habits
- Changes to personality and attitude
- Frequent or sudden changes in mood and temperament
- Angry and irritable
- Fearful, paranoid, and anxious without probable cause
- Changes to financial status (unexplained need for money)
- Use of object despite consequences to personal relationships

3. **Looking back, do you remember when this distorted pattern of thinking started in your life?**
   I get this question often as people explore their experience to see if they may be suffering from addictive thinking. One of the insidious components of addictive thinking is that, more often than not, it comes from childhood trauma and / or abuse. The thinking that served us as a child can harm us as adults. The very coping mechanisms our young mind created to survive the trauma can turn into addictive thinking as we get older. Therefore, it is important

to recognize these dysfunctional patterns of thinking and heal them. Through the rearview mirror of life, we can learn to identify unhealthy coping mechanisms and can get counseling to rewire our thinking patterns.

4. **How does an addiction or addictive thinking affect one's ability to reason and make healthy decisions?**

   Addictive thinking inhibits the ability to reason rationally. Yet, rational thought is an essential attribute of functioning adults. Many people who don't suffer from addiction wonder why an addict can't simply stop the addictive behavior. However, the brain's reward system is rewired like a rat hitting a button that gives them food. Pretty soon, it becomes compulsive and functions similar to an autopilot setting. This kind of learning usually is associated with basic survival needs and is subconsciously programmed through early childhood trauma experiences. This results in arrested development where the individual's emotional growth is stunted around the age at which the trauma was experienced. Therefore, I highly recommend seeking out a professional counselor to assist in the healing journey.

5. **Is addictive thinking the prelude to addictive behaviors and drug / alcohol abuse?**

   Yes and no. Addictive thinking does preclude other forms of addiction like sex, gambling, drugs, and alcohol. Yet, it doesn't mean someone with Addictive thinking will become an addict. I had never done a drug of any kind other than mild experimentation with marijuana when I was young. I have always guarded my use of alcohol with boundaries so I wouldn't become an alcoholic. My therapist asked me why I never tried drugs, and I said without thinking, "I was afraid if I did them once, I'd never stop." I learned that such a response is classic for those of us with Addictive Thinking whose subconscious is protecting them from going down those paths. Unfortunately, the object of our addiction can become things that gratify our ego and quiet the need to heal our wounds, such as work, accomplishment, and finances.

6. **How can an addiction affect people physically, emotionally, mentally, spiritually, and relationally?**
   Someone who has never experienced addictive thinking or addiction can have difficulty understanding how all-consuming it can be. Addiction is a disease that attacks all aspects of human psychology and physiology. The consequences of addiction are severe and can cause innumerable medical conditions including fatal lung and heart conditions. Addiction affects mental health and can elevate symptoms of depression, anxiety, PTSD, and ADHD. Gaining insight into the complex nature of addiction is helpful when developing a holistic treatment plan. Treatment for addiction that focuses on physical, mental, and spiritual wellness simultaneously is effective for a successful recovery.

7. **Where would you be today if you had not healed your thinking?**
   Had I not changed my thinking, done my healing work, and reprogrammed my subconscious, there would have been two options for my life. (A) I would have been living the same anxiety-filled, stressful life where I lived in the past and future; thereby missing out on living in the present. Had I not done the healing work, I would have continued working for employers I resented for taking advantage of me and used fear to keep me working for them. I would have continued to attract romantic partners who were living in cycles of their own dysfunction. Prior to my healing journey, I felt unworthy, lacked healthy boundaries, and could not self-soothe. (B) Like most addicts who hit what is called a Hard Rock Bottom, I'd be dead.

8. **Prior to your healing journey, how was your thinking attached to guilt and shame in your life?**

   There is a lot of talk in healing circles about how bad shame and guilt are. It's the same because folks miss so much by relegating them to the wrong category. The truth is there is positive shame and destructive shame. Like many addicts or those with addictive Thinking, I experienced both. We often feel guilt or shame when we do something wrong that compromises our soul and character. It's our soul telling us we did something we shouldn't have. It does not mean we are bad people. It means we did something wrong.

9. **Did your wounded thinking factor into you self-sabotaging your life?**

   Absolutely, yes! Wounded thinking impacts every area of our life. It begins gradually as our thinking patterns and self-talk subtly cope with surviving the trauma. It is why Transformational Thinking begins with healing work, taking responsibility for our lives, and acceptance. After that portion of the healing work is addressed, we can identify our *stinking thinking* and reprogram our subconscious minds with our conscious minds. The reprogramming gives birth to healthy beliefs and bears fruit in our actions. Prior to therapy, my beliefs and thoughts were atrocious. My father's abuse and his lack of even liking me created a hunger for approval and validation from authority figures. My issues included a lack of healthy boundaries and self-advocacy. Then I resented the other person for their actions, which I allowed.

10. **Did your pre-healed thinking influence your ability or lack of ability to trust others?**

    Yes. Trust is a foundational psychological component for humans. From our earliest days, we expect to be physically and emotionally safe and provided with food and shelter. This early expectation is not conscious; it is from a primitive, instinctual place. Experiencing early childhood trauma causes the body to produce adrenaline and cortisol, activating normal protective processes of fight, flight, or freeze. Unresolved traumatic experiences can stimulate these responses even in non-threatening situations. Yes, victims of trauma have trust issues. In my case, I trusted people to a point, but would not allow anyone past a certain level where the *wounded me* lived.

11. **Were you unable to control your thoughts like an alcoholic who cannot control their drinking?**

I get this question often. It is an early misconception for many. Here is why: The alcoholic is usually aware of their drinking. They may not acknowledge it is a problem, but they are aware of alcohol in their lives. Conversely, most of us never examine our thinking patterns or subconscious beliefs. Therefore, many of us with addictive thinking do not know we were on a dysfunctional autopilot setting heading for trouble. There was an unhealthy default setting after the virus of trauma entered our lives. It's only when we become aware that we can learn to control our thoughts. It's up to us to reprogram our subconscious and reset faulty beliefs. When that awareness comes, THEN our eyes are opened to the issues of our past thinking. It's one of those areas where a person can't know until they know…and then they can't unknow.

12. **Did you notice that your thinking patterns were different than others?**

The short answer is yes and no. <u>Yes</u>, I noticed my thoughts were different from an early age. But I also thought everyone else had it all figured out at home, school, and in the neighborhood. I thought I was the odd duck who didn't have it all figured out. It turns out no one has it figured out. I was a sensitive empath, hard-wired to care about others. I grew up with a father who didn't understand any of that and tried to beat it out of me. Conversely, the answer is <u>no</u> because negative thinking patterns became habitual over time and formed so subtly they are typically not noticed. By Harry calling my attention to them and writing them down, I could more easily identify the areas that required attention and those that were simply hogwash.

13. **What negative consequences did you experience prior to implementing transformational thinking?**

There were many consequences to my life and the lives of others. I have had two failed marriages. I lived in a constant, and I mean constant, state of stress and anxiety which was void of any real joy. I could not live in the moment with my attention bouncing frenetically between the past and future. My life had zero peace and very little deep, genuine, vulnerable connection with others. Additionally, I was hiding my best and most authentic self behind a mask of untreated pain.

14. **Do trauma and unhealed wounds predispose someone to stinking thinking?**

The short answer is yes. Trauma from childhood causes people to develop unhealthy thinking patterns and behaviors. These include victimhood thinking, emotional isolation, inability to form intimate relationships, and destructive habits (among others). This stinking thinking can be dangerous, as it influences (a) how we perceive ourselves, (b) our self-talk, (c) the choices we make, (d), our professional life, (e)the opportunities we pursue, and (f) the health of our relationships. Also, a byproduct of stinking thinking is we bury our emotions and lose touch with our authentic self. We live terrified that if we let the mask drop, we will no longer be cared for, loved, or accepted.

15. **Where do you go to get support on your journey to a healthier Thought Practice?**

I strongly encourage people to invest in a qualified therapist or coach to support their healing journey and work. When choosing a person to walk with you through your healing work, it's essential they have the right skills and experience to walk with you in your healing work. Look for a therapist with a background and experience working with clients with childhood trauma. I have found therapists and coaches from Cognitive Behavioral Therapy (CBT) or Rogerian therapy (i.e. Carl Rogers) tend to be the most effective. Too many therapists use a friendship style. You do not need a friend. It would be best if you had someone who will say hard things, ask penetrating questions, and push you to wrestle and do the work.

16. **What did and did not work in those early days of trying to change your distorted thinking?**

This is a common question and based on a fundamental misconception. It's not about what did or did not work. It all works based on proven principles. The key to applying the principles of Transformational Thinking is consistency and ongoing coaching. Having someone who can walk through this journey with you is imperative. It all works if you work it and follow the principles. Knowing the information and developing subconscious skills are two different things. I have yet to see someone follow the principles of responsibility, removing victimhood thinking, acceptance, and consistency of the transformational thinking process who does not heal and transform their life.

17. **As you implemented Thought Practice in your life, was this based on Mindfulness and the principles of Growth Mindset, or is different?**

That is another great question. Growth Mindset describes a way of viewing challenges and setbacks. People with a growth mindset believe their abilities are not set in stone, even if they struggle with specific skills. They think that with work, their skills can improve over time. Mindfulness is defined as the quality or state of being conscious or aware of something. It's a mental state achieved by focusing one's awareness on the present moment while calmly acknowledging and accepting one's feelings and thoughts.

These principles are essential components of transforming your thinking, but in and of themselves are not enough because they do not address healing our wounds, taking responsibility, and learning how to reprogram our default settings. That is why we often meet mindful people who practice meditation and are still struggling. They have not healed, taken responsibility, and reprogrammed their thinking.

18. **What guardrails are in place for you now to keep you from veering off track again?**

No guardrails or safety nets are needed when someone has developed the skills of genuine Transformational Thinking because they have a new normal. However, the same guardrails we used while healing our wounds and developing these new skills naturally help us process and continue living in a healthy Thought Practice. These include our intimate relationships as well as our therapists / coach. It also requires feeding our minds with the correct nutrition through various resources such as books, articles, podcasts, etc.

19. **What distortions of thinking have you been able to control through Thought Practice?**

Any technique to "control" thought distortions will fail to produce the desired results. We do not seek to control our thought distortions but rather to (a) heal the wounds that caused those distortions and then (b) reprogram the mind to live in truth rather than distortions. In physical medical terms, we are not teaching people how to live with cancer but seeking to eradicate cancerous thinking. If distorted thinking rears its head in my life, I can use Transformational Thinking techniques and trusted individuals in my life to assess and correct the thinking.

20. **Can you paint me a picture of where you are now, compared to where you were with addictive thinking?**

The most straightforward way to illustrate the differences is to chart them out in before and after comparison.

Before	**After**
Stress	Relaxed
Anxiety	Peace
No Intimacy	True Intimacy
Fear	Calm Courage
Need to Control	Non-judgmental thinking
Resentment	Forgiveness
Anger	Healthy Boundaries

21. **Can you share examples of how you transformed your self-talk?**

That is an excellent clarifying question. Too often, folks become discouraged simply because they miss a particular component of Transformational Thinking when retraining their brain. Namely refusing to indulge or give any millisecond of thought to the previously programmed lines of self-talk which did not serve you. We cannot bargain with, compromise our commitment to, or indulge ourselves with harmful self-talk. It isn't easy at first., I struggled for the first three months, and then all of a sudden, the ongoing practice paid off. Three months felt long, but then I had to remember that the preprogramming had been there for 40+ years. In that context, three months wasn't bad.

False Limiting Beliefs	Accurate Truthful Beliefs
I am such a loser.	I have strengths and weaknesses just like everyone.
I am such an idiot!	I am really good at working with people.
My only purpose is as a provider.	My purpose is to love people and support them on their journey.
You do not fit in with the masses, you do not belong here.	I am unique and the more I authentically live who I am, the more likely I'll find my people.
Someone hurts you, cut them off emotionally and don't let them in again.	You are learning how to advocate for yourself while establishing healthy boundaries.

Those are a sampling of the False Beliefs and the phrases I used to replace them. The more consistent we do this and the quicker we do this and refuse to give the false beliefs a foothold in our mind, the more rapid the reprogramming.

22. **What was your narrative then, compared to your narrative now about yourself, your life, your value, the people in your life, your future, etc.?**

In some ways, I am the same person. My drive, expertise, and skills in assisting others to transform chronic habits and roadblocks into pathways of profitability are as strong as ever. In other ways, I am a different person. My wounds have healed, and I understand how those wounds affected my decision-making and how to identify and prevent moral compromise. I have learned how to transform adversity into an advantage and now help others do the same.

The narrative that guided most of my life was that my value was in my work and provision for my family. As a child, I felt unworthy due to the abuse which carried me into adulthood. On this side of my healing work, I see my value in simply existing, being aware of my life and how it impacts others. I KNOW I am worthy of loving and being loved. I live anxiety-free, virtually stress-free, and in peace. My relationships are fewer but far more deeply intimate than before my transformative work.

23. **Do you sometimes get triggered to go back to your old way of thinking?**

Early in the Transformational Thinking process, as people are retraining their brains, it is common to experience triggering and some regression. It's two steps forward, one back, three forward, one sideways, non-linear experience. The better we get at the process, the less and less we are triggered to regress. However, as we navigate life, the gift of triggering is that those triggers call our attention to an area where we have more healing work to do. So in that aspect, our growth never ends. We don't "arrive," so to speak.

24. **What is a typical timeframe to retrain your brain with Transformative Thinking and Thought Practice?**

There is no common time frame. Each person, their thinking, the wounds from the past, their abilities in thinking, and emotional intelligence all combine to create a unique experience for each person in their Transformational Thinking. Retraining your brain takes consistency, vulnerability, responsibility, acceptance, support, and courage. That said, most people begin to see a difference within six weeks and feel a meaningful transformation in 12-16 weeks. Transformational Thinking is not a quick fix. This journey requires intentional effort and a reiterative process of ongoing personal growth and healing.

25. How would you finish this sentence? "I transformed my thoughts and my life by _____."

I transformed my thoughts and my life by taking responsibility for EVERY aspect of my life; working with an effective therapist/coach to teach me how to retrain my brain; and consistently feeding my mind the healthy nutrients it needs to experience newfound peace, joy, and love in my life.

26. Is there a symbol you think illustrates our ongoing iterative healing work and the results of our commitment to Transformative Thinking?

Yes, the chambered nautilus shell is very illustrative of this process. If you are not familiar with the chambered nautilus shell, google it. A soft-bodied cephalopod lives inside this hard shell in the deep waters of the Pacific and Indian oceans. The hard shell of the nautilus has many individual spiral chambers. As the chambered nautilus grows, it creates a larger chamber for itself, each one larger than the last.

27. Where can I go to follow you and your ongoing work?

- https://www.andrewhenryjacobs.com
- https://www.andrewhenryjacobs.com/blog
- https://www.rezults.net
- https://preparing4prison.com
- https://www.linkedin.com/in/drewjacobs

- Facebook: Andrew Henry Jacobs
- https://www.instagram.com/andrewhenryjacobs
- https://www.amazon.com/Transformational-Consulting-Bringing-Individuals-Organizations/dp/1098343166

Bonus: A Free One-on-One Coaching Session for You!

Healing is much more effective when we have a coach or therapist guiding us on our journey. Experienced guides support our work, challenge our assumptions, and encourage our growth. Are you ready for an experienced guide to accompany you on your healing journey as you:

- Heal your traumatic wounds, so they become a source of strength—instead of a hindrance?
- Cultivate valuable relationships that can support you for years to come?
- Change your subconscious and conscious thinking patterns, so they naturally work for you—instead of against you?

You are in luck! For a limited time, Drew is offering his readers an initial 45-minute coaching session via Zoom.

To schedule your complimentary session email Drew at DrewHJacobs@gmail.com.

Drew Jacobs speaks around the country on a variety of important topics including:

- Identifying and Healing Moral Compromise
- Creating a Culture Where Individuals and Teams Thrive
- How Unhealed Wounds Impact Individuals and Organizations
- The Most Important Conversation of Your Life

Additionally, Drew can tailor a specialized training for the unique needs of your team or organization.

If you would like Drew Jacobs to speak at your next event, please contact his business manager, Rhonda, at PetriniSolutions@gmail.com.

Use this code to access "all things Drew;" and to keep track of when Drew is speaking in your area.

Acknowledgments

There are so many people who have contributed to developing the ideas and thoughts in this book and my life. I cannot begin to thank you all. So, I would like to express gratitude for the lives and work of the following people: Richard Rohr, Peter Drucker, Wayne Dyer, Shep Gordon, and Brigitte Jacobs.

Thank you to my publishing team for being fantastic and patient. I am grateful for all the ways you help me get my voice out to the world and especially to my talented editor, Rhonda Petrini, for making sure my words are at their best. No way this could have existed without you, Doc!

My accomplishments are not mine alone. I have been encouraged, sustained, inspired, and tolerated by the greatest groups of friends anyone ever had. Thank you to my tribe for loving me just as I am and helping me become who I am becoming, for laughing with and at me, listening to my ideas, challenging the gaps, and encouraging me to find my voice. Thank you to my Nine, who loved me when I wasn't very lovable and loved me with accountability, practicality, and your presence. You know who you are, and I honor you by simply doing the next right thing every day, one day at a time.

Finally, thank you to those who walked away from my life when I was at my lowest. The lessons you taught me were transformational.

—Drew

www.ingramcontent.com/pod-product-compliance
Lightning Source LLC
Chambersburg PA
CBHW062321120626
46553CB00015B/133